Mark Twain's Audience

Mark Twain's Audience

A Critical Analysis of Reader Responses to the Writings of Mark Twain

Robert McParland

LEXINGTON BOOKS
Lanham • Boulder • New York • London

Published by Lexington Books
An imprint of The Rowman & Littlefield Publishing Group, Inc.
4501 Forbes Boulevard, Suite 200, Lanham, Maryland 20706
www.rowman.com

16 Carlisle Street, London W1D 3BT, United Kingdom

British Library Cataloguing in Publication Information Available

Library of Congress Cataloging-in-Publication Data

McParland, Robert.
Mark Twain's audience : a critical analysis of reader responses to the writings of Mark Twain / Robert McParland.
p. cm.
Includes bibliographical references and index.
ISBN 978-0-7391-9051-7 (cloth : alk. paper) -- ISBN 978-0-7391-9052-4 (electronic)
1. Twain, Mark, 1835-1910--Appreciation--United States. 2. Twain, Mark, 1835-1910--Influence. 3. Books and reading--United States--History. I. Title.
PS1342.A54M37 2014
818'.409--dc23
2014026723

Printed in the United States of America

Contents

Acknowledgments

Mark Twain saved many of the letters written to him across the years and a book like this can only be written because he did so. In my work I have sought the often fragmentary comments of dozens of people who have left journals, letters, or autobiographies. My research has benefited from the ways in which families and archivists have preserved these materials. I clearly owe a debt of gratitude to all book history scholars and principally to Jonathan Rose for his example and years of guidance. The Society for the History of Authors, Readers, and Publishing (SHARP) continues to make new strides in this field. I am also deeply indebted to the many scholars of Mark Twain studies and, most recently, to the fine beginning that R. Kent Rasmussen has made with *Dear Mark Twain: Letters from his Readers* (2013) into the search for Mark Twain's readers.

The continuing afterlife and energy of Mark Twain's legacy is sustained among us by the Mark Twain Papers project at the University of California, Berkeley, and the curators of the Mark Twain houses in Elmira, New York, Hartford, Connecticut, and Hannibal, Missouri. Mark Twain's writings, published before 1923, today are in the public domain. His correspondent's writings to him, likewise, fall into this period. Most letter writers likely never expected anyone to read their letters. Excerpts from many of these letters have now been published elsewhere, as in R. Kent Rasmussen's book, which, appearing after I had completed my initial research, has proved to be an invaluable stimulus to further inquiry. Care has been taken here to respect the words and the thoughts of these letter and journal writers and to learn something about their lives and reading. I have made efforts to locate the heirs of correspondents to Mark Twain. Those who I have reached have been generous in their cooperation with this project. I am grateful for the curators of the Mark Twain Papers at the University of California, who allow us to utilize the resources they so diligently preserve, and I wish to encourage you to consult the volumes of Twain's letters, autobiography, and journals that they expertly edit. Similarly, the preservation efforts of those libraries and archival collections that hold materials like autobiographies, journals and diaries, and nineteenth-century newspapers utilized here deserve acknowledgment as well, including those that have scanned and placed their resources online. These sources are indicated in the notes and include: the "Annie Adams Fields Papers," at Houghton Library, Harvard University, Cambridge, Massachusetts, as well as the "Annie Adams

Fields Papers" at the Massachusetts Historical Society; *Brooklyn Eagle* online; Documenting the American South, University of North Carolina, Chapel Hill; Harry Ransom Center, University of Texas; Harry S. Truman Presidential Library, University of Missouri; Hoag Mark Twain Collection, Minneapolis Public Library; James K. Hosner Collection, Minneapolis Library; Jewish Center for History, New York; Louis B. Nunn Center for Oral History, University of Kentucky Library, Lexington, Kentucky; Making of America online, University of Michigan and Cornell University; Middleton, New York Historical Society; Minnesota Historical Society, Minneapolis, Minnesota; Ohio Historical Society, African American Experience 1850–1920; Oregon Digital History Archive; Professor Stephen Railton's Mark Twain website, University of Virginia; Reader's Experience Database (RED); Rutgers University Oral History Collection, New Brunswick, New Jersey; University of California Bancroft Library Regional Oral History Collection; University of Mississippi Oral History Project, Hattiesburg, Mississippi; University of Southern Mississippi Oral History and Cultural Heritage; Virginia Polytechnic Oral History Collection.

My thanks go to my initial readers at Felician College, Sherida Yoder, Terry McAteer, Tony Demarest, George Castellitto, and to my students and colleagues at the college. The Felician College Library, the Drew University Library, and the New York Public Library also provided helpful resources. I would like to add my thanks to an astute reviewer for suggestions for revision and to Lindsey Porambo, Kayla Riddleberger, and Elizabeth DeBusk at Lexington Books for their editorial and production assistance.

The idea for a study of Mark Twain began, in part, with Debbie Cariddi's grandfather's set of Mark Twain books and in the laughter and cigar smoke of Carl "Doc" Martucci's gatherings. It is dedicated to the people who make us laugh.

ONE

America's Mark Twain

At times, Mark Twain seems almost like our contemporary. He is that kindly figure in a white suit, cigar in his mouth, squinting out across the ages. It was Mark Twain who once wrote that the public was the only critic whose opinion was worth anything at all. This book seeks Mark Twain's readers of his books and the listeners to his lectures. This is a study of Mark Twain's wide audience and of the many ways in which that audience has imagined Twain and encountered his literary output. In their great diversity, people throughout the world responded to Twain's work. In America, they interacted with his creativity throughout a post–Civil War era of great expansion. They read his stories, attended his lectures, and participated in creating his reputation. Those common readers lived in the midst of a publishing revolution. Twain's audience was worldwide and his audience includes many people who did not read his work but who certainly had heard of him, or heard his lectures, or heard his works read aloud. As Robert Darnton has pointed out, "for most people throughout most of history books had audiences rather than readers. They were better heard than seen."[1] So too with Mark Twain, who was a public lecturer and performer, a celebrity and a familiar image even to people who had not read his books. His audience has always included listeners and viewers as well as readers. It is this world-wide audience that made Mark Twain one of the most widely known literary figures that America has ever produced. This audience, so long in the shadows, merits our careful examination. They are a community of inter-preters whose reception of Twain's works must be discovered, so we may better understand Mark Twain's lasting impact.

In the late 1860s, when the young man with a shock of reddish hair and a mustache appeared to lecture to his audience, listeners expected to be entertained by an infamous Western humorist. Mark Twain began his career as a jesting lecturer, a comedian whose gift was that he could make people laugh. He wrote to his brother Orion: "I have a 'call' to a literature of a low order, ie. Humorous. It is nothing to be proud of but it is my strongest suit."[2] Twain, the writer, the speaker, the jokester, was instantly memorable. His audience is much less so. They laughed with delight. They turned pages with curiosity. Yet, much of the public memory of their lives has been eclipsed by the years. This study will provide a glimpse into their reading and their interaction with Twain's characters. Twain once commented: "My audience is dumb, it has no voice in print, so I cannot know whether I have won its approbation or its censure."[3] Twain's readership and lecture audiences are an important part of his story. As Martyn Lyons and Jay Arnold have asserted, "The history of the book, then, is dangerously incomplete without an investigation of the ultimate destination of books—their readers—and the ways they received and interpreted their texts."[4]

To search for actual readers' responses is to respect how historical meaning is retained in personal documents such as family papers, autobiographies, diaries, letters, and other cultural records. A reader's reactions to a text will provide fragmentary evidence of his or her reading. They do not tell us all we need to know about a reader's experience. However, since books are always transactions between authors and producers and their readers, the voices of actual readers ought not to be left missing from the critical and historical record. To better understand what a book means culturally, it is important to look at the audience whose responses are what most mattered in commercial terms. Letters and family papers suggest their social networks and their jottings in journals and diaries may help us to see readers' emotional responses, or their engagements with a figure or a specific passage in a text. Mark Twain saved many of the letters written by his readers to him and R. Kent Rasmussen's recent collection of some of these letters, *Dear Mark Twain* (2013), has provided a valuable beginning for scholars to investigate Twain's readers.[5] By considering this audience we may increase our understanding of Mark Twain and American culture. By listening to the voices of Twain's readers, we might come to be better able to know how Mark Twain's work intersected with their experience and why he was so very popular among them. It is through Mark Twain's audience that we may see Twain as a cultural phenomenon and a decisive influence upon American culture and world literature.

Mark Twain is a unique voice in American writing. He has been viewed in many guises: as a humorist, a writer, a businessman, an inventor, a husband, and a father. He was a traveler geographically across the reaches of the world and mentally across the reaches of time, a man of the South (Missouri and the Mississippi), the West (Nevada and San Francisco), and the East (Hartford, Elmira, and New York). With this writer, it is almost as if the terrain itself rises up to meet the physical reality of the book. *The Innocents Abroad* brought his readers to the ancient world and the Mideast in rich, lyrical language and generous illustration, under sturdy book covers. One can almost feel the dust of the West in *Roughing It*: the rough-edged voices and grinding fortunes of miners, the blinding sun on high mountain peaks. The book deserves a brown cover, or a deep forest green one, like some tribute to the land itself.

Mark Twain's popular audience was situated within a growing communications circuit that was essential to the distribution and reception of Twain's books. Publishers, agents, booksellers, retailers, librarians, and others brought his books to readers. They fashioned and distributed the material book, lifted its weight and designed its cover, its paper and text and illustrations. Twain's readers purchased his books, shared them in their families, or at work places, or they borrowed them from libraries. These were often subscription books. That is, they were purchased from sales agents who traveled into towns and rural areas to enlist readers. Many of Twain's audience were periodical readers, who met his characters in the *Century*, the *Atlantic, Harper's*, or any of the dozens of newspapers and periodicals in which his work was reprinted alongside a wide variety of articles and stories. These readers were part of the great upsurge in reading in America in the nineteenth century. Twain himself was representative of this growing book and periodical trade. He was a printer, a publisher, a journalist, a promoter, and an investor in a printing machine, as well as a prolific author. By locating Twain's contemporary audience, we begin to see what Twain and his collaborator Charles Dudley Warner called "the Gilded Age." The twentieth-century reception of Twain's work by his readers is also of interest, demonstrating the rise in popularity of *Tom Sawyer, Huckleberry Finn*, and *A Connecticut Yankee in King Arthur's Court*.

We still have a lot to learn about how Mark Twain's readers read his books. Twain's common readers may or may not have been technical readers, like scholars or critics, yet they interpreted the texts that they read. Readers make something personal of fiction and of essays, as they bring their lives to their reading. That is in evidence in the comments that Twain's readers have left in their journals, autobiographies, and letters. This study aims to bring us closer to the affective relationships of reader and writer by considering the responses of some of the common readers of Mark Twain.[6] We may ask about the attitudes and expectations that Twain's readers brought to his books. Was the reader accepting, flexible, and accommodating, or resistant? Did the reader identify with the characters in the story, or was the reader skeptical? Was there a willing suspension of disbelief and a receptive attitude? Did the reader enter the text imaginatively, or observe himself or herself in the act of reading? Was the reader attuned to irony, or was he or she taking things at face value? Is there a misreading? How did the reader actualize and realize the text?

Only further work in readers' letters, journals, and autobiographies can begin to tell us about their manner of reception. Up until now, we have had only a few broad surveys of Twain's readers. In the early 1930s, Charles Herrick Compton performed in St. Louis perhaps the most well-known of the surveys of readers of Mark Twain. Gathering results from library readers, he asserted, "Mark Twain's books are read because they offer an escape from modern life, our so-called civilization. In letters received from readers this desire for an escape was repeatedly brought out."[7] However, it remains to be asked, which of Twain's books offered these readers "an escape." Surely, later works like *What Is Man?* did not provide Twain's readers any escape from morbid contemplation. Yet, travel books like *The Innocents Abroad* may have provided readers with adventure abroad. Novels like *The Adventures of Huckleberry Finn* may have encouraged a reader's recollection of childhood as he or she followed Huck Finn and Jim on the Mississippi River. We can only begin to know how these readers responded by locating them within their families and communities, by finding them within library records, census records, newspaper accounts, reading groups, and literary societies.

Reading Twain's works was a historically mediated, social activity involving the interaction of readers and his texts. Twain's literary productions emerged from social and cultural forces that included his readers. Readers made meaning in their creative exchanges with Twain's stories. Their activity of reading occurred in social contexts, even when a single reader was being attentive to a single book. By looking to Twain's audience we can contextualize the place of books and periodical literature in peoples' lives. It is clear from the evidence of letters, journals, and the minutes of reading circles that his readers brought a set of experiences to their reading through which Twain's works were interpreted. We may gain insight into the habits and responses of readers to books from their comments about their reading of Twain's books in their letters, diaries, and autobiographies. The object of this study is to begin to investigate the responses of these readers to Twain's writings rather than to explore his texts, his celebrity, or the commercial marketplace per se.

Networks of readers in a specific locale suggest the social nature of reading. By gathering and layering their responses, we build a thick description of a community and its reactions to Mark Twain. In this study, readers and reading circles in Brooklyn, New York, Minneapolis, Minnesota, and Pontiac, Michigan are presented. This attention to local groups follows Roger Chartier's observation that reading occurs in "a specific act and habit, in specific places."[8] As critics from Christine Pawley to Ronald J. Zboray have pointed out, these places include libraries, schools, and reading circles. Through investigating these libraries, schools, and reading circles, we may look at the culture in which people read or shared Twain's works. Literary groups and clubs are noncommercial sites of reader interaction with texts. These are the "networks of kin, friends, and neighbors" that Ronald Zboray and Mary Saracino Zboray have seen in antebellum New England.[9] Through the records of reading circles and clubs, some insight may be gained if we can contextualize these readers' responses within their unique geographical context. Christine Pawley's study of Wisconsin communities and library reading in *Reading Places: Literacy, Democracy and the Public Library in Cold War America* (2010) and William Gilmore's study of Vermont readers, *Reading Becomes a Necessity of Life* (1989), serve as models for this ethnographic inquiry. In looking at the readers of Brooklyn, Minneapolis, Pontiac, and other locales, the goal is to begin to provide layers of thick description that may reveal habits or patterns of Twain appreciation. Among the challenges, however, is to recognize that there are generational cohorts and that the readers of one era may differ from those of another time. Consequently, the responses of western readers and readers in Brooklyn, New York, after 1900 have been separated from those of an earlier period of the 1870s and 1880s.

We must also recognize that literary reviews, booksellers' lists, and library records all give us information on readers and books and the mediating networks in which textual publication and reception occurred. A chapter is devoted to reading in our cultural institutions, schools, libraries, and churches, which were among these mediating networks. The extra-textual aspects of books, from print and paper to covers and illustrations are also important. The transmission of Twain's work included numerous appearances of his short stories or serialized fiction in periodicals. Twain's texts interacted with his audience through a series of social acts across what Robert Darnton has referred to as the communications circuit. Texts passed from publisher to printer to agents and from distributors to the reader.

Twain's books were intended to be sold, bought, and read by his nineteenth-century readers. However, for those readers his books may also have served as décor, paperweights, artifacts, status symbols, or something like furniture. Leah Price has said of the book, "it can serve as a gift, an investment, [...] even an engineering challenge."[10] A book may become a beloved object, like a child's stuffed animal or a boy's first baseball mitt. Nicholas A. Basbanes notes that the artist Maurice Sendak gave "particular prominence" in his Ridgefield, Connecticut, home to a copy of *The Prince and the Pauper* that his sister gave to him as a child. Sendak called the Twain volume "My very first book."[11] He told Basbanes that when his sister Natalie gave him the book, he "absolutely wept with joy" and brought the book to bed at night with him as a loved object. He was fascinated by the material book: its red cloth cover, its endpapers. He was filled with wonder at the book's design.

Others put Twain's works to more practical uses. S. Tillinghast of La Plume, Pennsylvania, used a copy of Twain's *A Tramp Abroad* as a scrapbook to paste items into. Twain's writing was erased beneath Tillinghast's project: glued in a worn copy of the book were clippings, flyers, correspondence, lists, and advertising items, creating a 'travelogue' of the compiler's own interests.[12] As Ellen Gruber Garvey has shown, such scrapbooks were a familiar feature of nineteenth-century life. Meanwhile, hefty subscription volumes of *The Innocents Abroad* and *Roughing It* were a valued possession in rural American homes. As Ronald Jenn has pointed out, some "cultural aspirants" in Victorian America viewed books as "objects and status symbols."[13]

Mark Twain sought a popular audience. He reached readers all across America and abroad through subscription sales and the periodical press, and such popular distribution suited him well. "Every book (Mark Twain) ever wrote, except *The Prince and the Pauper* and *Joan of Arc*, was constructed with its prospective sale as the important condition of its composition" notes Kenneth Andrews. [14] In his letters, Mark Twain often reports to his correspondents how many copies of his books have been sold and how much money he has earned. This suggests that he wrote deliberately to appeal to audiences. Twain's letters further show that he was ever concerned about his box office for his lectures. They reveal that the audience was often present in his awareness. Because his first books were marketed by subscription publishers, they were bound by the manner and exigencies of this form of publishing. These books were large because buyers equated heft with worth. Hamlin Hill observes that the subscription book did not only promote "padding" "[t]hey prompted several of the humorist's most familiar literary devices and techniques."[15] Hill asserts that Mark Twain "could not have been ignorant of the tastes of the special audience to whom subscription books—mid-nineteenth-century American style—made their appeal."[16]

As the *San Francisco Bulletin*, pointed out on March 14, 1885:

> Mark Twain long since learned the art of writing for the market. His recent books have the character of commercial ventures. He probably estimates in advance his profits. His books are not sold to a great extent over the counters of booksellers, but are circulated by subscription agents [...] Those who read "Tom Sawyer" and like it will probably read "Huckleberry Finn," and like it in less degree. No book has been put on the market with more advertising.[17]

Today the literary marketplace continues to be receptive to Mark Twain. In 2010, Mark Twain's *Autobiography*, Volume 1, was a triumphant best-seller. The *New York Times* reported that 275,000 copies had been sold by November 2010 and that the 500,000 word book had gone through six reprints. Volume 2 appeared in 2013. A St. Louis bookstore owner referred to the "attachment" of contemporary readers and "an enduring love affair with Mark Twain, especially around here." In Brooklyn, a bookstore proprietor called the *Autobiography* "the Dad book of the year" and added, "He's surprisingly relevant right now."[18]

On hearing that Mark Twain's autobiography would be sealed for one hundred years, a writer in the *Brooklyn Eagle*, at the turn of the twentieth century, wrote incredulously:

> There is no [likelihood] that the twenty-first century will pay any more attention to him than those of us who are less distinguished now. Civilization along the Congo will by that time have swept away more than a faint memory of the Mississippi Valley, and the antiquarians who consult the histories of Tom Sawyer and Huckleberry Finn in order to reconstruct the life of that distant era will get ideas as funny as any of Clemens's international jokes [...] But the chance that Mark Twain will be a name to conjure with in a hundred years hence is slight, and if Mr. Clemens has any reminiscences up his sleeve he would better play them now. [19]

To the contrary, today Mark Twain continues to be a highly recognizable figure, for children as well as for adults. Many people have read something written by him. Even those who have not read his books recognize his name and the image of a curly haired, mustached man in a white suit. Hal Holbrook's portrayals of Twain have reinforced this image. Mark Twain continues to be vividly present throughout American society. In Missouri, thousands of acres are preserved as the Mark Twain State Forest. In New Jersey, people sit down for a meal at the Mark Twain Diner in Union or at the Tom Sawyer Diner in Paramus. In Elmira, New York, people play golf on the Mark Twain Golf Course. Others attend classes at the Mark Twain School, of which there are some two dozen: from Brooklyn, New York, to Chicago and Kankakee, Illinois, and from Alexandria, Virginia, and Springfield, Missouri, to Los Angeles and San Diego, California. Twain's characters Tom Sawyer and Huckleberry Finn are similarly ubiquitous.

Across the years, Mark Twain's works have been a prime example of the fact that, "readers can read the same book in a variety of ways with important consequences" as Simon Eliot and Jonathan Rose point out. [20] Readers interpret writing and make texts of their own. This is true of Mark Twain's readers, who brought their lives and their concerns to their reading. We can see this in the comments that they have left in their letters, autobiographies, and journals. As Henry Wonham has observed, Mark Twain was quite aware of the community of interpreters and he "expressed his belief that interpretation is essentially a communal affair." [21] Thus, we need to consider the racial, ethnic, regional, and occupational variety of Twain's readers: female and male, black and white, British, American, and Native American. Twain arrived in these people's lives through a variety of mediums: the public lecture, the stage presentation, the film, or the classroom assignment among them. Twain's audience conspicuously provides a wide variety of responses. Books like *The Innocents Abroad* and *The Adventures of Huckleberry Finn* have generated controversy because of Twain's satirical approach to religion in the former book and the ways that race has been read in the latter. Other books, like *The Adventures of Tom Sawyer* and *The Prince and the Pauper,* while often considered children's stories, have been read by people of all ages.

The audience of Mark Twain is the focus of this study. However, any study of the readers of Mark Twain rests upon the shoulders of Twain's numerous biographers and critics. Equally, it relies upon the archivists of the Mark Twain collection at the Bancroft Library at the University of California in Berkeley, who preserve, organize, and maintain the public life of Twain's writings. Much of the twentieth-century critical discussion of Mark Twain proceeded in reaction to Van Wyck Brooks's *The Ordeal of Mark Twain* (1920) or to Bernard De Voto's response in *Mark Twain's America* (1932). As new materials have become available, much has been supplemented to those discussions and many new perspectives have arisen. The most significant of the biographies is Albert Bigelow Paine's *Mark Twain: A Biography* (1912), which was authorized by Samuel Clemens–Mark Twain, whom Paine assisted and with whom Paine briefly lived toward the end of his life. This book is some 2,000 pages long; often dictated by Twain to stenographer Josephine Hobby or to Paine, it is close to the life and the myth of the man. It has served as a basis for biographers and critics ever since. Among the distinguished biographies of Twain are those of Justin Kaplan, *Mr. Clemens and Mark Twain* (1966), a winner of the Pulitzer Prize and National Book Award, and Ron Powers' notable *Mark Twain: A Life* (2005). To this must be added dozens of studies from the past decade or two that fill in for us the final years of the writer's life. This study is indebted to the recent work of R. Kent Rasmussen, who has gathered readers' letters from the Mark Twain collection and has vigorously begun the inquiry into these reader's lives and their appreciation of Twain. This work is also indebted to Twain himself: he is one of the few authors who saved letters from readers.

The curators of the Mark Twain collection at the University of California and those who supervise the Twain memorials in Elmira, Hartford, and Hannibal deserve much thanks for keeping Twain's legacy alive for us. In recent years, critical studies from Shelley Fisher Fishkin, Bruce Michelson, Peter Messent, Ann Ryan, Laura Skandera Trombley, and many others have broadened Twain studies, highlighting issues of race, Twain's distinctive uses of vernacular speech, Twain's relationships with print culture, and his relationships with women. As Andrew Hoffmann has pointed out, each generation deserves a new look at Mark Twain because of its different conceptions of "a remarkable person."[22] However, the goal here is to provide that new look at Mark Twain through the perspectives of people who were Mark Twain's audience. We will look at the impact of Twain's writings upon both nineteenth- and twentieth-century readers. By listening to these readers, as well as to the voice of Mark Twain, it is hoped that we will gain a further glimpse into Twain and his audience, and into a remarkable piece of American cultural history.

The reception of an author's works by common readers provides important indicators of a writer's impact. The social significance of an author is often measured only by critical comment in major periodicals. Wide claims about a writer's popularity are made on the basis of a journal or magazine's book review. A more complete assessment will include the voice of the common reader, when possible. As we look at Twain's reception, Twain's audience may provide us with further insights into the identity of the American people in their process from the Civil War to the turn of the twentieth century. Freedom, justice, democracy, boyhood or girlhood, the American landscape, and the age of machines and American development are reflected in Mark Twain and his readers. We may consider how Twain impacted upon their world. "Mark Twain was an emblem of the United States' rise to prominence" and, as Andrew Hoffman points out, in this process, he changed from a humorist to a distinguished American writer and a social philosopher without losing his audience.[23]

The reading experiences of Twain's contemporaries are available in hundreds of letters to the author, as well as in diary entries, reading circle minutes, and other sources. While Twain's critics and biographers have explored the critical reception of Twain's novels, the investigation of his ordinary readers, the thousands of everyday persons who read and responded to his work, remains an important missing piece. To understand an author's cultural impact, in addition to considering the writer and his works, one must also assess popular reception. The study of common readers was once thought to be beyond retrieval. However, the methodologies developed by historians of the book, from Jonathan Rose, David Vincent, Janice Radway, Kate Flint, to Ronald Zboray and others, have shown that it is increasingly possible to recover the common reader. An investigation into the reception of Mark Twain's texts by his audience can give us valuable insights into nineteenth-century American culture. As Ronald J. Zboray and Mary Saracino Zboray point out, while snippets and terse phrases from nineteenth-century readers cannot tell the whole story, "they do point out some ways that people felt about the books, pamphlets and news items they read."[24] Readers and listeners who were not professional literary critics or editors, but were rather, workers, homemakers, immigrants, former slaves, and business people, as well as writers, clergy, or teachers, were the people who made Mark Twain's books popular. This study attempts to begin to reclaim the forgotten voices of this diverse American audience of Mark Twain.

While there have been many books about Mark Twain, few have looked in any sustained way at his audience. Our fascination with the man and the writer has overshadowed our concern with his readers. Mark Twain left reams of manuscript, letters, and notes and most of this is carefully tended by the curators of the Mark Twain Project (MTP) in Berkeley, California. Critics roaming amid this vast legacy recognize that it is difficult to write about Mark Twain. After all, there was Samuel Clemens the man and there was Mark Twain the writer. One immediately encounters a persona, a construction. There are also apocryphal stories about Mark Twain. Some of them have become folklore. One has to trust that Twain's biographers have, in their various ways, separated fact from fiction. The textual legacy of biographical discourse on Twain includes the deployment of these often repeated stories. An analysis of Twain's audience must include a historical genealogy of the facts, including the context in which these facts were expressed. Twain biographers have given us helpful and often entertaining representations of his life. In some cases, as in the writing of Justin Kaplan and Ron Powers, these are masterful literary works in their own right. Yet, one must tread carefully across the many stories about Twain via the work of a long line of scholars who have studied him in order to understand his work, his audience, and his era.

The method here is to explore Twain's audience through letters, diaries, autobiographies, reading circles and literary societies, library records, newspapers and periodicals, and other personal and public documents. As critics have often pointed out, there are some tensions or differences between an experienced life and a recollected one. The duality of Samuel Clemens/Mark Twain highlights this. When one investigates the accounts of reading left by people in their diaries, journals, letters, or autobiographies, it is necessary to recognize the possible distortions of time and recollection. Whereas a letter or notebook might offer us an immediate response, the autobiography, or oral recollection, may be colored by forgetfulness or rationalizations, or at least by subsequent experience. As Barbara Hochman (2011) has pointed out, "Readers comments always trail behind the reading experience—they are produced when the reading stops."[25] While facts can be assembled and tangible evidence of reader response can be produced, there remains our interpretation of those facts and of these writers' often brief jottings.[26] Interpretation and analysis of these fragmentary writings is a necessary aspect of a study of this nature.

The study of the audience of a popular writer holds a key to our understanding of that author's cultural impact. In 1932, Bernard De Voto asserted that "Since 1869 Mark Twain is more widely read than any other American." Surveys from the 1930s bear out the general accuracy of that comment. In his introduction to *Mark Twain's America*, De Voto approached the question of whether anything more was needed about Mark Twain. He responded with a resounding yes: "it is cried aloud for." That remains the case today, even after landmark books such as DeVoto's study and those of Justin Kaplan, Ron Powers, and others. De Voto wrote in his introduction, in a letter to Robert Forsythe: "Mr. Arthur Schlesinger has suggested that I am writing the social history of Mark Twain, but history aspires to a comprehensiveness I have not attempted."[27] That is likewise true here. This inquiry into Twain's readers is intended as a starting place for further research into Twain's audience.

This is an attempt to approach a familiar literary figure from a less than familiar angle. As Ronald Jenn has pointed out in *Book History*, French translations of Mark Twain's *Tom Sawyer* and *Huckleberry Finn* reflect Meredith McGill's statement that "publishing history is most valuable to literary history when it dislocates its subject—when it redraws the boundary between the literary and what lies outside of it."[28] This is what I intend to do with this study of Twain, who himself redrew literary boundaries. Here the reader, or audience, is placed in the foreground. Most of Mark Twain's readers have left little lasting record of their reading. Some have left only a sparse record of their actions. They attended a Twain lecture. Or, they checked out a Twain book from a library. Others, like Indiana teacher and bookseller Charles Powner, simply "checked out." Powner reportedly died in bed reading Mark Twain. And what are we to make of that?[29]

Mark Twain's readers have left traces. Twain received many letters and those he did not discard remain in the Mark Twain Papers.[30] There one sees that some of Twain's readers wrote about their lives and mentioned their reading. Publicly, Twain commented that it was tiresome to respond to all the letters he received. One reader, who recalled Twain's comment about this, decided to write to him anyway:

> Dear Mark, I don't care if letters are a bore to you either to answer or receive. I've had so much amusement & c. I want to thank you for it and I'm going to do it. Accept then the hearty gratitude of one who feels indebted in a higher degree than his subscription to The Galaxy or purchase of 'The Innocents Abroad' cancels. Sometimes I think the balance between you writers and we readers is most unfair and while you are racking your brains out to amuse us, we in our selfishness swallow it all and also all amusing things that happen to us [...][31]

We know that readers fashioned autobiographies, or kept commonplace books and scrapbooks. They copied passages from the books that they most cherished and they added their observations.[32] This tells us something about their reading. Others have left brief journal entries. Such bits and pieces gathered become something like an epistemological field. One may look at a reading 'community' and ask if there is a pattern in its reception of a prominent writer's work. The variety of these responses further emphasizes the cultural importance of Mark Twain.

Mark Twain is an important figure for us to look at because he was at the center of the post–Civil War publishing industry, both as a writer and a publisher, during the years he dubbed "The Gilded Age." The world of Mark Twain's books is filled with publishers, printers, shippers and distributors, bookstores, subscription book agents, periodical reviewers, and common readers. Those common readers were unique—culturally, occupationally, and in gender, race, ethnicity, and a host of other qualities. They were active participants in the construction of meaning and memory. Critics have recognized this, as they have referred to Twain's community of readers. Here we attempt to enter, with a glimpse, the world of Mark Twain's nineteenth century. Like Twain's Henry Morgan in *A Connecticut Yankee in King Arthur's Court*, we travel in time.

When Samuel Clemens was born, the Missouri town that his family moved to was lit by oil lamps. The antebellum world of his childhood was tended to by small business owners and farmers whose slaves lived in small, wooden houses within blocks of the river. Jacksonian America, while politically independent, still modeled its literature and culture on British writing and culture. By the time he died in 1910, the writer we know as Mark Twain had seen cities rising, America aglow with invention, and a rich literature that had at last found its voice. American literature now reached out to readers across the world. This book addresses how the reception of Mark Twain was partly responsible for the emergence of American literature as a viable world literature and it considers carefully his contact with his contemporaries on the page and on the stage.

We will explore here the reception of an iconic figure that represents America in the late nineteenth century. This study intends to show his significance within that historical moment through Twain's audience and how they experienced his works and his public persona. Indeed, the goal of this research is, through audience reception, to consider the myth of Mark Twain and to show, through his readers, his literary and historical importance to America. Through Mark Twain, a transatlantic author, American literature gained a unique presence in the world with the publication of his book *Innocents Abroad* (1869).[33]

In the first section, attention is given to responses to Mark Twain's first books of travel, *The Innocents Abroad* and *Roughing It*, by his readers of the late 1860s and the 1870s. Twain's first book concerned travel to Europe and the Mid-East, a journey to the ancient world. The second book provided portraits of the American West. *The Innocents Abroad* sold more than 70,000 copies in its first year and many more afterward. *Roughing It*, likewise, had strong sales. We may ask what it was about the concerns and interests of people in this period that made these books so popular. Was there a need for laughter in the years following the Civil War and for books characterized by humor and keen observation? Was vicarious travel attractive to American readers at a time when print, shipping, commerce, and new technologies were opening their thoughts out to the world? Was Twain's satirical and irreverent approach to religion provocative for these readers? Did Twain's books suggest that the new world of America held a brash difference from the old world at a time when there was a renewed assertion of American vitality?

Mark Twain's initial audience in the West is as difficult to uncover as a speck of gold in the high Sierra Nevada hills. However, his beginnings as a writer for newspapers are an important part of his story. It is apparent that *Roughing It* and his vignettes of western life served as models for subsequent writing by others on the American West. Letters increasingly arrived to Twain after the publication of *The Innocents Abroad* and *Roughing It*. We hear comments from miners, ranchers, and of immigrants, whose visions of America were influenced by Twain. Next, we will turn to an examination of the subscription audience for these books and for Twain's first novel, *The Gilded Age*. This audience begins to become visible through the comments of members of the subscription sales force: those people who sold Twain's books door to door in towns and rural communities. The subscription sales ledgers posted by Professor Stephen Railton on his Mark Twain website are examined through census records, local publications, maps, and other archival sources that provide us with some further idea of who the buyers of Twain's books were.[34]

This is a writer who appealed to all ages and the investigation of the audience for Twain's renowned classics of childhood is an important one. *The Adventures of Tom Sawyer*, *The Adventures of Huckleberry Finn*, and *The Prince and the Pauper* have been a part of many children's lives. Not only boys but girls also have been drawn to the books. This raises the difficult question of what happens when a girl reads a boy's book. Responses to *The Adventures of Tom Sawyer* from children include those from boys and those from girls across the years. Educational institutions and public libraries also played a role in advancing or attempting to discourage the dissemination to young readers of Mark Twain's books. We will look at the impact of schools and libraries on Twain's readers.

The following section ranges widely, categorizing Twain's readers by gender, race, and region. The matter of race and reading in African American reading circles has been capably explored by Elizabeth McHenry in *Forgotten Readers: Recovering the Lost History of African American Literary Societies* (2002). Taking its cue from her work, this section includes a look at an African American reading group in Brooklyn. Newspaper accounts of the circle's meetings, meeting minutes, and African American newspaper comments on Twain are presented. The controversial reception of this novel across the years includes its history of being banned for alleged impropriety by the Concord library. Reception of this novel is noted in surveys and in interviews, comments by writers, and accounts of its censorship in educational settings. The novel has been prized by some critics for Twain's use of dialect and vernacular speech. It appears to have been most esteemed by readers for the memories of childhood it evokes.

Twain provided a scathing treatment of medievalism and modernity in his novel *A Connecticut Yankee in King Arthur's Court.* The audience for this novel in America and in England is examined, including the Catholic audience for a novel that held that church to be an archaic bastion of medievalism. Immigrants arriving from Europe could also be identified by their religious affiliations. Their encounters with Mark Twain's books are mentioned here. Issues of regional response are also considered. Early in his career, Mark Twain discovered that he needed to bridge his western and Midwestern audience with the elite audience of the northeast. In exploring these issues of regional response, we begin with responses from women of the Northeast and follow this with a voice from the South that is critical of Twain. Following this is a brief investigation of Mark Twain's audiences who heard him lecture and watched him perform. Considerable work on Twain's lectures has been accomplished by Fred Lorch, Charles Neider, and others. It is possible to begin to see this audience indirectly through newspaper accounts of these lectures. In this chapter, I add something further with a consideration of people in clubs and literary societies in Brooklyn, New York, and their response to humorous Twain stories.

Finally, we come to the global audience for Twain's writings. The transatlantic nature of Twain's work was enhanced by his many visits to England and the European continent. The world lecture tour of 1895 brought his lectures to a global audience. Howard G. Baetzhold has written of Twain's interaction with England and Carl Dolmetsch has explored his time in Vienna. To locate Twain's audience in these places remains a challenge for researchers. This study notes Twain's overseas adventures and follows Twain home to New York, where reading circles were involved with his stories during the years of his absence. Mark Twain's final decade as a highly visible author is the subject of the final section. Twain's last visit to Hannibal, Missouri, his time in New York City, and the breadth of his national and international following is considered. As newspapers worldwide kept images of Twain in front of the public, this was a period in which Twain wrote sharp social criticism and highly imaginative works that did not all reach the public. Archives in Missouri and in New York show his continuing popularity through the twentieth century. Public surveys indicate Mark Twain's developing place in the American literary canon.

This book, while it includes the responses of writers, editors, ministers, and political figures, is intended as a movement toward uncovering Twain's popular audience: his common readers. It is by no means comprehensive. The hundreds of letters to Mark Twain in the Mark Twain collection at the University of California in Berkeley will offer scholars further material to explore. This study considers the social meaning of print, viewing reading as a collective activity that supported values and self-definition. In this endeavor, I have explored archives with specific questions about Twain's audience. For example, we may ask, to what extent can we recover middle-class and working-class readers' responses and did these differ from each other? Did the gender of a reader matter when a female reader read *Tom Sawyer*, or *Huckleberry Finn*? Why was Twain's travel book *The Innocents Abroad* so attractive to the nineteenth-century reader but less so for the twentieth-century reader? It is difficult to arrive at any clear answers to such questions. However, in seeking such answers, it is useful to compare responses of males and females, blacks and whites, immigrants, and people of different classes and occupations. In addition, possible regional variations in the audience of Mark Twain can be explored: his audience in rural areas of the Northeast, the South, and the West.

In Twain's case, a history of his audience cannot be limited to readers alone. Twain's audience includes the viewers and listeners to his public lectures. It also includes people who were read to, or who heard of Twain's characters second-hand. Today, commercial advertisers define an "audience" as a "market" and for Twain, the writer and publisher, his audience was this also. However, within this marketplace there were specific readers and they are our concern here. As the industry of print developed with steam rotary presses, increased transportation, and broadened commerce, Twain's audience grew as a result of technical improvements, education, and a movement toward mass communication. Even as a mass audience was emerging, Twain retained some degree of personal contact with his public. This public consisted of individuals: his largely forgotten common readers, viewers, and listeners.

While Mark Twain has achieved lasting celebrity, his nineteenth-century readers have drifted into anonymity and silence. To return them to our attention, nineteenth-century American reading circles, particularly those of the latter part of the nineteenth century, are explored through each group's records and minutes. I have focused primarily upon reading circles in Brooklyn, New York, which received coverage in local newspapers, and reading circles in Michigan, whose records are available through the Making of America online resource provided by the University of Michigan. Papers from the Mark Twain Project (MTP), Bancroft Library, University of California, Berkeley, have been consulted. Many of the selections compiled by R. Kent Rasmussen in *Dear Mark Twain* (University of California Press, 2013) have been repeated here and they can be read in their entirety in his fine book. The collections of the New York Public Library and the New York Historical Society special collections have been explored for autobiographies and other relevant texts. Likewise, I have consulted the New York Society Library's circulation records and catalogues of several other nineteenth-century libraries. The library archives in other regions of the United States have also been examined. Historical societies' records of reading circles have been obtained by correspondence. Publishers' records at the Princeton University Library and

Columbia University Library (Harpers), as well as useful sources at the Morgan Library (Miscellaneous American collection) and Cornell University Library have also been considered. Online autobiographies, letters, and books from the University of North Carolina, and the University of Michigan and Cornell University Making of America collection have been useful. In these collections are autobiographies, letters, or other materials in which individuals in Twain's audience mention the author or his texts. Creative writers, book- and sermon-writing ministers, educators, reporters, and people who recorded meeting Twain are among the writers of these texts. Newspaper accounts of Twain's public lectures in various American cities have been examined to locate audience members' recollections.

Mark Twain's readers display a great diversity in their responses to him and his writings. Correspondents who wrote to Twain told him that they identified with him, or that he had helped them in their lives. Others sought advice on writing and they sought his autograph. Some readers, like Jacob E. Hemmell of Baltimore, told Twain that they felt a bond with him. In February 1882, he wrote:

> Permit me, an admirer of yours and a scribbler at times to address you in a friendly way for I feel I am an intimate and long acquaintance of yours. My addressing you is to satisfy a long pent-up desire that has been filling my bosom for months— nay—years.
>
> I have read with the keenest pleasure all the books that you have written and published, I believe, and have just finished your last— "The Tramp Abroad" and was extremely edified.

The letter writer soon betrays a lack of knowledge about the Clemens family and the son of Olivia and Samuel Clemens, who died as an infant. He refers to Olivia Clemens as "Mrs. Mark": "Dear Mark, I love you dearly and want you to write me an autograph, only let me know how Mrs. Mark and all the little Marks and Markesses are getting along."[35]

Some of Twain's readers discovered a keen eye for description and sure sense of reality in his work. The poet James Whitcomb Riley, for example, heard Twain's careful attention to sound and dialect in his writing. He commended Mark Twain in a letter from Indianapolis on February 25, 1885:

> Dear Sir: Your sketches in which real characters and their varied dialects occur have interested and delighted me for many years and in thanking you, as I want to now, I ask you to accept as well the little book of Hoosier dialect I mail with this."[36]

Some envisioned the practical effects of Twain's books upon American society. In January 1890, Twain's chapter in *A Connecticut Yankee in King Arthur's Court* titled "Political Economy" caught John Richards' concern with social issues. The chapter contrasts free trade with the medieval "protection system" of the lords and their serfs. Richards's reading was clearly connected with his personal interests with protective tariffs and American industry. He wrote:

> Pardon the privilege a stranger takes in writing. I have just been "reveling" in your inimitable "King Arthur" and on reaching the 33rd chapter bethought me of how you could, more than a thousand others with philosophy, alter our financial policy with, Satire, or humour. [37]

Other readers of Twain's works insisted on distinguishing fact from fiction. Charles W. Rhodes, a cheese merchant in New York City, wrote on December 13, 1880:

> I have read "Roughing It" "Innocents Abroad" "Gilded Age" "Scetches Old and New" and am just finishing "Tramp Abroad" What I want to know is by what rule a fellow can infallibly judge when you are lying and when you are telling the truth. I write this in case you intend to afflict an innocent and unoffending public with any more such works. I would suggest the next volume be published with the truth printed in italics. They usually have small fonts of these in printing offices. [38]

Readers who wrote to Twain sometimes spoke of how helpful his books had been to them personally. Frank L. Eaton wrote on January 3, 1903, from Ypsilanti, Michigan:

> I have just finished reading that portion of your Life on the Mississippi describing your crossing that Island 66. Each time I read this, I gather greater force from the lesson, which it teaches, of the value of unshaken confidence in what one knows.
>
> I have been the proud possessor of a set of your works for more than a year, and I think that the lesson to be learned from that one particular chapter is worth the full value of the books, and I know of nothing that I have read in recent years, which has done me as much good, or has been as helpful to me at various times, as that particular instance. I have, therefore, taken the liberty of writing you and tell you how much I appreciate it, and of my earnest wish that the youth of the entire land might read the story and grasp its full meaning. [39]

Perhaps even more poignant were letters from readers who said that Twain's writings provided healing in their lives. Emerson O. Stevens, a fifteen year old writing from Cleveland May 5, 1881, insisted that reading Twain's work was healing and renewing. He struggled with paralysis as a teenager and later became a teacher of English:

> Perhaps you will excuse me for writing to you, when I tell you that for the last three years, although unknown to yourself, you have been one of my physicians. A physician ought not take offense at hearing from one of his patients.
>
> For the last three years I have been confined to the house with paralysis of the lower limbs, nearly two years of the time having been unable to walk. Now that I am somewhat better, I wish to thank you for the pleasure which your writings have given me. I firmly believe that

the good solid laughs I have had over them, have done me more good than all the medicine I have taken. And if it be a comfort to know that you have helped a boy pass three dreary years of illness, may that comfort be yours.[40]

Likewise, from Baltimore, "Benj Ochiltree," on October 17, 1906, wrote:

I want to thank you for the pleasure your books have given me during many years of confinement in my room. Life would frequently have been dull indeed had it not been for the companionship of Huck Finn, Col. Sellers, et. al. When I get to Hell the greatest torture that I will have be the possible knowledge that you shall have written something else I shall not be permitted to read.[41]

The restorative effects of Twain's books were mentioned by Dr. Andrew Brown, who had been a resident of Hannibal and wrote to Twain on June 7, 1909:

When you kindly permitted me to call on you about a year ago, merely because I happened to be a native of Hannibal, you did not allow me to thank you as I wanted to, for the great amount of good your books have given me from the time you wrote the first one. . . . Really tho, in giving you thanks, I did not want to claim the small distinction of having been a boy in Hannibal. I was a poet too (albeit a dumb one) for I remember at the age of fourteen (thirty five years ago) discoursing to the effect your books had the power to lift me from any depth of melancholy and that they helped me to be good because they showed that to be good was sensible."[42]

The 'moral' impact of Twain's books on Brown may be seen in contrast with the ban that the Concord Library placed on his work. Brown's father had started a drug store with money he made in the California Gold Rush, Rasmussen tells us. After working in his father's store as a clerk, he trained in allopathic medicine and became a surgeon in Birmingham, Alabama.

Similarly, on November 14, 1906, Dr. A. J. Williams wrote to Twain:

I am an admirer of you, and as this admiration is cumulative it has at last got beyond my control, and I am obliged to resort to that solace of all affectionately perturbed spirits, a letter. . . . And while my pen is wet, I will, in a professional way, express my gratitude for that quiet humor which has done more good in the world than all the doctors physic. Please keep on making people laugh.[43]

A doctor from Ohio, George W. Galloway wrote Twain that *The Adventures of Tom Sawyer* was responsible for his marriage. He married Flora M. Schneider of Akron, Ohio, his second wife, sometime after reading the novel aloud with her.

While confined to my room the result of a runaway accident a year ago, a young lady the granddaughter of the proprietor of the hotel, brought me your work, Tom Sawyer, to read. I read it aloud to her. it took us an awful long time to read it and- well, we are married now, & she thinks we ought to have a nicely bound copy of it on our table, as it was indirectly responsible for our marriage. not knowing where to procure it, I thought I would ask you to tell me. Hoping that you will pardon me for troubling you.[44]

These examples and many others show how Mark Twain and his texts have been interpreted and used in various ways by his readers. The variety in reading texts that has been observed by reader-response critics is certainly in evidence here. Twain has been interpreted by critics, by publishers, by newspaper reporters, periodical writers, speaker's bureaus, and advertisers, and in a variety of social settings like readers' circles and classrooms. His characters have appeared in films, television, anthologies, stage plays, radio plays, and comic books. Huck Finn and Tom Sawyer now live in a world of the Internet and e-books, on websites, e-mail, podcast, hypertext, and recorded books. One can surely write of Mark Twain and American culture with the same sense of this individual's literary importance as Marjorie Garber has seen in Shakespeare's continuing relevance, in *Shakespeare and Culture* (2008). Twain is an enduring presence among us.

The making of Mark Twain's audience has much to do with the making of American literature following the Civil War. Twain used the vernacular speech of Midwesterners, African Americans, and Western miners and he offered distinctly American stories and scenes to a global public. The goal of this study is to provide a look at Mark Twain's audience through the perspectives of people who have read his work, those who have attended his lectures, or people who have simply been entranced by his public persona. By listening to Mark Twain's audience, we may gain a glimpse into their lives as readers and into a remarkable period in American cultural history.

NOTES

1. Robert Darnton, *The Case for Books: Past, Present, Future*, New York: Perseus, 2006. p. 206. Darnton has provided a model for considering how books are produced, distributed, and circulated through society. See Darnton 2006, p. 10. He also discusses the communications circuit in *The Kiss of Lamourette: Reflections in Cultural History*, New York: W. W. Norton, 1991, rpt. 1996. pp. 65–83. Following the work of Jonathan Rose, I make use of the term "audiences," which includes readers and those who listened to books read to them, or who heard lectures or saw theatrical versions. An audience is here defined as the listeners to Twain's lectures, as well as his readers of all ages, across class, gender, race, ethnicity, region, and occupation.

2. Mark Twain, Letter to Orion Clemens, October 19–20, 1865, *Collected Letters of Mark Twain*, Vol. 1, pp. 6–7.

3. Twain's comment to Andrew Lang is noted by Frederick Anderson in *Mark Twain: The Critical Heritage*, London: Routledge, 1971, p. 15. His comments on February 15, 1887, also appear in A.B. Paine's biography of Mark Twain, Vol. 1, Part 1.

4. See Martyn Lyons and Jay Arnold, *History of the Book in Australia, 1891–1948: Toward a National Culture in a Colonized Market*. St. Lucia: University of Queensland Press, 2001, xvi. James L. Machor observes a "lack of sustained inquiry into the experience of reading as a historically grounded dynamic." See Machor, "Fiction and Informed Reading in Early Nineteenth-Century America," *Nineteenth-Century Literature* 47 (1992): 320–48. This inquiry attempts to begin to excavate the historical meaning embodied in letters, diaries, journals, reviews, advertisements, and other sources.

5. Readers' letters to Mark Twain have been preserved by the Mark Twain Project (MTP), Bancroft Library, at the University of California in Berkeley. Several of these letters have been collected by R. Kent Rasmussen in *Dear Mark Twain: Letters from His Readers* (2013). This is an important source for seeking Twain's audience, which I have utilized here.

6. Stephen Railton points to this challenge on his useful website Mark Twain and His Times. Reader response critics observe that readers make meaning. See authors like Louise Rosenblatt, Wolfgang Iser, and Stanley Fish for more on reader response criticism. Wolfgang Iser speaks of "the response-inviting structures of the text" (*Prospecting*, p. 50).

7. Charles Compton, *Essays on the Readers of Mark Twain, Hardy, Sandburg, Shaw, William James, Greek Classics*. New York: H.W. Wilson, 1934. Compton's library study was one of the most significant investigations of Mark Twain readers.

8. Ronald J. Zboray and Mary Saracino Zboray, "'Have You Read . . . ?' Real Readers and Their Responses in Antebellum Boston and Its Region," *Nineteenth-Century Literature*, Vol. 52, No. 2 (September 1997): 139–170. See also, xiii.

9. Roger Chartier in Guglielmo Cavallo and Roger Chartier, eds. *A History of Reading in the West*, trans. Lydia G. Cochrane. Cambridge: Polity, 1995.

10. Leah Price, "Reading: The State of the Discipline," *Book History* 7 (2004): 305.

11. Maurice Sendak is quoted in Nicholas Basbanes, *A Splendor of Letters*, New York: Harper, 2003, p. 234.

12. S. Tillinghast Scrapbook, University of California, Santa Barbara Archives, SC 843. Ellen Gruber Garvey, in *Writing with Scissors* (Oxford 2012), has offered a study of nineteenth-century scrapbooks. Her second chapter focuses upon public response to Mark Twain's self-pasting scrapbook.

13. Ronald Jenn, "From American Frontier to European Borders: Publishing French Translations of Mark Twain's Novels *Tom Sawyer* and *Huckleberry Finn* (1884-1965)," *Book History*, Vol. 9 (2006): 243.

14. Kenneth Andrews is quoted in Hamlin Hill, "Mark Twain's Audience and Artistry," *American Quarterly*, Vol. 15, No. 1 (Spring 1963): 25.

15. Hamlin Hill, "Mark Twain: Audience and Artistry," *American Quarterly*. Vol. 15, No. 1 (Spring 1963): 25–40, p. 25.

16. Hamlin Hill, Ibid, p. 25.

17. *San Francisco Bulletin* (March 14, 1881): 1, (CR 269).

18. *New York Times* (November 20, 2010): C1.

19. *Brooklyn Eagle* (May 29, 1899): 4.

20. Simon Eliot and Jonathan Rose, *A Companion to the History of the Book*, Malden, MA: Blackwell, 2007. p. 1.

21. Henry Wonham, *Mark Twain and the Art of the Tall Tale*. Oxford University Press, 1993. p. 15.

22. Andrew Hoffmann, *Inventing Mark Twain*, New York: William Morrow, 1997, xiii.

23. Andrew Hoffmann points this out in *Inventing Mark Twain*, xvii. See also Louis J. Budd, *Our Mark Twain: The Making of His Public Personality*, Philadelphia: University of Pennsylvania Press, 1983. p. 243.

24. Ronald J. Zboray and Mary Saracino Zboray, "'Have You Read . . . ?' Real Readers and Their Responses in Antebellum Boston and Its Region," *Nineteenth-Century Literature*, Vol. 52, No. 2 (September 1997) 139–170. p. 142.

25. Barbara Hochman, *Uncle Tom's Cabin and the Reading Revolution*. Amherst: University of Massachusetts Press, 2011. p. 6.

26. A reception study has to balance interpretation and presentation. My objective here is to allow the reader reactions that are being presented to largely speak for themselves.

27. Bernard De Voto, *Mark Twain's America*, Boston: Little Brown, 1932. ix.

28. Ronald Jenn quotes Meredith Mc Gill in "From American Frontier to European Borders," *Book History*, Vol. 9 (2006): 235–260.

29. Marvin Mondlin and Roy Meador, *Book Row: An Anecdotal History of the Antiquarian Book Trade*. New York: Carroll and Graf, 2004. p. 41.

30. There are letters that Twain did discard, which are lost to us. One may ask if those that have been retained tend to support a particular image of Twain and whether discarded letters might disrupt this image. Twain cultivated his public persona and, following his death, Twain's daughter Clara Clemens and his literary executor Albert Bigelow Paine sought to preserve a positive public image of Twain.

31. Letter from Anonymous Reader to Mark Twain, MTP, University of California.

32. For a fine study of readers' uses of scrapbooks see Ellen Gruber Garvey, *Writing with Scissors*, Oxford University Press, 2012.

33. Meredith McGill, *American Literature and the Culture of Reprinting, 1834–1853*. University of Pennsylvania Press, 2004, Robert Weisbuch, *Atlantic Double-Cross: American Literature and British Influence in the Age of Emerson*. Chicago: University of Chicago Press, 1986, Larzar Ziff, *Return Passages, Great American Travel Writing, 1780–1910*. New Haven: Yale University Press, 2001.

34. "Mark Twain and His Times" is maintained by the University of Virginia. See htt://twain.lib.virginia.edu/marketin/mrkthp.html.

35. Jacob Hemmel, Letter to Mark Twain. Baltimore, Maryland, 1882. MTP, University of California. See R. Kent Rasmussen, *Dear Mark Twain*, University of California Press, 2013, p. 84.

36. James Whitcomb Riley, Letter to Mark Twain. February 22, 1885. MTP, University of California. See Rasmussen, 110.

37. John Richards, Letter to Mark Twain, January 12, 1890. Rasmussen, 145–146.

38. Charles Rhodes, Letter to Mark Twain, December 13, 1880. MTP, University of California.

39. Frank L. Eaton, Letter to Mark Twain, January 13, 1903. Rasmussen, 208. Rasmussen notes that it has been difficult to locate this attorney in the Yypsilanti city directory for 1903.

40. Emerson O. Stevens, Cleveland, Letter to Mark Twain, May 5, 1881. MTP, University of California.

41. Benjamin Ochiltree, Baltimore, Letter to Mark Twain, October 17, 1906. MTP, University of California. R. Kent Rasmussen, who has made efforts to locate letter writers, comments that this letter writer has not been found. He has located a Benj Ochiltre in the Bronx, who was an agent for the American Refrigerator Transit Company. However, no person by that name appears in the Baltimore directory.

42. Andrew Brown, Letter to Mark Twain, June 7, 1909. MTP, University of California. See Rasmussen, 265–266.

43. A.J. Williams, Letter to Mark Twain. November 14, 1909. MTP, University of California. See Rasmussen, 121.

44. George W. Galloway. Letter to Mark Twain. March 24, 1885. MTP, University of California. See Rasmussen, 111.

TWO

The Innocents Abroad and the American Reader

Mark Twain's nineteenth-century audience was built by his books of travel. Audiences were invited to make imaginative journeys to far-off places—the Sandwich Islands (which we now call Hawaii), the storied American West, and the fabled deserts of the Holy Land. They were welcomed to make travels in time to the medieval realms of *The Prince and the Pauper* and *A Connecticut Yankee in King Arthur's Court*. They went on these imaginative journeys laughing, sometime uproariously. For each visit to these places was filled with Mark Twain's humor and his keen eye for social parody. This audience knew Twain as a humorist and began to develop a friendly acquaintance with his writings. As Barbara Hochman has pointed out, the nineteenth-century reader was engaged in "friendly" reading relations, in which readers found a connection with authors.[1] The book was a reader's friend and readers before the 1880s could feel that they were engaged in a conversation with the writer. The evidence, from the letters of readers to Mark Twain, suggests that they felt a familiar bond with the author and that these readers were looking for not only humor but something more. Free from the turmoil of the Civil War, America was turning outward to the world. An audience whose lives were permeated by religion could laugh at Mark Twain's jests about it. They could enjoy his unique observations of the old world while sensing the promise of the new era that was beginning to emerge.

A. *THE INNOCENTS ABROAD*

The Innocents Abroad was the most popular travel book of its time. Mark Twain, the book's author, was, in the broadest sense, a "travel writer."

23

With *The Innocents Abroad,* a travelogue of Europe and the Mid-East, Twain's readers traveled imaginatively with him. Their America was on the move after the Civil War toward commercial growth, westward expansion, and frontier dreams. These nineteenth-century readers most frequently identified Mark Twain as a humorist and as a travel writer who complemented their search for new horizons. With *The Innocents Abroad,* Mark Twain connected with a trend in American culture. The time was ripe for travel books. There was an audience for them who craved journeys to far off places, although many would never leave their armchairs. Twain's book appeared in a period in which there was, as Harold H. Hellwig observes, "nostalgia about a disappearing frontier perspective, a growing concern about the assimilation of native cultures [...]" and a search for "stable moral beliefs."[2] Twain's method in *Innocents Abroad* was to contrast old world European culture with "new world" Americans. That "new world" grew in political and economic power throughout the gilded age, gaining what Jeffrey Alan Melton has called "increasing muscularity."[3] It was also filled with thousands of new readers and a growing publishing industry that responded to them.

First year sales of *The Innocents Abroad* have been estimated at 70,000 copies. This figure was only exceeded by the earlier sales figures for *Uncle Tom's Cabin,* the bestselling book of the century. Within a decade of its first printing, Twain's book had sold more than 125,000 copies.[4] The book received generally favorable reviews and it made readers laugh. As one reader wrote, "Marco Polo, Mark Twain, and all the other great travelers of the world love to tell tall ones once in a while"[5] This reader's comment reflects both Twain's reputation as a humorist and the notion of travel and discovery.

Other readers responded quite personally to the book. Six or so years after the book's publication, a letter to Twain from an Alabama woman, Louise Rutherford, indicates that she is quite familiar with *The Innocents Abroad* and that Twain's book has become a matter of discussion in her family. On November 21, 1875, Rutherford wrote to Twain about her attempts to get a book of her own published. Why, she wondered, had Twain succeeded with his book?

> My cousin Willie (I live with him and his wife) says it is because your writings are sensible; which is a polite and delicate way he has of expressing his opinion of my own. He paid me a dubious compliment the other day. I happened to quote you on something we were discussing; and he said I was the only woman he knew who had sense enough to appreciate Mark Twain.[6]

Louise Rutherford's cousin Willie applies criteria ("sensible") that she may or may not have agreed with. She seems able to absorb Willie's disparagement of female readers and her book, while regarding Willie's comment on the merits of her reading of Twain. However, one might regard Willie as suppressing her view, in the solicitous and heavy-handed manner of the narrator's husband in Charlotte Perkins Gilman's *The Yellow Wallpaper*. Rutherford is clearly ambitious to write and Willie seems to be calling her efforts not "sensible," while claiming that her reading of Twain was, to the contrary, a sensible use of her time. This woman is curious and perhaps romantically oriented. She proceeds to ask Twain about the current state of affairs of the men he traveled to the Holy Land with:

> Where are Dan and Jack? Are they married? If not, I will send them a valentine if you will tell me where and how to direct, and keep the secret. I don't want to get up a flirtation. I am not sweet sixteen. I am practical twenty-six; but I like a little innocent fun; and a valentine from this far away place would puzzle them. Moreover, I am sorry for Dan; he is so awful ugly; and there is a bond of sympathy between Jack and I, on account of that turtle. I found him a fraud too. . . .[7]

Twain's characters were often memorable and they prompted thoughts of "a little innocent fun." Yet, even as his humor entertained readers, his burlesque, Bruce Michelson points out, "has its roots in indignation." Throughout his career, Mark Twain was a social critic. In Michelson's view, *The Innocents Abroad* moved readers "toward laughter arising from recognition of the absurdity of the world."[8] Today, we do not read Twain in the same context as his contemporaries read him. We may wonder just how they did read *The Innocents Abroad*. Did those readers want to take an imaginative voyage by reading Twain's account? Did they become curious about the book because their friends, family, or co-workers talked about it? Were these travelers, or the readers that read this story of travel, concerned with national assertion and America's place in the world? Did they merely want to laugh? Is the appeal of *Innocents Abroad* its opportunity for imaginative play, or for tourism as play? What are we to make of this voyage that was promoted as a religious pilgrimage but appears to have been essentially tourism? The records of their responses, while brief, may provide us with some answers to these questions.

B. THE *QUAKER CITY* VOYAGE

Mark Twain's manuscript for *The Innocents Abroad* arose from a deal he had made with the *Alta California*, a newspaper in San Francisco, and with the *New York Tribune* for letters about his trip to the Holy Land, Egypt, and Greece. This was the first group voyage of American travelers to the Mideast and the newspapers thought their readers would be interested. It would also be a momentous trip for Twain. From it would come not only his first book, but also his first look at the image of his future wife. In Smyrna he saw the face of Olivia Langdon, the sister of one of the passengers, Charley Langdon. He wrote, "I saw her in the form of an ivory miniature in her brother Charley's stateroom in the steamer *Quaker City* in the bay of Smyrna, in the summer of 1867, when she was in her twenty-second year." [9]

The trip was the inspiration of Henry Ward Beecher, the renowned pastor of the Plymouth Church in Brooklyn. Beecher, the brother of Harriet Beecher Stowe, had arranged with his congregation for a pilgrimage to the Holy Land. Indeed, Beecher himself had arranged for some famous personages, like General William Tecumseh Sherman, to join him on the voyage. However, that passenger list quickly changed. Beecher declined from going on the trip and so did many in his congregation and soon about the only famous—or infamous—name signed up on the register for the voyage was "Mark Twain." Arriving at the shipping office with his friend Edward House, he had introduced himself to Captain Duncan of the *Quaker City* as the Reverend Mark Twain. [10]

Twain boarded the *Quaker City* on June 9, 1867, with Charley Langdon and about seventy-five other passengers. His account of their journey would become less a travelogue than a comedy. The passengers on this voyage represented a new American middle class and upper middle class. Whereas the excursion had been heavily advertised in Henry Ward Beecher's Plymouth Church in Brooklyn, most of that congregation bowed out when Beecher himself was unable to go. Instead, the passenger list became largely filled with hardworking Midwestern evangelicals. Twain wrote, "I basked in the happiness of being for once in my life drifting with the tide of a great popular movement." [11] In his view, these passengers, who he dubbed the "American Vandal" lacked in cultivation and refinement. It appears that the parochialism of many of the ship's passengers bothered him. So he satirized his fellow travelers.

Twain's audience appears to have sensed how his book highlighted the "American" difference from old world Europe. The tension between "new world" and "old world" that is present in *The Innocents Abroad* and in 1870s American culture is suggested in the comments of some of his readers. Mrs. Mary B. Ingham writes of a statement by a traveler from Cleveland on the *Quaker City*. That traveler claimed that a member of the Russian royal family found meeting with the visitors from America rewarding: "Whenever I meet an American I meet a brother," the Russian noble said. [12] There may be a suggestion here of some correspondence between visiting Americans and the old world of the czars. However, the old world fell under the scathing satire of Twain. Of the art of the great masters, he wrote that he would not pay a dime for their art. A recollection of Twain's jibes at old world art is clearly in evidence in 1873, as Penina Williams writes in *Appleton's Journal*:

> As to pleasure! O, Mr. Editor, my life is a burden to me because of pictures and statues! Thank Heaven we in this country are spared from

much infliction of the old masters (vide Wilkie Collins *Miscellanies* and
Mark Twain *Innocents Abroad* for particulars concerning the affliction).
But I, being a commonplace person [...] (prefer) food and good eat-
ing.[13]

As Mrs. Williams pursued gustatory delights, other American readers
were looking out at the world. American travelers and explorers are portrayed as sensible Americans in *Ladies' Repository* in 1875. Stanley's writing of missionaries in Africa and Twain's writing in *The Innocents Abroad*
is cited: "Stanley—like Mark Twain, whose 'Innocents Abroad' is one of
the best books of travel extant, notwithstanding its broad waggery—
wields a most sensible American pen."[14] We can see travel and discovery
linked in this comment. Twain and travel was also on the mind of Benjamin Franklin Taylor in *The World on Wheels* (1874):

> A man needs about as many resources on a long railway journey as
> Robinson Crusoe needed on that island of his. He wants a man Friday
> of some sort. If, like Mark Twain's Holy Land mud-turtles, he cannot
> sing himself, he must know how to make others sing.[15]

The very title of Taylor's work suggests mobility, even as his comment
recalls the outward expansion in Daniel Defoe's novel of travel and discovery, *Robinson Crusoe*. Taylor recognizes the necessity of human community, "a man Friday of some sort," even if the people who comprise
this community are less than ideal companions, as were Twain's fellow
passengers.

Other Americans positioned their American distinctiveness against
old world forms and the European landscape. A kind of American "one-
upmanship" appears in a book by Samuel Kneeland, who recalls that
Innocents Abroad pointed to the landscape of America as well as that of
Europe. For Kneeland, Twain provided an ideal description of Lake Ta-
hoe that suggested that the beauty of America's landscape superseded
even the magnificent sights of the European continent. "[T]his is the lake
that Mark Twain extols above the Italian lakes in 'Innocents Abroad,' to
which admirable burlesque the reader is referred for fuller description."[16] Reader observations like this bring out the contrast between the
"old world" of Europe and upstart culture of America that Twain presented in his book. After the all-consuming turbulence of the Civil War,
increasing numbers of Americans had begun looking outward to the
world. With reference to food, landscape, and culture, they insisted upon
drawing clearly their distinct difference from Europe and cherishing the
unique beauty of the American continent.

These American readers were told of a journey that began when the
Quaker City sailed out of New York harbor in June 1867. On board the
ship, Twain, who smoked, played cards, and drank with the men in
Room #10, appeared scandalous to the more abstemious, religiously austere passengers. Twain's critique of the pilgrims is at the center of his

book. He distinguishes the passengers by calling them the "saints" and the "sinners." The "pilgrims" are acquisitive tourists who grab after souvenirs. Mary Magdalene's house is among the locations that are victimized. Arriving at Bethel, "The pilgrims took down portions of the front wall for specimens as is their honored custom" (*The Innocents Abroad* [TIA] 234). "The pilgrims took what was left of the hallowed ruin" of Jacob's pillows (TIA 264). From the Plain of the Shepherd near Bethlehem "the pilgrims took some of the stone wall and hurried on" (TIA 300). At the Church of the Holy Sepulchre, they are "out of luck" because they cannot procure "any collections worth having"[17] Twain took secular notes rather than holy objects. *The Innocents Abroad* was built from journal entries and newspaper dispatches. Twain provided his readers with vicarious travel and described for them the "old world." Readers could imaginatively join the voyage, disembark at Beirut, and imaginatively spend almost a month in Palestine. They also could have a good laugh.

Mark Twain's narrative in *The Innocents Abroad* is characterized by humorous anecdotes, flippant satire, and informative passages. Readers become acquainted with a narrator who has "assumed the well-defined identity of the genteel tourist," as Henry Nash Smith points out. Twain's use of newspaper dispatches likely influenced his narrative voice to sound much like them. This narrator, says Smith, "resorts to comic deflation"[18] For example, Twain writes that Leonardo da Vinci's *The Last Supper* was "a perfect old nightmare of a picture." He wouldn't pay forty dollars for a million like it. He observes that, judging by the prices for a tourist to go sailing on the Sea of Galilee it is no wonder that Jesus walked.

Twain knew that the old world was an important topic for his audience. He set out to record his own reactions to it. Henry Nash Smith has concluded that Twain felt a need to protect himself "against the crushing weight of history." He was impatient with conventional attitudes toward these places, objects, and artworks. In *The Innocents Abroad*, the narrator's telling has "the implication that the history is but a burden to be cast off by the man of the new world."[19] Yet, he realized that scriptural history had to be recognized, so he later added revisions in a section about the Sphinx and descriptions of Galilee. Nineteenth-century readers, living in a generally religious and nonsecular society, were partial to such descriptions.

Twain opened the imaginations of his readers to the American innocent's pilgrimage to the old world. The "American Adam," was encountering the past while trying to escape from it. The actuality of the Holy Land was dry, parched desert and hardly romantic. Even so, the Biblical past and the European past meant a good deal to Mark Twain's audience. He would seek through history in his other travel journals, and in *The Prince and the Pauper, A Connecticut Yankee in King Arthur's Court*, and *Joan of Arc*. Twain appears to have seen that in modern America's contact with the "old world" American ingenuity and uniqueness could arise. Twain echoes, as Justin Kaplan recognizes, "Emerson's call for Americans to cease listening to the Muses of Europe and "speak their own minds, make their own past."[20] We hear the assertions of his narrator:

> You cannot think in this place any more than you can in any other in Palestine that would be likely to inspire reflection. Beggars, cripples, and greasy monks compass you about, and make you think only of the bucksheeth when you would rather think of something more in keeping with the character of the spot. . . . I have no "meditations" suggested by this spot where the very first "Merry Christmas!" was uttered to all the world, and from whence the friend of my childhood, Santa Claus, departed on his first journey to gladden and continue to gladden roaring firesides on wintry mornings in many a distant land forever and forever. I touch, with reverent finger, the actual spot where the infant Jesus lay, but I think- nothing.

In his text, Mark Twain develops the idea of the historical sublime, as Henry Nash Smith has pointed out.[21] However, like the stand-up comic, he practices bathos: the absurd drop from the sublime to the ridiculous. He tells stories laced with impatience for old world art and mannerisms. In Venice, the gondolier's singing is annoying and he threatens to throw the man overboard. In Florence, he writes: "we tried indolently to recollect something about the Guelphs and the Ghibellines and other historical cut-throats [...]"[22] Contemporaries laughed, or grumbled at his irreverence.

Modern readers may see in *The Innocents Abroad* Twain's objections to the ways that conformity may stifle human freedom. It is clear that he did not care for the evangelical tendency to take facts to demonstrate Biblical prophecies. In his critique, the pilgrims' "cult of pious respectability" was revealed as self-centered. Counter to them were "the sinners": Twain and his compeers in Room #10, who refused to buy into any of it. Their contact with each other was more like that of members of a secret community. This social dichotomy reappears in *Huckleberry Finn*, in which Huck and Jim are community and the "respectable" and "Christian" feuding families are satirized.

Readers appear to have focused on the humor in *Innocents Abroad*, not on its structure or shifts in voice and point of view. One reader saw the book as therapeutic: it brought healing laughter. In the edited manuscript of Susy Clemens's journal we read this person's letter from Virginia:

> Soon after the war, a dear friend in Baltimore sent me a copy of Mark Twain's "Innocents Abroad," it was the first copy that reached the valley, possibly the first in Virginia. All of our household read it. I lent it to our friends, and at length nearly everybody in the village had read it. The book was so much enjoyed by people who were sick or sad, that it came to be considered a remedy for all cases where it could be taken,

and we sent it about to people, who as the prayer book says were
troubled in mind, body, or estate.... [23]

In Twain's book, realism clashed with ideality. The book was irreverent toward Europe, or sentimental versions of the continent's treasures,
and some readers evidently liked that. Twain wrote to Elijah Bliss: "The
irreverence of the volume appears to be a tip-top good feature of it." [24]

The *Syracuse Standard* defended Twain's approach to Jerusalem:

> If we had written such a book as "The Innocents Abroad" we would
> consider it the highest praise if we were told that we were not a bit
> reverent in it. Other travelers have been reverent- reverent over old
> traditions in which they could not possibly have had the slightest inter-
> est [....] And thus the book becomes a transcript of our own senti-
> ments. [25]

It is doubtful that this one review shows "strong and widely shared
feelings" in Twain's audience, as Henry Nash Smith claims. Yet, it seems
logical that American readers did wish to assert the prospects of their
own country and its institutions.

Twain "contrasted the dreamlike unreality of the European past with
the American workaday world of technology and progress," observes
Smith. "This pattern of ideas was so familiar in the United States and was
connected with an aggressive nationalism." This view holds that the
American audience was less concerned with ideas than it was concerned
with pragmatic technological progress. This perspective was supported
by the "ideology of republicanism," which is connected with American
nationalism. In calling his character the American vandal, Twain presented an image that includes the democratic "image of the self-educated
average man against a cultivated elite." [26] Comments from Penina
Williams and Benjamin Franklin Taylor, as we have seen, appear to echo
this attitude. In the *New York Herald*, Twain's missive read: "We always
took care to make it understood that we were Americans- Americans!"
He writes in the same passage: "The people stared at us everywhere, and
we stared at them. We generously made them feel rather small, too, before we got done with them, because we bore down on them with America's greatness until we crushed them." [27]

Reader interest in *The Innocents Abroad* continued into the first decade
of the next century, as we shall later see. With changing times and cultural transitions, Twain's book would fade from view in the new century.
However, his story of travel was one of the most popular books of nineteenth-century America. Through this book, Mark Twain, a name that
Samuel Clemens had invented for himself in Virginia City and San Francisco, became familiar to readers. As he stepped out onto the lecture
platform, he began to meet some of his audience and to share more of his
humorous tales of western life. Mark Twain's audience soon became acquainted with his experiences in the American West, as he recalled them

in *Roughing It*. These stories became central to his audience's perception of him as a humorist.

C. WESTERN READERS

In the 1870s, *The Innocents Abroad* and *Roughing It* met with different readerships. Mark Twain discovered that he needed to appeal to an East Coast literary establishment, as well as to his Western readers. His Western readers lived amid the rugged terrain from Virginia City to the West Coast, where he had first come to attention through his articles in newspapers. In contrast were Twain's East Coast readers, those in Hartford, the literary elite of Boston, and readers in New York, which was fast becoming the principal publishing center of the country. In our search for Mark Twain's audience, we begin by looking for Twain's western readers. Then we will look at reading circles in Brooklyn, New York, the site of Twain's first meetings with Henry Ward Beecher and the launching point for his *Quaker City* journey.

While he was a newspaper writer in San Francisco, Mark Twain jested that part of his audience was disembodied or spectral. As he prepared to leave for Hawaii, for a newspaper assignment for which he had arranged, he wrote a piece in which he imagines hearing from one of his readers who was a ghost. On March 11, 1866, there appeared in *The Golden Era* his account of a séance:

> I stumbled upon a private fireside séance a night or two ago, where two old gentlemen and a middle aged gentleman and his wife were communicating (as they firmly believed) with the ghosts of the departed. They have met for this purpose every week for years. They do not "investigate"- they have long since become strong believers, and further investigations are not needed by them.[28]

He notes the use of something like a Ouija board:

> The First ghost that announced his presence: spelled this on the dial: "My name is Thomas Tilson; I was a preacher. I have been dead many years. I know this man Mark Twain well!"
> I voluntarily exclaimed: "The very devil you do?" That odd, dead parson took me by surprise when he spelled my name, and I felt cold chills creep over me. Then the ghost and I continued the conversation:
> "Did you know me on earth?"
> "No. But I read what you write. Every day, almost. I like your writings."
> "Thank you, But how do you read it?- do they take the *Territorial Enterprise* in h-, or rather, heaven, I beg your pardon?"
> "No. I read it through my affinity."
> "Who is your affinity?"
> "Mac Crellish of the Alta."

In this sketch, the "ghost" proceeds to say that he influenced Mac Crellish, owner of the *Alta California*. "If he starts to do what I think he ought not to do, I change his mind." Twain then refers to the ghost of William Thomson, an assistant teacher in New York on Mott Street who knows him also. Twain writes that this ghost "said he was with me constantly." "Well, you get into some mighty bad company sometimes, Bill, if you travel with me," he replies. He concludes, "I am not afraid of such pleasant corpses as these ever running me crazy. I find them better company than a good many live people."[29]

The audience for Mark Twain became more palpable in the following years. His images of the American West entered the lives of readers who lived in rural communities in other regions of the United States. Seldom visiting a book store, they bought Twain's books through the subscription publishing method. After scanning through a prospectus provided by a door to door subscription salesperson, they agreed to purchase *The Innocents Abroad* or Twain's next book, *Roughing It*. Through these books, Twain brought them imaginatively to Europe and to the Holy Land, or to the American West, Virginia City, and California.

Mark Twain may have considered his audience spectral and unseen, but for them he was company. This audience emerged from all occupations and walks of life. They included the people that he often wrote about as a journalist in Virginia City and San Francisco. Assigned to write about an opera, he wrote about a furniture mover at the opera: "I was particularly impressed by the able manner in which Signor Bellindo Alphonso Cellini, the accomplished basso-relievo furniture scout and sofa shifter, performed his part." He writes of a woman at the Pioneer's Ball blowing her nose. Her performance, he says, "marked her as a cultivated and accomplished woman of the world; its exquisitely modulated tone excited the admiration of all who had the happiness to hear it." We see here Mark Twain turning his attention not to the performance featured on the stage but to the human comedy in the audience and cultural life around him. He commented on the new fashion trend of hoop skirts: "to critically examine these hoops- to get the best effect- one should stand on the corner of Montgomery and look up a steep street like Clay or Washington [...] It reminds me of how I used to peep under circus tents when I was a boy and see a lot of mysterious legs about with no visible bodies attached to them."[30]

The early audience was engaged in a kind of conversation with a young writer who looked at incongruities. Twain had a keen eye for human behavior and an ear for the sound and patterns of human speech. He was wise to the paradoxes of the world: "Behold, the same gust of wind that blows a lady's dress aside and exposes her ankle, fills your eyes so full of sand that you can't see it."[31] He became a proficient writer of humorous anecdotes. For example, in *Roughing It*, he recalls a San Francisco area earthquake and the minister who informed his congregation: "Keep your seats! There is no better place to die than this." After the third shock wave, the minister changed his tune: "But outside is good enough."[32]

In 1865, the audience for Twain's humor broadened. Twain's biographers tell us that in December 1864 he left the city for Angels Camp, where he did some mining and listened to the stories of the miners. Mostly he had gone there just to escape for a while. There he began formulating the idea that would become his most popular early story. Mark Twain's national reputation emerged with the publication of his story "Jim Smiley and His Jumping Frog" (1865). The story, told by his character Simon Wheeler, reflects southwest storytelling style.[33]

On November 18, 1865, the story appeared in an East Coast newspaper. About a year following the publication of "The Celebrated Jumping Frog of Calaveras County," Mark Twain left San Francisco. He brought with him jokes, the tall-tale, the parody, and a tendency toward fantasy. Narrative voice is one of the keys to Twain's manner of telling the story of the jumping frog. "The humorous story is told gravely," Twain wrote, "the teller does his best to conceal the fact that he even dimly suspects there is anything funny about it [...]"[34] As Henry Nash Smith points out, "The oral culture of storytelling in the United States was replete with comical anecdotes, tall tales of vernacular heroes. In the decades before the Civil War, these stories began to be printed and circulated in newspapers and magazines." There was a use of local dialects. Smith adds that "uncouth manners and speech could easily become a mask for homely wisdom and rugged honesty."[35] Twain imported images from tall tales into his work. Smith notes that American "vernacular characters" appear in Twain's newspaper articles of the 1860s: the stage coach driver crossing the Sierra Nevada in September 1863, the Virginia City newspaper editor unable to whistle difficult tunes.

Mark Twain was introduced to readers in the East on November 18, when the New York *Saturday Press* printed "Jim Smiley and his Jumping Frog." He had sent the story to the humorist Artemus Ward in New York for Ward's upcoming travel book. It had arrived too late: Ward's book had already been published. However, with Ward's encouragement George W. Carleton, the publisher, sent Twain's story along to Henry Clapp, editor of the *Saturday Press*. The story was reprinted widely in periodicals on the East Coast and then in newspapers across the Midwest. The *Alta California* in San Francisco claimed that New York was "in a roar." In December 1865, the *Alta California* reprinted the story as "The Jumping Frog of Calaveras County." Mark Twain had become a national phenomenon.

Mark Twain's success was not lost on aspiring humorists, who now wanted to imitate him. At Promontory, Nevada, John Hanson Beedle speaks of "an old copy of the *Cincinnati Commercial*" that he saw at a railway station. A piece that he had written had appeared in the newspaper. "An old monte-checker, whose acquaintance once I had made at Benton the previous year, soon hastened to take me by the hand with many compliments," he writes. "Capital, sir. Capital! Almost equal to Mark Twain; good burlesque; much pleased with your account of how we raped the old Californians."[36] Beedle clearly wanted to be associated with Mark Twain and is self-congratulatory in his comments. Twain's notoriety is evident; he is a model for this would-be humorist. Beedle consciously employs the comment of the "old monte-checker" to affirm that his burlesque is "almost equal to Mark Twain." It is clear from these comments that Twain had already developed a considerable audience as a humorist.

D. *ROUGHING IT*

Mark Twain's narrative of the West, *Roughing It*, appeared in the winter of 1872. There were 20,000 orders for *Roughing It* before the publisher began distribution. Initially, its sales moved at a quicker pace than *The Innocents Abroad*. In its first six months it sold "about sixty thousand copies."[37] *Roughing It* provided vivid images of the American West, descriptions of mining camps and towns. Readers met with a world of violence, money, social and racial hierarchy, and memorable, archetypal characters. This novelty catapulted the book toward sales. However, the book did not reach the same figure in sales as *The Innocents Abroad* in its first year. *Roughing It* sales were at 67, 395 by midsummer and by the end of the year had reached 75,168.[38] Twain's first check from his publisher Elisha Bliss was for $10,562.13. The book eventually earned Twain more than $20,000 in the first year.

"They like a book about America because they understand it better," Twain wrote to Bliss. And "it isn't a great deal of trouble to write books about one's own country."[39] Twain had limited the number of review copies of the book that were sent out. In contrast, there had been two thousand review copies sent out for *The Innocents Abroad* and one might speculate whether the distribution of fewer promotional copies affected sales of *Roughing It*. Reviews such as the one that appeared in the *Atlantic* were positive. William Dean Howells called the book "singularly entertaining."[40] "This is a goodly volume of nearly six hundred pages"; the *Overland Monthly* wrote of *Roughing It*, "and if mirth is indeed one of the best medicines, as we have somewhere read [...] *Roughing It* should have a place in every sick-room and be the invalid's cherished companion. In taking in Clemens' jokes, however, for hygienic purposes, it behooves the patient to exercise great caution in regard to the strength of the dose."[41]

Audiences in the early 1870s associated Mark Twain, the writer of "The Jumping Frog" and *The Innocents Abroad*, with the American West. The images that Mark Twain produced in *Roughing It*, his account of life in the West, influenced the autobiographical writings of miners and pioneers who lived in the Western United States. Twain's descriptions also affected how the American West was seen by immigrants who came to live in the United States. Mark Twain once told a reporter from the *Baltimore Gazette* (April 27, 1877): "The men who dig gold out of the Black Hills have got to work for it and earn it. The glitter gets into print; the tales of hardships and bitter disappointment don't."[42] Miners in the West knew that hardship firsthand. One of Twain's readers wrote recalling *Roughing It*:

> A Rocky Mountain mining camp, indeed, is about the newest and roughest place, at its beginnings, to be forced upon the world. The kitchen requisites consist of copper pails, tin cups, and iron knives and forks, the library of a pack of cards, a copy of "Mining Code," and perhaps a well-thumbed copy of Bret Harte's "Luck" or Mark Twain's "Roughing It." Once found Byron's poems, Dickens's "Nicholas Nickleby," Shakespeare's plays and an old Harper's magazine, as the entire library of a Colorado camp.[43]

In this writer's attention to specifics, we can see a panhandler's careful gaze as he identifies the items in camp. He sifts them out like the rocks in a stream; he observes tools and cards and books as if they were like shining bits of glitter in the dirt of the Western hills. Reading is significant, at least in this one camp, and books may be found amid the rugged simplicity of a miner's life. A pack of cards and the stories of Bret Harte and Mark Twain are signs of entertainment amid the homely details and tools of the mining trade.

Mark Twain shaped the image that some people had of the American West. Immigrants imagined America through Twain's books. Miners and would-be humorists referred to him as they fashioned their own stories. Among those who read Twain's work and recognized his growing reputation was Thomas "Pet" McMurray, who had been a printer at the *Hannibal Courier* in the 1840s when Samuel Clemens was there. In a letter of July 16, 1872, he wrote to the author:

> Dear Sam, you may call this a piece of presumption- but I can't help that- so few, so very few of my boyhood acquaintances have become Literary Lights in the world, that I must not fail to keep up some kind of intercourse with those who have made their mark- the cat you know may smile at the King—that is I mean to keep up an intercourse, if I kin. If your memory extends so far back, you will recollect that when a boy, a little sandy-haired boy, nearly a quarter of a century ago [...]
> It always affords me a great deal of pleasure to read your productions- consider them the natural offspring of that brain that was always so chock-full of fun and mischief when a boy..."

He describes himself as the father of five and says that, as of 1854, he has been in a mercantile business. He describes his family's reading:

"the boy is a great book-worm, and a fond admirer of yours- never fails to read all the productions from your pen that his eye catches. If he should get hold of "Roughing It" he would at once be of the same turn of mind that the Southern people were in '61 'want to be let alone until he devoured it."

He added a "P.S.": "Don't get vain of your reputation. Your reputation don't extend to every nook and corner yet." He informed Twain that a female acquaintance had stopped into his store and he had told her he was writing a letter to Mark Twain.

"Who is Mark Twain?" was the reply. Had she been a man, should have taken her to be of that class who still persist in voting for Gen. Jackson. . . . So you see there is a great work for you to do yet before your name is a universal household word, particularly in the rural districts.[44]

Mark Twain, of course, did develop a reputation that extended to nearly every "nook and corner." Twain's account of the west, *Roughing It*, reached people living in the cities of the Northeast of the United States, as well as readers in the West. The American Publishing Company sent subscription agents out to procure sales of the book in rural areas all across the country.

Twain's books also reached former Civil War soldiers. On February 17, 1876, Twain asked Bliss to donate copies of his books to the National Home for Disabled Soldiers. A letter had come from Edward Hastings, Librarian, Reading Room, National Soldiers Home, Elizabeth City County, Virginia. Twain told Bliss "These go to disabled soldiers of the US" and wrote "Answered" on the envelope.[45] There is no record of library circulation for those readers. However, we do know that former Civil War soldiers were reading Mark Twain a decade after the war. Books by Mark Twain could be found in the library of the Soldiers' Home in Milwaukee, Wisconsin, beginning in 1865. Twain's books were also at the Soldier's Home in Grand Rapids, Michigan, where Reverend Riley Crooks Crawford, who was briefly their chaplain, recalled in an autobiographical article: "Meanwhile, I had done some successful canvassing for some valuable books."[46]

Roughing It brought images and experiences of life in Nevada, California, and distant Hawaii to readers who otherwise would never visit these places. S.T. Crowell and E. Gayle of Cape Cod, who were sisters, wrote to Twain from Dennis on August 27, 1877. They indicated that they had read, in *Roughing It*, Twain's account of how he had experienced stage fright before his first lecture. They applauded the book as better than Dickens:

We read "Roughing It" all last Winter wept each time we came to the end- if you had only kept on writing more of it, it would have be the best book in the World it beats Dickens works all "holler."[47]

The sisters make an appeal to Twain because they want to publish a local story. The letter begins curiously with what one might call a Freudian slip:

> We are two sin twisters (we meant to write twin sisters) of Cape Cod, have lived here all our lives with a few interruptions; we never went to a big city, never saw a publisher, are afraid of big cities and publishers. But something happened in this locality a while ago that we have written into a book and want dreadfully to publish. So we want to know if you will let us send you the M.S.S. and read it and approve it and send it to that unknown animal the publisher and tell him to put it in print. . . .

The Innocents Abroad had been a weighty book of many pages. As a subscription book, *Roughing It*, likewise, required some further heft. So, Mark Twain increased the page count by tacking on a record of some of his adventures in the Sandwich Islands. After all, the Pacific paradise of Hawaii was in the west too: the very far west. To most Americans, the islands across the sea were new and exotic. Going there had been yet another adventure for the young Mark Twain. From his early adulthood, he was a restless traveler. He had traveled west by train and stagecoach and gone east as a journalist. He had lived in Virginia City and San Francisco. Early in 1866, when Twain learned that the California Steam Navigation Company had begun to sail from San Francisco to Honolulu, he had encouraged the *Sacramento Union* to send him to the Sandwich Islands. He arranged a deal in which his travel letters would be printed in the newspaper.

While he was in Hawaii, Mark Twain's first major news story arrived unexpectedly. On June 15, a life-boat filled with exhausted sailors came in on the surf at Laupahoehoe, about two hundred miles south of Honolulu. The crew of the *Hornet*, a clipper ship ravaged by fire, had drifted for forty-three days across four thousand miles of ocean. Mark Twain interviewed the men and sent their story to the *Union*. It was published on July 19 and began to be reprinted across the United States. Mark Twain just happened to be in the right place, when the starving but resilient sailors at last reached the safety of land. Of course, Twain was never one to rely upon serendipity or inspiration for relevant material. To fill out his accounts for the *Sacramento Union*, he took a Honolulu chaplain's copy of James Jarves' *History of the Hawaiian Islands* (1849). This supplied him with facts about the Polynesian world that so much had stirred his senses. Upon returning to California, he worked his account of the incident into a magazine article. This he presented to the *Union* along with a bill for twenty dollars per letter for his Sandwich Islands letters. His article sold to *Harper's Monthly* and it was titled "Forty-Three Days in an Open Boat." The editors mistakenly called the author "Mark Swain." Thirty years later "Mark Twain" would be the most recognizable pen name in the world and Harper and Brothers would be yearning for a publishing deal for his collected works.

Mark Twain's skill for descriptive writing, invention, and humor was already creating an audience when he left for Hawaii. Yet, he would not see the faces of his audience until he began lecturing later that year. Twain brought something exotic and new to his audience by adding his adventures in the Sandwich Islands to *Roughing It*. To trek through Hawaii, or Nevada, in the 1860s was challenging. However, as a young man, Mark Twain had no need of comfort or safety. His life was an ongoing adventure and it was an adventure toward far-off places that his readers and his lecture audiences craved.

E. READING CIRCLES AND LITERARY CLUBS

Mark Twain's readers of the early to mid-1870s extended across the entire United States and across the ocean to England. His stories of the American West, Hawaii, and the old world interested an increasing number of people who gathered in groups and heard Twain's stories read aloud. By this time, Mark Twain had become a subject of interest in literary clubs in the East. Among these literary reading circles were several in Brooklyn, New York. Twain had enjoyed a growing following in Brooklyn, ever since his visits to Henry Ward Beecher at the Plymouth Church and his later lecture performances there.

In 1873, the *Brooklyn Eagle* reported that "Professor Raymond read from Dickens, Mark Twain &c. in the lecture room of Plymouth Church before well-pleased audiences." Several other speakers in Brooklyn read Mark Twain's writings aloud to audiences during the 1870s. At the Mite Society of the Union Tabernacle Church, Williamsborough Lyceum, "a humorous reading from Mark Twain by Professor Upham kept the audience in a continual roar of laughter."[48] At the Atheneum, on the corner of Clinton Street and Atlantic Avenue, members of the New York Teachers Association were entertained by readings from Mark Twain by A.P. Burbank. The *Brooklyn Eagle* reported: "Mr. A. P. Burbank closed the first part of the programme with the reading of 'Our Guide in Rome' from Mark Twain's 'Innocents Abroad.'" When he read "A Boy's Composition on a Horse" he "fairly convulsed the audience with mirth." According to this report "the ladies were in a large majority."[49] Within this gathering was Algernon S. Higgins, the principal of Public School 9, who lived at 150 Sixth Avenue. He would become a member of the Brooklyn Board of Education.

Twain's humorous short stories and passages from *The Innocents Abroad*, *Roughing It*, and *The Gilded Age* were read aloud at several Brooklyn gatherings. At the Westminster Church on the corner of Clinton

Street and First Place in Brooklyn, "the audience filled the room to over-flowing." The *Brooklyn Eagle* wrote:

> The inevitable reading from Mark Twain, which one always encounters at gatherings of this sort, came next. The selection was from "Roughing It" and was given by Mr. Frank B. Jackson. The spirit of the piece was caught up better than could be anticipated, for reading Mark Twain as it should be read is not always an easy thing to do. In this case the reader achieved a fair degree of success. [50]

Dr. James L. Farley was another public reader of Mark Twain, who shared those readings with audiences in Brooklyn. At the Ingell Literary Society of Browne' Business College, 295 Fulton Street, he read Mark Twain alongside works by Shakespeare, Henry Ward Beecher, Trowbridge, Louver, and Dickens. Irving T. Astin and S. McClure both received prizes that night for excellence in how they read selections from Mark Twain and Samuel Louvar. [51]

Dr. Farley and A.P. Burbank were regularly featured as readers and raconteurs of all things pertaining to Mark Twain. The Everett Literary Society met on Monday evening at the Hanson Baptist Church, where Mr. A.P. Burbank presented "Literary Nightmare" by Mark Twain (February 20, 1878). Across town, Twain's fiction was featured at the Clinton Commandery, March 31, 1878: "The xylophone came in again and Dr. Farley read 'Love in Oyster Bay' and followed with that exceedingly funny story by Mark Twain about the hired man, the cat on the roof and the candy pull. It was capitally rendered and the audience fairly roared with laughter." [52] In November 1878 Dr. Farley read Mark Twain's essay on cats at Tuscan Lodge. A few years later, a note appeared that "Dr. (James) Farley slightly resembles Mark Twain in both figure and manner. He seems to understand the secret of holding the attention of his audience. He seems most at home rendering the work of the humorists." [53]

Such events featured Mark Twain as a humorist who could be imitated. The reader, Mr. Burbank or Dr. Farley, substituted for Twain and took on the role of the humorist within the community. It appears that the humorous sketches by Twain were more popular in reading groups and literary societies than the serious social criticism in the Warner and Twain collaboration, *The Gilded Age*. The popular reach of *The Gilded Age* was maximized through its stage versions rather than by public readings. Unauthorized stage productions of *The Gilded Age* brought the vivid characters of Colonel Sellers and Laura Hawkins to local gatherings across America. However, it was Twain himself, as a lecturer and stage performer, who galvanized popular attention for his works. Potential readers were introduced to Mark Twain by his presence in their towns on any of several indefatigable lecture tours. The wit and charm that appeared in his books was also available to them in person. Mark Twain traveled up and down the North American continent telling them stories. And yes, how he could make them laugh!

NOTES

1. Barbara Hochman, *Getting at the Author.* Amherst: University of Massachusetts Press, 1964.
2. Harold H. Hellwig, *Mark Twain's Travel Literature* (Jefferson, N.C.: McFarland, 2008). p. 2. Mark Twain's travel writing is also considered by Jeffrey Alan Melton in *Mark Twain Travel Books and Tourism: The Tide of a Great Popular Movement* (Tuscaloosa: University of Alabama Press, 2002). Richard Bridgman explores Twain's travels in *Traveling in Mark Twain*, (1987). One might also look at the work of Thomas Tinney on Twain's travel writing. Larzer Ziff's *Great American Travel Writing, 1700–1900* (Yale University Press, 2001) has a section covering Twain's books. "Travel writing was a perfect vehicle for Twain's imagination," writes Ziff, p. 174.
3. Jeffrey Alan Melton, xv. Melton views Mark Twain principally as a travel writer. "For readers in the late nineteenth century," he says, "Mark Twain was first and foremost a travel writer instead of a novelist" p. 1. The reception of Twain as a travel writer can be substantiated by looking at book sales and the responses to Twain by his nineteenth-century readers. *Innocents Abroad* was the best selling travel book of the nineteenth century and, as Melton points out, "all of Twain's five travel books are closely linked" (xiv).
4. Mark Twain fully recognized the sales potential of his travel books. *Innocents Abroad* sold more than 70,000 copies in its first year. *Roughing It* sold 76,000 across its first two years and had sold 96,000 by 1879. *A Tramp Abroad* sold 62,000 copies in its first year. *Life on the Mississippi*, which many critics regard as one of Twain's strongest works, sold only 32,000 copies in its first year but continues to command attention throughout the twentieth and early twenty-first centuries.
5. George Ack, *In Pastures New.* New York: McClure, Phillips, 1906. p. 174.
6. Louise Rutherford Letter to Mark Twain, November 21, 1875. See Rasmussen, 42–43.
7. Ibid.
8. Bruce Michelson "Tourist," p. 387. In Michelson's view, "Mark Twain was gathering an audience with expectations of being entertained by a humorist" and his name was "sure to bring more business in the bookshop." Michelson writes, "The readers he had won expected clowning." p. 388.
9. *Autobiography of Mark Twain*, ed. Harriet Elinor Smith. Berkeley: University of California Press, 2010. p. 320.
10. This story may be apocryphal. It is mentioned in *Mark Twain Letters*, Vol. 2, ed. Edgar Branch, Michael B. Frank, Berkeley: University of California Press, p. 16, and in Sara deSaussure and Philip Beidler's *The Mythologizing of Mark Twain*, Tuscaloosa: University of Alabama Press, 1984. p. 140, and many other volumes. Justin Kaplan offers a slight variation in *Mr. Clemens and Mr. Twain*, New York: Simon and Schuster, 1966. p. 28.
11. Mark Twain, *The Innocents Abroad*, Chapter 2.
12. Mary B. Ingham, "Alexis: His Home and His Religion," *Ladies Repository*, Vol. 9, Is. 3 (March 1872): 216–22. p. 218.
13. Penina Williams, "The Plaint of a Commonplace Person," *Appleton Journal*, Vol. 10, Is. 228 (July 17, 1873): 82.
14. "Africa," *Ladies Repository*, 165.
15. Benjamin Franklin Taylor, *The World on Wheels and Other Sketches*, S.C. Griggs, 1874.
16. Samuel Kneeland, *Wonders of the Yosemite Valley and California.* New York: A. Moore and Boston: Lee, Shephard, and Dillingham, p. 34.

17. Mark Twain, *The Innocents Abroad*, pp. 234, 264, 300, 269–70. Robert Regan offers the view that Twain's division of "pilgrims" and "sinners" in *The Innocents Abroad* carries through his other books. "The Reprobate Elect in *Innocents Abroad*," *On Mark Twain: The Best from American Literature*. Ed. Louis Budd and E.H. Cody, Durham: Duke University Press, 1987. p. 225–27. Regan believes that Twain created this inversion so that the pilgrims "held up" by society appear as sinners and the sinners, who are "kept down" are shown to be otherwise. Twain points to the pilgrims and "represents them as deficient in the qualities of true religion" p 226. Regan notes three times in his text that Twain criticizes "their lack of spontaneity and independence." pp. 226–27. Justin Kaplan writes: "Their sharp trading and acquisitive drive were, when they were abroad, just about equaled by their gullibility." *Mr. Clemens and Mr. Twain*. New York: Simon and Schuster, 1966. p. 42.

18. Henry Nash Smith, *Mark Twain: The Development of a Writer*. Cambridge: Harvard University Press, 1962. pp. 30–31.

19. Henry Nash Smith, *Mark Twain: The Development of a Writer*. p. 42, p. 31.

20. Justin Kaplan, *Mr. Clemens and Mr. Twain*, New York: Simon and Schuster, 1966. p. 49.

21. *The Innocents Abroad*. Henry Nash Smith, *Mark Twain: The Development of a Writer*. p. 29.

22. Mark Twain, *The Innocents Abroad*. p. 60.

23. Susy Clemens, *Papa: An Intimate Biography of Mark Twain*. ed, Charles Neider. Garden City: Doubleday, 1978. pp. 221–22.

24. Mark Twain's letter to Elisha Bliss is quoted by Henry Nash Smith, *Mark Twain: The Development of a Writer*, p. 37.

25. *Syracuse Standard* (October 5, 1869).

26. Henry Nash Smith, *Mark Twain: The Development of a Writer*. pp. 37–38, 39, 40.

27. Mark Twain, *New York Herald*. Also see quoted in Justin Kaplan, *Mr. Clemens and Mr. Twain*, p. 55.

28. Bernard Taper, *Mark Twain in San Francisco*, p. 232. *The Golden Era* (March 11, 1866).

29. See *The Golden Era* (March 5, 1866) and (March 11, 1866).

30. *Autobiography*. Vol. I, MTP. Berkeley: University of California Press, 2010.

31. Bernard Taper, *Mark Twain in San Francisco*, New York: McGraw-Hill, 1963. xviii.

32. Ibid, xix. Twain places the church in Oakland, rather than in San Francisco.

33. Mark Twain, *Early Tales and Sketches*, Vol. II, pp. 68–69.

34. Mark Twain, *How to Tell a Story*; Louis Budd, *Our Mark Twain: The Making of His Public Personality*, Philadelphia: University of Pennsylvania Press, 1983. p. 17.

35. Henry Nash Smith, *Mark Twain: The Development of a Writer*. Cambridge: Harvard University Press, 1962, pp. 4, 8.

36. John Hanson Beedle, *The Undeveloped West, or Five Years in the Territories*. Philadelphia and Chicago: National Publishing, 1873, p. 54.

37. Ron Powers, *Mark Twain: A Life*, p.148.

38. Ron Powers, p. 322.

39. Justin Kaplan, *Mr. Clemens and Mr. Twain*, p. 148.

40. "Recent Literature," *Atlantic*, Mark Twain Letters, Vol. 5, 95.

41. "Current Literature," *Overland and Out West Monthly*. Vol. 8, Is. 6 (June 1872): 571–81. p. 580.

42. *Baltimore Gazette* (April 27, 1877), rpt. *New York World* (April 28, 1877).

43. Ernest Ingersoll, *Knocking about the Rockies*, New York: Harper and Brothers, 1883.

44. Thomas "Pet" McMurray, Letter to Mark Twain, MTP, 31816. University of California.

45. Mark Twain Letter to Edward Hastings of National Soldier's Home, February 17, 1876, MTP. Bancroft Library, University of California.

46. Reverend Riley Crooks Crawford briefly served as the chaplain for the soldiers' home in Grand Rapids, Michigan.

47. S.T. Crowell and E. Gayle, Letter to Mark Twain, August 27, 1877. MTP, University of California. Rasmussen, 49.

48. "Local Brevities," *Brooklyn Eagle*, February 27, 1873.

49. *Brooklyn Eagle*, November 11, 1875; *Brooklyn Eagle*, December 9, 1877, p. 3–4.

50. "Literature and Music: Second Annual Reception of the South Brooklyn Literary Society," *Brooklyn Eagle*, Friday May 25, 1877. This article appeared on the Friday before 'Decoration Day,' or Memorial Day, which began in New York in 1873.

51. *Brooklyn Eagle*, Saturday, May 6, 1876. p. 6.

52. *Brooklyn Eagle*, February 20, 1878; March 31, 1878, p. 3; 31. *The Brooklyn Eagle*, (Sunday, March 31, 1878), p. 3.

53. "Tuscan Lodge: The Second Annual Parlor Entertainment," *The Brooklyn Eagle*, (November 22, 1878), p. 4.

THREE

Marketing Mark Twain

Mark Twain was advertised as "the people's author." He decided that subscription publishing would be his best opportunity to reach many readers. It appears that he was right.[1] The American Publishing Company, dedicated to this form of marketing and bookselling, sent agents out throughout the country. They went "door to door" to buyers and a broad audience began to discover Mark Twain. This audience can be discovered by tracing the path of these book agents. Mark Twain's early books—*The Innocents Abroad, Roughing It*, and *The Gilded Age*—were illustrated, bulky, eye-catching volumes. The publishing company knew that these potential book buyers often believed that the bulk and weight of a volume meant that they were getting their money's worth. Subscription publishers also recognized that it would be harder to get book reviews for their books. However, limited press runs were not in Twain's interest. He told William Dean Howells, "Anything but subscription publishing is printing for private circulation." Howells wrote: "No book of literary quality was made to go by subscription except Mr. Clemens's books, and I think these went because the subscription public never knew what good literature they were"[2]

Subscription publishing was one of the factors that set Mark Twain on the path to wide popularity. He once described his subscription book audience as one of people who were not in bookstores: "the factory hands and the farmers. They never go to a bookstore; they have to be hunted down by a canvasser."[3] These were working people, what we would call the common reader. By following the trail of subscription agents we may begin to discover who they were. Justin Kaplan writes that "Bliss's army of book agents [...] invested every town and hamlet."[4] Surely this is hyperbole. However, it is true that "Bliss believed in saturation, repetition, and persistency." As Kaplan points out, "Bliss concentrated on

towns instead of cities, on popular papers instead of literary journals."[5]
The people in these towns, readers of those popular papers, became a
fundamental core of Twain's readers.

A market model of book circulation sees readers as the final destination of the communications circuit that Robert Darnton theorized. Yet,
another way to view the circulation of the book is to look for individual
readers. Indeed, it is difficult to find the actual individuals who bought
Mark Twain's books. Yet, if we can manage to find records, in empirically
grounded study we may follow methods like those of Jonathan Rose in
The Intellectual Life of the British Working Class and ask the reader about his
or her reading. In this way we may begin to analyze the real common
readers who were targeted by Twain's publisher's subscription book
campaigns. One way of locating these readers is to trace the activities of
the subscription agents who sold Twain's books to them and to examine
their sales ledgers.

Subscription agents were recruited by the American Publishing Company, whose offices were on Asylum Street in Hartford, a city that was, at
this time, a major publishing center. Elisha Bliss, the company's owner,
had several methods for recruiting subscription book agents. The primary one was newspaper and book ads. For example, this ad appeared in
the *Tolland County Press* in Connecticut: "To Agents, or any who need
work. American Publishing Company Hartford. Dan De Quille's new
book, with an introduction by Mark Twain, is just ready [...] Go for this
one. It will fill your pockets with money for sure! Don't delay and lose
territory you want, send for circulars at once. It costs nothing to see
them."[6]

One of the company's many book agents was Mrs. J.W. Likins, who
sold engraved portraits of Ulysses S. Grant and several books. She left
Akron in 1868 and traveled with her family to California. She became a
book agent when her husband became sick and he could no longer work.
She specifically recalls selling Twain's *The Innocents Abroad*. "On my way
I passed the book store of H.H. Bancroft, then on the corner of Montgomery and Merchant streets. In the window I noticed a card with the words
'Agents Wanted' on it. I asked him, 'Do you employ ladies agents?' 'Yes,'
he replied, 'allow me to take you to the Subscription Department.'"[7]

Mrs. Likins writes: "I called on one gentleman I pitied very much; he
had to use crutches. He told me he was a cripple, from rheumatism. Still
he seemed energetic, and full of business, carrying on a drug store and
keeping the Post-Office, and was contented and happy. He said, when I
came around again, he would take Mark Twain's 'Innocents Abroad,' if I
would bring it to him, as he was a great reader."[8]

Mrs. J.W. Likins sold Mark Twain's books in Santa Clara County,
California. In her autobiography, she says that she received "many orders
for Mark Twain's 'Innocents Abroad.'" Soon after beginning work as a
subscription agent, at Mayfield, in Santa Clara County, Mrs. Likins called

upon a prospective customer. "I would bring it to him as he was a great reader. I called at the blacksmith shop above his place. There was a man working there, an apprentice, I think, who was so low as to be abrasive and vulgar, forgetting he ever had a mother."[9] Leaving the blacksmith shop, Mrs. Likins walked through working class areas of the town. She met with people at the wharfs, in lumber businesses, and at a tannery. The books she carried were reaching buyers. She says, "I had sufficient employment to keep me busy for several months amongst the shipping, wharf-ingers, and lumber merchants. In this way I finished my first twelve months [...]"[10]

This entrepreneur, Mrs. Likins, was not alone in her efforts. There were other subscription agents at work in the area and she had to define her work district. Mrs. Likins reports that she began to sell Mark Twain's *Innocents Abroad*, "which had just been published. This was a very popular book. The City was divided into three districts, making two agents in the City besides myself. With that I had some trouble, as I did not understand the rules and regulations in the business [...]"[11] There were apparently some territorial tensions between the agents. "When I commenced on Mark Twain's 'Roughing It' I found the small lady had the district in the City adjoining mine [...]" There was a man selling "on one side of Market and one of Mission, from Bay to Sixteenth Street"[12]

When she called on Mr. Roman's bookstore in March 1872 "to secure territory for Mark Twain's book 'Roughing It,'" they had given her Santa Clara County and a part of the city. "The book was not expected from the East for several days," she writes. "The citizens of San Jose knew me well by this time, and patronized me liberally. In this place, in three weeks, I sold one hundred and five copies, which was the largest sale ever made there on one book by any canvasser. With this book I visited Los Gatos [...] The town consisted of one street; on the lower side of it were many dwellings; at some of them the entrances were lower than the sidewalk [...]"[13]

It is clear that Mrs. Likins worked hard at selling Mark Twain's *Roughing It* and that the book reached many readers in Santa Clara County. In January 1872, anticipating a sale at an office, she watched as people came and went. "I secured four copies of the books, in two styles of binding, and watched the office for several days before I could catch them all in. When I did, I marched through the rooms with my four books, into their office. I addressed them politely, calling them [...]"[14]

Others she met, however, were not inclined toward reading, or toward purchasing the book. Mrs. Likins recalls: "While I was working on this same book, I called in a store where there were two proprietors; as I entered, one was standing in the doorway; when I asked him to buy, he gruffly said, 'I don't want any books.'" She says that this man then added, "What in h-l are you doing here? There are getting to be too many of you women strolling around here, but it is only an excuse to get amongst the men. You are getting most too old; you won't stand much show in picking up a man to live with." [15]

Not to be deterred, she persisted on her sales route. Mrs. Likins asked more potential customers if they would like to buy a book. She tells of meeting a man who said: "I would be pleased to do so, to assist you, but I have already subscribed for a copy." Her narrative follows: "'You will please to excuse me, sir,' I replied, 'but where did you buy, and who of?' He had not time to reply, when I heard a peculiar noise, something like a big bullfrog croaking." She then says that a man who looked like a frog began speaking gruffly with her. He asked what the point was of caring who sold the book to the man with whom she had been speaking. [16] Despite such unpleasant encounters, she affirms the success of the mission to sell Twain's book: "[T]his was the most saleable book I had ever worked on. In many of the stores on Front Street, I took from three to five orders a day. In canvassing Battery [S]treet, I went upstairs in a building occupied by Government employees." They told her that their wages were too small for them to buy the books. There she met with the man who had already subscribed. [17]

Mrs. Likins also sold Twain's *Gilded Age*, in the same region, two years later. "Taking my basket of books, I called on Mr. R. at his residence; was introduced to his wife and son; found them very pleasant. The latter bought Mark Twain's 'Gilded Age.' Thanking him, it now being dark, [I] hastened to the boarding house." [18] On one of the days afterward, she passed Mrs. S.'s saloon. There she had received an order for Joseph Johnson's book. She went on to a tannery and then turned back into town. "Called at the store, but had no success; crossed the street to the telegraph office; sold one of Mark Twain's 'Gilded Age' to the operator, who, by the way, I found to be a very kind-hearted gentleman. I next called on the butcher. He recognized me immediately and seemed very glad to see me but would not buy." [19]

Who was the telegraph operator and what did he think of Mark Twain's collaboration with Charles Dudley Warner? Who were those book buyers on Front Street? If one hundred and five copies of *Roughing It* were sold in three weeks in San Jose, who read those copies? Which workers for the lumber merchants and which shipping workers by the wharfs in Santa Clara read Mark Twain? This information is lost to us. It would be interesting to know what they thought of Mark Twain's books.

The American Publishing Company's ad for Twain's book appeared in other books as well as in newspapers:

> Selling Books By Subscription/ The American Publishing Company/ of/ Hartford, Connecticut/ are engaged in the publication of rare and valuable/ Standard Works/ selling them by/ SUBSCRIPTION ONLY/ By this method they reach directly the whole reading public, multiplying sales tenfold, and place the works in the hands of thousands whose attention otherwise would not be called to them.

At the bottom is an ad that attempts to entice readers to become subscription agents: "We want agents throughout the country."[20]

Prospective agents received coaching from manuals on making subscription sales. In 1857, J. Walter Stoops wrote *The Art of Canvassing or, the Experience of a Practical Canvasser*. (New York: Privately Printed, 1857). On the back of J.S. Ingram's *Centennial Exhibition, Philadelphia* (1876), there is an ad for subscription book agents enticing people to this business as an income source. Agents were given pamphlets on how to sell, such as the *Agent's Companion: A Manual of Confidential Instruction*. However, these guides to salesmanship were soon criticized by writers like Bates Harrington, who saw through "the tricks of the trade" in *How 'Tis Done: A Thorough Ventilate of the Numerous Schemes Conducted by Walking Canvassers, Together With the Various Advertising Dodges for Swindling the Public* (Chicago: Fidelity Publishing, 1879).[21]

The *New York Times* (March 10, 1873) states that female agents were drawn into this business by false promises from publishers.[22] Elizabeth Lindley wrote anecdotes in her diary about her experiences as a book agent that may support this view. She was one of many agents who spent money on room and board in their attempt to make money and who barely broke even, if that. She begins her short-lived diary on July 7: "I have just returned from answering an 'ad' for a book agent. Am perfectly delighted with the contract I made, and now feel that I was very stupid to have wasted so much time grieving in poverty on account of my pride."[23]

Book agent Harriet Wason writes: "I had examined my prospectus sufficiently to know that it was a book intended for youthful minds, and all in reading- life clean through to the oldest age, and I felt capable of giving it a possible showing."[24] With a sense of targeted audiences, subscription book agents reached into rural areas and pitched books to readers of all ages. The agents showed their customers differently priced bindings. In the year that *The Gilded Age* was sold by subscription, the John E. Potter Company issued to its agents the *Grand Combinator Prospectus* that offered samples of 150 titles, with two sample book spines. Mark Twain surely remembered this. When he began acting as a publisher with his own firm, Charles Webster and Company, he also made use of subscription book agents. Some 10,000 canvassers were sent out to sell Grant's *Memoirs*. The *New York Times* (December 3, 1885) claimed that "1,000 tons of paper" was used for copies of this book.[25] However, by the time Twain published Grant's *Memoirs*, some people had grown tired of subscription book agents calling on them. In Mount Pleasant, Iowa, the *Free Press* cast one of their readers, Kate Merrybee, as "A Lady Tormented by Canvassing Agents." She wrote to the newspaper that the people who came to her door arrived with "So many things a person don't really need."[26]

Turned away, subscription book agents wrote in their diaries of their trials and tribulations. Frank Kelly of Maine used wrapping paper for his diary and he not only wrote of his experiences, he also drew them. Next to an entry of 1894, dated "Tuesday, October 2" Kelly drew "A discouraged agent." In this drawing, a man, with a cat near his feet, holds a book in one hand and tips his hat toward a woman in the doorway. The woman, standing ramrod straight in a long dress, has her hair in a bun and a scowl upon her face. The agent seems to tip a bit forward, almost apologetically. On the opposite page, to the left, there is an entry for "Monday, October 1, 1894. Canvassed at Jonesport." Beside it is Kelly's drawing of a stagecoach, or "express wagon" on which he has traveled, wearing his father's long overcoat.[27]

The American Publishing Company provided its subscription agents with an advertising pitch for book customers. Mark Twain's notoriety was insisted upon. "There is no occasion for me to talk to you about Mark Twain; there is not a man, woman, or child in the United States that does not know him as AMERICA'S GREATEST HUMORIST." How many agents actually made use of this ad copy is unknown. Yet, one can imagine a subscription agent standing on someone's doorstep repeating verbatim the phrase: "Everybody has laughed with him hundreds of times."[28]

Twain became the centerpiece for the publishing program of the Hartford company. By the 1840s, Hartford had become a center for subscription book publishing. Case, Tiffany and Company procured a building and the means for stereotyping and they proceeded to print Bibles. The firm of Elisha Bliss emerged from this context. Like other subscription publishers, he padded his books with thick covers and illustrations. The company recruited agents through newspaper ads filled with promises of commission on sales. The prospect of work and income appealed to women who were otherwise limited in employment in the public sphere. The company's ads for agents for Twain's *Innocents Abroad* were directed toward "disabled Soldiers, aged and other Clergymen having leisure hours, Teachers and Students during vacation, &c., Invalids unable to endure hard physical labor, Young Men who wish to travel and gather knowledge and experience by contact with the world, and all who can bring industry, perseverance, and a determined will to the work."[29]

Subscription agents frequently carried their wares into rural areas, where nearly three-quarters of the American population lived. These customers seldom, if ever, visited a bookstore. They were sold subscription books for a price higher than books available in stores. The prospectus that the agent carried included a sales pitch, a table of contents, chapter titles, a cover with sample bindings, some dramatic copy from the book, and a set of illustrations. The subscription agent would usually solicit the signatures of buyers and keep a ledger. The bulk of the physical book may have appealed to those who wished to have a big, apparently expensive book in their home.[30]

Upon creating his own publishing company, Twain followed this practice.[31] For Grant's *Memoirs*, his family would receive 70 percent of the profits from the book. Twain set forth an appeal to patriotism with his prospectus, an appeal to sentiment and to history. He asserted that "Grant should be dear to all Americans" and offered a simple down payment of $1. Some 650,000 copies were sold, netting royalties of $415,000 for Julia Grant and her family.[32]

The presence of agents selling Twain's books throughout the country was complemented by Mark Twain's own far-flung travels. When Twain was planning *Life on the Mississippi*, he traveled north on the river for the first time. To Livy he wrote of being "upon this hideous trip to St. Paul, with a heart brimming full of thoughts."[33] The residents of St. Paul had been reading Mark Twain's writings for many years. A canvas for *The Gilded Age* began in St. Paul early in 1873. At the same time, two thousand miles away, the *Brooklyn Eagle* offered this note to its readers: "A Minnesota legislator went into a St. Paul book store the other day. He inquired for the head clerk. He spent two hours in looking over the works of Scott, Dickens, Macaulay and Mark Twain, but finally satisfied his literary longings with a dime novel and went away happy."[34] Twain did not write dime novels. Yet, in 1873 his first novel, *The Gilded Age*, had appeared.

St. Paul residents bought subscription copies of *The Gilded Age* in 1873, as Stephen Railton's website indicates.[35] The subscription ledger that Railton offers us draws upon the Barrett Collection and reprints several signatures of subscription customers. Three sections of a subscription agent's sales prospectus are reprinted. Railton notes that this agent sold 140 copies of *The Gilded Age* to customers in the St. Paul-Minneapolis area. He provides about eighty names and notes that two names are identified as "Mrs." However, many of these customers made use of their initials rather than their proper names. Census records and birth and death records in St. Paul suggest that several of these patrons were women. Generally, the lack of signed first names makes it difficult to trace them.

It is clear that one key area of this agent's territory was a mixed business and residential district near the Mississippi River. The agent sold many books along East 3rd, which is today Kellogg Boulevard. This main thoroughfare extended past St. Peter Street, where the Greek Revival cathedral stood near the Presbyterian Church. It continued by the intersections of Wabasha, Cedar, Minnesota, Robert, and Jackson Streets to the Union Depot at Sibley Street. The area on Third between Robert and Jackson had been rebuilt in the past decade following a March 1860 fire. Businessman Louis Robert and Governor Ramsey had lived in this area and A.R. Larpenteur had been a store clerk there. A few three-story buildings that had been recently built were in the area.[36]

George Acker was probably sitting in his office when the subscription agent came to visit. Acker bought a copy of *The Gilded Age*. It appears that Acker himself was living a Gilded Age story. His business partner in the fuel company was James Jerome Hill, who would become a railroad baron and a transporter of coal and wood from St. Paul to the Pacific Northwest. George S. Acker handled much of the firm's correspondence. Near the levee on the Mississippi River, in 1867, the James J. Hill warehouse was a low building with a large door near the water. The second floor was on a level with the railroad tracks serving a line toward the nearby Union Depot. A grain elevator stood just behind the warehouse. The subscription agent who visited Acker would have recognized this location as the depot for the La Crosse and Milwaukee Railroad. James Hill had recently been a passenger agent for a transportation company and he had purchased a warehouse near the St. Paul and Pacific railroad terminal at riverside. Across the years, this became a major terminus. Nine railroad lines eventually came together where the St. Paul Union Station was built. It is no surprise that the subscription agent looked for business here.

George Acker likely could have heard the train through his office window. It had sped past the Presbyterian Church that overlooked the river at Third and St. Peter Street. It went past the Catholic Church with which his business partner, James Hill and his wife Mary Theresa Mehegan and their ten children, had a special relationship with Fr. Caillet. In March 1873, Hill's diary records that his family was sick with colds that winter. The Hill family had grown even as his business operations expanded. The fuel business was held in a partnership with Chauncey Griggs. William Newcombe and John Armstrong were partners in the firm for a time. By 1871, the business grew to a point where a new partner was needed and on January 1, 1872, George Acker had become partner.

The Gilded Age appeared in 1873. By this time the business of Hill and Acker was in full swing. On May 3, 1873, Hill wrote in his diary: "and BH [Brice Hall] coal as called for 500 tons @ $11. Had regular collision in p.m. with Griggs about above." One Sunday, Hill found George Acker playing poker with two company employees. He wrote in his diary: "Told Acker I hoped he would never let himself indulge in any such game."[37] Acker presumably found other amusements: including the writings of Mark Twain.

Years later, Hill's business records show that there are several memos regarding George Acker and the purchase of the *Denver* steamer. In 1878, Hill writes: "I have recently become the owner of the steam ferry boat *Denver*, and in making the transfer, I find she stands at St. Joseph, Missouri, in the name of a former owner Mr. Blakeston who sold to Munger and Acker, Munger to Acker, and Acker to Hill and Armstrong."[38] The *Denver City* (Denver #1) was owned by the Hannibal and St. Joseph Railroad Company. This burned at the wharf at St. Joseph in 1867. *Denver* #2 was built in Pittsburgh and operated from St. Joseph, Missouri, until March 13, 1880, when it was wrecked on the ice.

Also in the St. Paul-Minneapolis areas was R. \T. Spofford, who bought a copy of Mark Twain's book. He lived at 219 Nicollet Avenue in Minneapolis. Later, at 219–221 Nicollet Avenue, the Dolly Varden Building was built in 1882. Back in the 1830s, the French geographer Jean-Nicholas Nicollet had mapped the upper Mississippi and pointed out the source of the river. Several place names were named after him, including Nicollet Avenue in Minneapolis.

The new attention to Mark Twain in Minneapolis-St. Paul seems to have been rivaled by the lingering impact there of the British author Charles Dickens. The upper Mississippi had gained a curious association with the name of Charles Dickens's character "Dolly Varden" in *Barnaby Rudge* (1841). By 1872, the name had become attached to many things. Dolly Varden was a flirtatious locksmith's daughter who dressed in cherry color hat ribbons and polonaise dresses and attracted many men. In 1872, "Dolly Varden" had become a dress craze and a fashion fad. Dolly Varden costumes were mentioned in *Harper's Bazaar* (July 15, 1871) in "New York Fashion." Upon the opening of the Lord and Taylor department store, the *New York Times* (March 29, 1872) speaks of Dolly Varden dresses. On July 12, 1872, the *New York Times* printed an article about seaside recreation at Long Branch: "Every Day Life, Dolly Varden." Indeed, by 1872, the name Dolly Varden was applied to dress style and hats, paper dolls, a mine in Nevada, a horse racing track at Prospect Park in Brooklyn, and, most enduringly, to a fish. The story has been told that a woman in the western United States, familiar with Dolly Varden fashions, compared the lightly spotted trout to Dolly Varden. The trout reminded her of a beautiful woman in a striped gown. The name Dolly Varden for this trout has lasted to the present day.

On June 4, 1872, Julius Chambers, a reporter and editor for the *New York Tribune*, was visiting Minnesota in search for the origins of the Mississippi River. He had called his canoe the *Dolly Varden*. Designating Elk Lake adjoining Lake Itasca as the origin of the great river, he called the lake Dolly Varden also. The *New York Herald* on July 6, 1872, reported that Chambers paddled his canoe *Dolly Varden* up Nicollet Creek. The *Brooklyn Daily Eagle* reported on July 17, 1872, that Chambers had given up his journey on *Dolly Varden* and gotten on the steamer *Rob Roy*, named after Sir Walter Scott's character.

"The Dolly Varden Letters" were composed by Linda Warfel Slaughter for the *St. Paul Pioneer Press*. The editorial offices for that publication were on Cedar Street between East 4th and East 5th. This was in the same district that the American Publishing Company subscription agent was at work seeking subscriptions to Mark Twain's book. Linda Warfel had married Dr. Benjamin Franklin Slaughter and had followed him to his assignment at forts on the frontier, where their children were born: Rosalynd, Jessamine, and Linda. Her papers indicate that she read both Dickens and Twain.[39]

Mark Twain's books were available at the Minneapolis Public Library, which merged with the Atheneum in 1884. The library was described in 1894 as "one of the most beautiful library buildings in the country… and it houses one of the best of city libraries."[40] Curiously, the Minneapolis Public Library shows all of Twain's works in its catalogue in 1901 except *Huckleberry Finn*. Evidence compiled by Bernadette Lear from 758 locations and 1,200 sources indicates that *Huckleberry Finn* was not widely censored and that the novel appeared in United States libraries more often than other Mark Twain books.[41] However, this was not the case in Minneapolis. A study of Hibbing, Minnesota, readers at this time indicated that *The Adventures of Tom Sawyer* was among the most popular books for school children. Most of the children surveyed were from immigrant families where English was spoken alongside Swedish, Norwegian, Italian, or another European language.[42]

A. MIDDLETOWN READERS

The New York and Hartford book trade sold Twain's books to readers in the suburbs north of New York City. On Stephen Railton's Mark Twain website, he has provided ledgers for a subscription agent in Middletown, New York. Professor Railton's site shows fifty book sales of *Life on the Mississippi*. The first names that appear on the ledger are those of individuals named King and Vail. These are members of the families that jointly owned the local pharmacy, King and Vail Drugs and Medicine on Main Street. There were many members of the Vail family throughout Middletown. This M. Vail may be Maria, who would have been about fifty-three years old at the time of the book purchase. (Jacob and James Vail were with the Orange County Milk Association.) Next on the list is Leander Brink, who sold carpets and furniture at North and Orchard. The Brinks include William, who was about sixty years old, and Alice and Christina, who were in their thirties. J.W. King, who is next on the list, is likely James King, who bought two copies in cloth binding. Julia Van Deusen, who was about forty-one, appears to be the next person on the list.

Many names follow on the subscription ledger list and it is often difficult to trace these people. Some, however, can be identified. Mrs. H. B. Ogden, the wife of hotel keeper Henry B. Ogden, purchased a copy in Half Morocco. Edwin Little, a miller at a nearby mill, bought a cloth bound copy. A copy was purchased by Ida Conkling, whose family were lumber dealers. Mrs. Dekay was the wife of George Dekay, a wagon maker at Houston and Main.

We can see from this sample that this agent apparently targeted businesses. The people who purchased the novel represent a range of business occupations and trades. D. Houston is a member of the Houston family that included William and N.D., the town's sheriff and assistant sheriff. One of the copies of Twain's book was purchased by Peter Hornbeck. Gertrude Hornbeck was a dressmaker. Aaron Hornbeck would become the mayor of Middletown in 1904. The name of another book buyer, Levi Robinson, shows up eight years earlier as a farmhand at William North's estate near Walton Park in 1875. It is certainly possible that Robinson had moved to nearby Middletown by 1883.[43]

Middletown was along the Erie Railroad. It was the site of the Exchange Building and the Gothic Hall. Bull's Opera House had opened back in 1871, with a lecture by P.T. Barnum. On an island in the road at Orchard and North, a statue was dedicated to the Civil War soldiers of Wallkill. While Middletown residents were reading *Life on the Mississippi*, Dr. Julia Badner started the Old Folks Home in town. People began skating at a newly built roller rink. They had recently started using telephones. Back in 1840 the Middletown Lyceum had a library of three hundred volumes. The 1857–1858 Directory reported that the reading room had several hundred volumes. However, interest fell off after the Civil War. The library ceased to exist in 1877. Mary K. Van Keuren, a librarian, reported in 1913 that the Orchard School library, where people had once borrowed books served as the start of a local library. She wrote that "books were gathered together and brought to the Board of Education, and a subscription started for new books." In January 1901 the Thrall Library was dedicated.[44]

B. *THE GILDED AGE*

The book that the Middletown residents were reading, *The Gilded Age*, was Mark Twain's first novel and his only collaborative effort. It turned out to be quite popular on the stage, running for more than one hundred performances. As a topical work filled with contemporary references it aimed at the readers of its time. It gave a name to the era in which it was written but the novel has by now largely faded from view among Twain's better-known books.

In Hartford, an after dinner conversation at Nook Farm turned into a challenge to Charles Dudley Warner and Twain from their wives. Twain's biographer Albert Bigelow Paine noted that Twain recalled to him that the men had been criticizing "the novels in which their wives were finding entertainment." If you think those books are so bad, their wives said, write one that is better.[45] This challenge might be likened to the prompting given to James Fenimore Cooper by his wife, who said something similar when he criticized the fiction of Jane Austen. As a result, Cooper wrote his first novel, *Precaution*. For American authors, there remained the implicit challenge to write novels that were as good as the novels of English authors.

Livy Langdon Clemens and Susan Warner had intervened in a conversation in which their husbands criticized current problems in America. In Justin Kaplan's words, they "suggested that writing was better than criticizing."[46] So, *The Gilded Age* became a curious mixture of story and social critique offered by two very different authors who attempted collaboration. It was Mark Twain's first attempt at writing a novel. "You want to know what I'm doing? I am writing two admirable books" he wrote early in 1874 to Mary Fairbanks.[47] He was now mixing ideas with those of another author, much like he was mixing drinks at the time. Twain had fallen away from his temperance vows to Livy. He made cocktails, noted Charles Warren Stoddard: bourbon, whiskey, sugar, lemons.[48]

Neither Twain nor Warner had written a novel before. Yet, they were sure that their audience would gravitate toward a story that was topical and sensational. Warner was six years older than Clemens. He had worked in business in Philadelphia, as a railroad surveyor for two years in Missouri, and practiced law in Chicago. He had been a newspaper editor in Hartford since the start of the Civil War. He brought these experiences to his part of the collaboration. Warner had recently completed two travel books: *My Summer in a Garden* (1871) and *Saunterings* (1872). It appears that Twain and Warner found fault with the sentimentality in women's novels and insisted upon a need for realism.[49] They shared a skeptical view of America and a common experience of Missouri. They decided that they could put together their resources.

Twain began to work with Warner on a novel with the sharp edge of social satire. *The Gilded Age* (1871) emerged as an experiment in collaboration and novel writing. Its title became the designation for a historic period. At a time when railroads were expanding along with the U.S. economy, the novel appeared as a tale of unsuccessful schemes and political corruption. It appealed to a contemporary audience and their sense of current events. Twain drew upon his family history, stories of Tennessee land, and of the Mississippi steamboat explosion that had killed his brother Henry. The melodrama featured the impractical business of Colonel Sellers and a woman named Laura Hawkins, an impulsive romantic and political lobbyist who murders her lover.

At Nook Farm, each evening Twain and Charles Dudley Warner read the day's work on their manuscript aloud. Their wives, Livy Clemens and Susan Warner, were astute listeners and commentators who were treated to an ongoing serial. "They have done a power of criticizing, but have always been anxious to be on hand at the reading & find out what has been happening [...] since the previous evening," Twain wrote to Mary Fairbanks.[50] The public, meanwhile, appears to have wanted another funny book from Mark Twain. *The Gilded Age* would be something quite different: a melodramatic indictment of corruption.

J.J. Winthrop did not like the book at all:

> I have read it through—& what have you done? Instead of a choice slander on English manners & their infernal "I beg your pardon" &c, it is an unjust libel on the fairest government on which the sun ever shone (which is not saying much) And who in heavens name is your "colleague" Some ___ who no one ever heard of whose name is made illustrious by coupling it with yours & to what purpose To ruin your brilliant reputation. . . .

The critic acknowledges there are some good pieces in the novel and credits Twain for them. However, most are "idiotic," he says.[51]

The reduced sales figures for this book, compared with those of Twain's previous books, may be attributed to audience expectations of humorous content. However, they may also be the result of a slump in the economy, or a response to the sometimes awkward structure of the narrative. Warner and Twain brought their diverse backgrounds to the book. Mark Twain had reported on territorial politics while in Nevada. He lived briefly in Washington, DC, and he wrote of his experience of politics there. Later, in 1890, he recalled: "Was reporter in a legislature two sessions and the same in Congress one session, and thus learned to know personally three sample bodies of the smallest minds and the selfishest souls in and the cowardliest hearts that God makes."[52] At the center of the novel was a political exposé featuring the character Laura Hawkins. This was worked out by both men in collaboration. Colonel Sellers was the creation of Mark Twain, who wrote the first eleven chapters, to page 399. He contributed other blocks or single chapters later, on prospecting and mining and on political corruption. There were "differences in method and temperament" between the men.

The social and historical context in which Twain and Warner wrote is an important aspect of the book they created. It is the context in which their audience encountered their story. What has come to be called the Gilded Age may be characterized by immigration, the notion of progress, trends toward political corruption, the growth of cities, settlement of the West, the experience of African Americans post–Civil War, temperance, women seeking a place in public society, a concern about the theories of Darwin. It was a second industrial revolution: the age of the machine, the spread of railroads, the growth of investment capital, and increasing movement to the cities. After the Civil War American commerce grew. It also became increasingly impersonal. Machine technology reduced the costs of labor. More capitalization was needed for businesses. There were dislocations in money supply. The nation grew in overall wealth and wages rose some 50 percent in manufacturing from 1859–1890. However, there was the depression of 1873–1879 and it affected the American book trade.

Twain and Warner could expect that their audience was aware of a January 1873 scandal in the Grant Administration. Senator Samuel C. Pomeroy, Radical Republican representative for Kansas since 1861, had been suspected of vote buying in two previous elections. This time he was caught. In Topeka, Kansas, he had bribed an official for a nominating vote. Twain and Warner created Senator Abner Dilworthy—the exact image of Pomeroy, as an archetype of corruption. Jim Fink, Boss Tweed, and Credit Mobilier are all recognizable in their novel. Twain also drew upon the case of Laura D. Fair, who walked away from a murder charge on the grounds of "emotional insanity." An acquaintance from Twain's Mississippi River days, M. Jeff Thompson, a state engineer for Louisiana, thought he recognized the origins of several characters and wrote to Warner to tell him so. He added that he supposed that Colonel Sellers and Laura Hawkins were "friends of Clemens."[53]

The book was aimed specifically at contemporary readers. Postwar America witnessed the growth of centralized capital and business inclination toward the exploitation of any opportunity. President Ulysses S. Grant's administration allowed speculators to rig stock shares and divert public wealth to their own purse strings. The Credit Mobilier Scandal shook the nation as Union Pacific stockholders fixed shares with the help of members of Congress, who over-budgeted railroad construction costs. This was the age of Boss Tweed, a notoriously corrupt political machine schemer in New York. *The Gilded Age* exposed Washington workings. The book looked at the social and the political—and the criminal. It also included Twain's first look at race relations.

Twain planned to return to Britain to secure the British copyright and to work on his expected book on England, which he never wrote. The goal was to be on British soil when *The Gilded Age* was published there, to claim copyright. On February 28, 1874, Twain wrote a letter to John Brown in which he claimed that the first two months sales of the book were larger than any other American book. He says in this letter that in the eight weeks since publication they have sold 40,000 books.[54] However, sales were not equal to those for *The Innocents Abroad*. The American Publishing Company bindery records indicated 110,843 copies of *The Innocents Abroad* since July 1869, 85,699 copies of *Roughing It* since January 1872. There were 47,557 copies of *The Gilded Age* distributed since December 1873 and some of these volumes were review copies, rather than sold copies. G. T. Ferris, writing in *Appleton's Journal* (July 4, 1874) repeated these figures and stated that the aggregate sale of Twain's books had reached 241,000 copies and earned some $950,000. This, he said, was a figure "so remarkable as to be almost unparalleled."[55]

Upon reading Twain's book, some readers felt a bond with the author. However, the motives of at least one reader went beyond this. Will Clemens of Akron, Ohio, sought Twain's patronage and continued to write to Twain, as if the author owed him something because they shared the same last name. In his first letter, he wrote: "I have just finished the *Gilded Age* for the second time and I am determined to write to you, not, for the sake of the book but to form an acquaintance with yourself." There were thirteen letters in all from this newspaper writer, R. Kent Rasmussen points out.[56]

The Gilded Age embodied a conscious thrust of political criticism. Ulysses S. Grant was then beginning the second term of his presidency. Grant's vice-president, his private secretary, his bother-in-law, his secretary of war, and his secretary of the treasury were all to be marked by abuse of office and influence. Corporations and combinations were creating monopolies to force out competition. The government was filled with bribery. American cities grew into settings of crime and alienation. This was a time of financial panic as well as a time of reform. The United States experienced the emergence of labor unions. Railroads added powerfully to commerce and brought people across the miles, even as men struggled and railroad baron wars persisted. The United States began to prosper and to gain industrial power. This was also a time of immigration. There was increased social and economic mobility. Amid all of this energetic movement, Twain and Warner wondered: was democracy failing?

In the Hartford community where the men lived, others were wondering less about democracy than about stories of infidelity. In November 1872, Henry Ward Beecher had an affair with Elizabeth Tilton, a Sunday school teacher. She was married to Theodore Tilton, a religious journalist and church member. The affair was blown up into a great scandal. Victoria Woodhull, a proponent of "free love" and of the women's rights movement, a former fortune teller and stockbroker backed by Vanderbilt, had been condemned by Beecher from the pulpit for her own lax relationship standards. She sharply criticized Beecher. Years after her criticism of Beecher, she would begin a quixotic campaign as the first female candidate for the U.S. presidency. The reading audience for the book appears to have most liked the character of Colonel Sellers and only secondarily the other elements of drama in the book: bribery in Washington, lobbying, the promotion of a railroad, coal mining, surveying, the jury system and insanity pleas, business and banking. Twain and Warner had written about corruption schemes in Philadelphia, conflicts between Quaker morality and the marketplace, the Negro and the carpetbaggers, emancipation of women, credit, and frontier life.

The Gilded Age was published in London by Routledge on December 22, 1873, and in the United States by the American Publishing Company. The immediate critical response to the book was mixed. In his review of Mark Twain in *Appleton's* (July 4, 1874), G.L. Ferris wrote, "Like most American humorists, Mark Twain depends chiefly on exaggeration as the effective element in his art."[57] This article follows one titled "The Tyranny of a Republic." By juxtaposition, Twain appears as the democratic image of the American: "He strolls in the open breezy sunshine, happy go lucky fashion, yet with a keenness of vision that allows nothing in his horizon to escape him." Some reviewers panned the novel; its political satire had no precedents no tradition. By spring 1874, some 240,000 copies of Mark Twain's "latest" books had been sold and nearly a million dollars had been made by the American Publishing Company.[58]

Mark Twain, at this time, began to distance himself from the racial prejudice present in the views of his childhood context in Missouri. He recognized the dehumanization that had been enacted and how this had affected both slaves and their owners. To *The Gilded Age* he brought images of pre–Civil War Missouri. He and Warner examined post–Civil War political corruption. Their vision of the ideals of the American Republic cast a satirical look at a troubled period of Reconstruction. Meanwhile, the authors recognized that in post–Civil War America, the nation was moving into a Gilded Age of increasing economic prosperity, technological development, and growth. Railroads were crisscrossing the land backed by investment capital. It was a time of business risks. The nation had moved westward and international trade had vigorously expanded.

Colonel Sellers was perhaps the most entertaining and memorable character in their book. He is the character that readers most recalled in their own references to the novel. In William Dean Howells' view, Colonel Sellers was one image of a representative type: the American character aspiring, bombastic, optimistic. George Escol Sellers of Bowlesville, Illinois heard that his name was being used in the novel. Newspapers claimed he was the model for Colonel Sellers. He was not. But the threat of a lawsuit came with this claim. The Escol in the name was dropped and Warner and Clemens escaped any litigation. Colonel Sellers would become most popular among Americans who saw the theatrical version of *The Gilded Age*.

Mark Twain, by now, had become quite popular, including among the elite of the Eastern literary establishment whose respect he had worked hard to gain. He was invited to a dinner hosted by the *Atlantic Monthly*, which was now published by H.O. Houghton. James Fields had sold the firm to James Osgood, who would become Twain's publisher. In the financial panic of 1873, Osgood had sold off the magazine to Houghton. The magazine remained at the center of the Boston cultural world and William Dean Howells, who much liked Mark Twain and his work, was its editor. At Parker House in Boston December 13, Twain was one of the speakers at this dinner, held by the *Atlantic* to recognize its first years under new owners Henry O. Houghton and George Mifflin. Across the way sat a young man who would soon become the foremost writer of American literature, Henry James, an author who wrote from a different aesthetic than that of Mark Twain. His novel *Watch and Ward* had been published but had quickly faded. *Roderick Hudson* was still in manuscript and not yet published. In the next decades, across many novels and stories, Henry James would reinforce the connection of American literature with the "old world" of Europe, even as Twain was tugging it in a different direction. Twain represented democracy, vernacular speech, comedy, moral and political awareness, and writing stories for the masses. James was a craftsman who offered character study, psychological depth, European settings, resonant symbolism, and challenging prose. Twain's audience might be called "popular" and James's "literary" but such distinctions hardly capture the enduring worth of their writing.

NOTES

1. Justin Kaplan, *Mr. Clemens and Mr. Twain*. New York: Simon and Schuster, 1966. p. 61.

2. Ibid, 62.

3. Michael Winship, "Publishing in America: Needs and Opportunities for Research" (61–102) in History of the Book: America, 1639–1876, ed. David D. Hall and John Hench. Worcester: American Antiquarian Society, 1987. 61–102, Ronald Jenn, "From American Frontiers to European Borders: French Translations of Tom Sawyer and Huckleberry Finn," *Book History* 9, 237–38.

4. Justin Kaplan, *Mr. Clemens and Mr. Twain*, p. 105.

5. Ibid, 106.

6. *Tolland County Press* (August 31, 1876).

7. Mrs. J.W. Likins, *Six Years Experience as a Book Agent. San Francisco, 1874 in California as I Saw It: First Person Narratives of California's Early Years, 1849–1900*. San Francisco, 1874. California State Archives. Library of Congress. www.memory.loc.gov

8. Mrs. J.W. Likins, 79.

9. Ibid, 79.

10. Ibid, 89.

11. Ibid, 102.

12. Ibid, 103.

13. Ibid, 124.

14. Ibid, 110.

15. Ibid, 111.

16. Ibid, 113.

17. Ibid, 116.

18. Ibid, 147.

19. Ibid, 156.

20. American Publishing Company advertisement, 1869. A variation of this appears on the Stephen Railton's "Mark Twain and His Times" website at University of Virginia. Inno3.html.

21. These materials are in the Zinman Collection, University of Pennsylvania.

22. "Ambiguous Advertisements," *New York Times* (March 10, 1873).

23. Zinman Collection, University of Pennsylvania, Philadelphia Area Consortium of Special Collection Libraries.

24. Harriet Wason, *Facts, by a Woman*. Oakland: Pacific Press Publishing House, 1881. Ronald Jenn quotes this from online sources. p. 237. Amy Thomas notes the need for reevaluation of nineteenth-century subscription books. Amy Thomas, "'There is Nothing So Effective as a Personal Canvass': Revaluing Nineteenth-Century American Subscription Books," *Book History* I (1998): 140–55. Distribution of Mark Twain's nov-

els has been looked at since the 1940s, with attention to *The Innocents Abroad* and *A Connecticut Yankee in King Arthur's Court.*

25. *New York Times* (December 3, 1885). The figure of 10,000 subscription agents is provided by Friedman, p. 69. *The Grand Combinator Prospectus* is in the Zinman Collection.

26. Kate Merrybee, "A Lady Tormented by Canvassing Agents," *Free Press* (March 25, 1875).

27. Frank Kelly in Zinman Collection, University of Pennsylvania, Philadelphia Area Consortium of Special Collections Libraries.

28. Stephen Railton, "Mark Twain and his Times," website, http://twain.lib.virginia.edu/index2.html.

29. Leon T. Dickinson, "Mark Twain's Revisions in Writing *The Innocents Abroad,*" *American Literature*, Vol. 19, No. 2 (1947): 139–57.

30. Donald Sheehan, *This Was Publishing: A Chronicle of the Book Trade in the Gilded Age.* Bloomington: Indiana University Press, 1952.

31. C.E. Miller, "Give the Books to Clemens," *American History* 34 (1990): 40–44.

32. G. Carson "Get the prospect seated… and keep talking," *American Heritage* Vol. 9, No. 5 (1958): 38–41, 77–80; D.P. O'Hara, "Book Publishing in the United States to 19012, Subscription Books and Their Publishers," *Publisher's Weekly* 115 (May 11, 1929): 2244–2246.

33. *Mark Twain Letters*, Mark Twain Papers, MTP, University of California, Bancroft Library, 14497.

34. *Brooklyn Eagle* (Friday, February 7, 1873). The distance from Brooklyn to St. Paul is 1,197.7 miles.

35. Stephen Railton, "Marketing Twain," "Mark Twain and His Times" website, University of Virginia.

36. Information on residents obtained from Minnesota state census records and local publications. Also useful were maps from the John L. Borchert Map Library, City of St. Paul.

37. James Hill Diary and Notebook. May 3, 1873, James Hill Family Papers. Minnesota Historical Society.

38. James Hill Letter Book, April 11, 1878–January 16, 1879, p. 261. The James J. Hill-George Acker Letters are in the collection of the Minnesota Historical Society, Roll 19, Roll 20.

39. Benjamin and Linda Slaughter Papers, State Historical Society of South Dakota. Linda Warfel Slaughter became a deputy superintendent of schools, a temperance union leader, and the vice present of a women's suffrage association. Besides this, she was the writer of *The Freedmen of the South* (1869), *Fortress to Farm, Twenty Three Years on the Frontier, The New Northwest,* "My Soldier," (1904) and "The Surrender of Sitting Bull" (1904).

40. William Isaac Fletcher, *Public Libraries of America.* Boston: Roberts Brothers, 1894, p. 93.

41. Bernadette Lear, "Were Tom and Huck on the Shelf?" *Nineteenth-Century Literature* 64 (September 2009). p. 213. Lear points out that her findings show "diverse reactions" of librarians in Scranton and Wilkes-Barre, Pennsylvania, and that most libraries did not ban *Huckleberry Finn.* She reject's Geller's assertion in *Forbidden Books* that *Huckleberry Finn* was "widely censored" and demonstrates that the novel was seldom censored and was widely available.

42. Reading in Hibbing, *English Journal* (1918): 474–487.

43. Information on residents obtained from Middletown publications, New York State Census records. The census data for Middletown appears inexact. John H. Hasbrouck's 1857–1858 *Middletown Directory* is a useful source, although its listings of residents are from more than two decades before the time this subscription agent canvassed this area. The growth of Middletown from a village to its incorporation as a city in 1888 is evident in Hasbrouck's publication and library records. In the 1857–1858 Directory we see ads for "Horse Thief Detecting Societies," "Truss: the Utero-Abdomi-

nal Supporter," the F.B. Hulse Coal Yard, and T.C. Royce-Dental Surgeon "Satisfaction Guaranteed." Identification of book buyers through these records is, in some cases, uncertain. For example, was W.A. Horton, who purchased the Twain book, related to Eugene Horton, who had a mansion on South Street?

44. Barbara C. Chumard, *Thrall Library, 1901–1960, A Historical Study of a Small Town Library.* SUNY-Albany, MLS thesis, 1996.

45. Albert Bigelow Paine, *Mark Twain: A Biography. Mark Twain Letters*, Vol. 5, 259.

46. Justin Kaplan, *Mr. Clemens and Mr. Twain*, p. 159.

47. Mark Twain, Letter to Mary Fairbanks. April 1873. *Mark Twain Letters*, Vol. 5. The second story was, apparently, the beginning of *The Adventures of Tom Sawyer.*

48. Ron Powers, *Mark Twain: A Life*, p. 340.

49. Female reformers like Isabelle Hooker likewise rejected the images of the Victorian woman promoted by these novels.

50. Mark Twain, Letter to Mary Fairbanks, 1873, *Mark Twain Letters*, Vol. 5, University of California Press, p. 171.

51. J.J. Winthrop, Letter to Mark Twain, August 10, 1874. Mark Twain Papers, University of California, Bancroft Library. See Rasmussen, 29.

52. Justin Kaplan, *Mr. Clemens and Mr. Twain*, p. 159.

53. Justin Kaplan, *Mr. Clemens and Mr. Twain*, 161. James Lampton became Colonel Sellers. Other people made claims for this character's origins. Twain later received the rights to make this a character in a play adapted from the novel.

54. Justin Kaplan, *Mr. Clemens and Mr. Twain*, 163. M. Jeff Thompson letter to Charles Dudley Warner (February 20, 1874), MTP UCLC 39061. Mark Twain Letter to John Brown (February 28, 1874), Mark Twain Letter to Elisha Bliss (May 22, 1874), G. L. Ferris, *Appleton's Journal*, Vol. 12, Is. 276 (July 4, 1874): 15–18. p. 17.

55. G. L. Ferris, *Appleton's Journal*, Vol. 12, Is. 276 (July 4, 1874): 15–18. p. 17.

56. Will Montgomery Clemens, Letter to Mark Twain, Akron, Ohio, November 26, 1877. University of California, Mark Twain Collection, Bancroft Library.

57. G.L. Ferris, *Appleton's Journal* 16.

58. Ron Powers, *Mark Twain: A Life*, p. 350.

FOUR

The Trouble That Began at Eight

Audiences for Twain's Lectures

The stage was a natural place for Mark Twain. Interaction with his audience through his lectures fostered the sale and reading of his books. The popularity of Twain's lectures suggests an important interaction between the writer and his audience and between written texts and oral culture. This interaction can be explored through letters to Twain and newspaper accounts that sometimes reveal the presence of audience members at his lectures. In journals and diaries, often there is only a mere mention of attending a lecture, as in the diary of Ezra Pabody, who went to a Twain lecture in Minneapolis:

> Saturday, January 24, 1885—I was quite hoarse this morning when I got up but it soon passed away. . . . At two o'clock Aunt Myra and I went to hear Mark Twain at the grand opera house. I thawed out the water pipes in Mr. Harrington's this evening.[1]

This passage is characterized by the absence of any obvious reaction to Twain. Twain's lecture and Mr. Harrington's water pipes appear equally important to Mr. Pabody. Newspaper accounts that mention audience responses often suggest that Twain made captivating contact with the people in his audience. "He [....] seeks to establish a sort of button-hole connection" said one reviewer.[2] Even so, news accounts usually focus upon Twain rather than his audience. They also show that reporters sometimes held contrasting views about the same lecture. It is difficult to know if the opinions of these reporters were representative of the views of a varied audience.

Twain critics like Fred Lorch have done extraordinary work in broadening our knowledge of Twain's lecture audiences. Even so, we still have much to learn about their responses to Twain's narrative voices from the stage. Henry B. Wonham has convincingly pointed out that, in the case of Mark Twain, the author who reads his work to his audience is something of "an artifice" who tells his narrator's story and establishes, through voice and gestures, "a community based on shared understanding and experience."[3] Wonham observes that "Individual members of a living audience are knit together both by cultural ties and the simultaneity of their responses."[4] There is also the "inherent difference between oral and written presentation" that Wonham recognizes. The onstage presentation is a form of communication that approximates folk narrative performance. Or, as Walter Ong has observed, the "narrator in an oral culture . . . normally and naturally operated in episodic patterning" and practiced a style that was "aggregative" and "additive" rather than "analytic."[5] We know that Twain's narrative performance was interactive and had these characteristics. Yet, we may ask how audiences received and interacted with Twain's lectures. A gathering of audience comments in a given locale might be placed alongside library records, newspaper reviews, reading circle minutes, and other documents to help us to gain a more personalized account of Mark Twain's audience in different communities.

Mark Twain was a performer. That much was obvious to his audience. After seeing Charles Dickens present his public reading on December 31, 1867, Mark Twain made a significant note about Dickens that he later applied in his own work: "He did not merely read, but also acted."[6] That kind of performance was Twain's manner of lecturing also. Although his presentations were called "lectures," most often Mark Twain read aloud from his works. He adapted these readings to his audiences. His humorous anecdotes came as digressions. He believed that "narrative should flow as flows the brook down through the hills and leafy woodlands, its course changed by every bowlder."[7] He wrote, "To string incongruities and absurdities together in a wandering and sometimes purposeless way, and seem innocently unaware that they are absurdities, is the basis of the American art."[8]

To his first audiences, Twain was recognizable as a humorist. He was frequently compared with comic lecturers and storytellers like Artemus Ward. In 1868, Twain stood five feet, ten inches, and he had long legs, the kind that dangle, step broadly, and make a conspicuous entrance on stage. He had curly reddish brown hair, a full moustache, and bright eyes. As a lecturer, he was developing a public personality and there is little doubt that his lecture tours stimulated future sales of his books. People attending Twain's lectures expected him to be funny. He responded by combining serious information with comic anecdotes. In 1867–1868 publications he is described as slouching, shifting moods, and using description.

Twain's first lectures could be situated within a tradition of lecturing that had been popular for several decades. He worked with the power of his personality to enchant and move a crowd. Through these lectures, Twain sustained a sense of contact with his reading audience at a time when an increasingly industrialized publishing business took aim at a mass readership. At first, some of his lecture audiences were small. He recalled a sparse audience in St. Louis early in his career as a lecturer: "Behind them stretched that fearful row of barren benches. It was like talking to people on the edge of the great Desert of Sahara, but we had a good time."[9] However, more often, Twain's lectures were well-attended. As a showman, he was ever conscious of developing the promotional means for drawing a crowd to his lectures. In 1869, he took out newspaper ads in San Francisco newspapers for his first lecture, famously noting that the doors would open at seven and "The trouble begins at eight." He arranged to have men who could laugh loudly planted in the audience.[10] Later, in 1876, he encouraged his lecture manager James Pond to print handbills and posters and to have men with sandwich board announcements walk across busy intersections.

A. THE FIRST LECTURE

Lecture audiences first encountered Mark Twain in San Francisco. Upon returning to the city in 1866 from the Sandwich Islands, which we now know as Hawaii, he became a performer. He rented Maguire's Academy of Music, a hall on Pine Street near Montgomery seating 1,500 to 2,000 people. For Twain's lecture debut, on October 2, 1866, Thomas Maguire agreed to rent the hall for half-price on credit and fifty percent of the gate proceeds. Twain enlisted three men to sit in the hall and laugh uproariously. He spent $750 on publicity handbills and ran notices in the local newspapers that have become legendary. These concluded with the phrase: "Doors Open at 7 o'clock. The Trouble to begin at 8 o'clock."

Twain's concern with his image and reception are immediately evident. On October 2, 1866, he arrived early at the Academy of Music and wandered nervously backstage. When the lights came up, he was surprised to see that the house was full. Twain's lecture on Hawaii was as informative as it was humorous. For example, he gave attention to sugar production in the islands: "I have dwelt upon this subject to show you that these islands have a genuine importance to America—an importance which is not generally appreciated by our citizens. They pay revenues into the United States Treasury now amounting to over half a million a year [...] The property has got to fall to heir, and why not the United States?"[11] He encouraged his listeners to imagine standing atop Haleakala looking down at "the seething world of fire that once swept up out of the tremendous abyss ages ago." His audience was brought to Hawaii imaginatively through descriptive writing and perspective:

> These bushes look like parlor shrubs from the summit where you stand, and the file of visitors moving through them on their mules is diminished to a detachment of mice almost; and to them you, standing so high against the sun, ten thousand feet above their heads, look no larger than a grasshopper.
>
> This in the morning; but at three or four in the afternoon a thousand little patches of white clouds, like handfuls of wool, come drifting noiselessly, one after another, into the center, like a procession of shrouded phantoms, and circle round and round the vast sides, and settle gradually down and mingle together until the colossal basin is filled to the brim with snowy fog, and all its seared and desolate wonders are hidden from sight. [12]

Mark Twain brought descriptions like this east with him, trying them out on audiences in New York and Brooklyn. A newspaper noted one of the performances:

> A choice audience appeared last night to hear Mark Twain, the California humorist [...] In California, Mark Twain is well-known and draws like a poultice, but among us he is a stranger. Notwithstanding this he will soon win his way to public favor. [13]

Twain realized that most of his audience had come to expect humor from him. In the lectures there was an instructive vein and vivid description but people attended his lectures for his humor. While he entertained successfully, he may have also had a suspicion that he was not reaching everyone in his audience. He conveyed this humorously in a sketch, "How the Author Was Sold in Newark," which he wrote sometime in 1869. In this essay he writes of being invited to speak to a society, where one member, aware of his reputation as a humorist, asks if the humorist can do something to cheer his uncle "who had grown bereft of all emotion." He states that he believes that he can. "My son, bring the old party round. I have got some jokes in that lecture that will make him laugh, if there is any laugh in him [...]" Unfortunately, the jokes are unsuccessful ("but I never moved him once"). Feeling puzzled that his jokes did not move the man, he speaks to the president of the society: "I was going to make that confounded old fool laugh, in the second row." The society's president replies, "Well, you were wasting your time, because he is deaf and dumb, and as blind as a badger." [14]

Twain began his first tour lecturing on *The Innocents Abroad* on November 17, 1868, in Cleveland, where some of the travelers who had been on the *Quaker City* voyage lived. Anticipating a challenging audience, he wrote to Mrs. Fairbanks: "I would like you to write the first critique on this lecture—and then it wouldn't be slurred over carelessly, anyhow." [15] Mrs. Fairbanks advertised nine days before the Cleveland lecture with notices, followed by "reminders." She reprinted three of Twain's pieces. Her own comments appeared in the *Cleveland Herald* November 18, the day after the lecture.

Mark Twain's lecture audiences appear in the background of most newspaper reviews. At times there is a brief description of this woman, or that man in the crowd, but their names seldom, if ever, appear. Those reviews of Twain's lectures cover the entire spectrum of good to bad and they focus upon Twain. Two days before Christmas, in Detroit, a reporter criticized Twain for a "fake" drawl (Dec. 23, 1868). Shortly after the New Year, a journalist in Indiana compared his images of Europe to "a string of pearls from which the string has been lost."[16] The next day, a reporter in Indianapolis said that if anyone doubted it would be a fun night and expected boredom, once he or she heard the drawl that soon changed.

> The awakening from this error comes so suddenly, so thoroughly and so pleasantly too, that from this point on to the close of the lecture, the doubter at first, is a willing and delighted captive, drinking in every word.

However, the *Indianapolis Daily Sentinel*, published the same day, had a different opinion:

> [O]f all the miserable speaking ever heard, Mark Twain certainly can get up the poorest. Imagine a singsong snuffling tone from the nose, never varying six notes, and frequently mumbling out so that no one could understand it, and imagine that tone proceeding from a rather good looking young man, who wears good clothes, but is apparently afraid of making a gesture, and who generally keeps one hand raised above him and resting upon a desk that no one but Goliath could have read from with ease, and you have Mark Twain.[17]

In late March, 1869, the *Chicago Tribune* described him: He "hangs around loose […] leaning on the desk or flirting around the corners of it; then marching and counter-marching to the rear of it." The *Chicago Tribune* reporter observed that Twain's humor often arrived at the end of a sentence or phrase, after a pause.[18] As in most other reports, we receive descriptions of Twain and few descriptions of audience responses to him.

At the time Mark Twain first stepped onto the lecture stage, lectures had become a popular form of entertainment. The postwar years saw the rise of industry and the growth of cities and the postwar lecture circuit was fairly vibrant. Mark Twain, who was becoming familiar to audiences as one of America's great humorists, joined that lecture circuit. Comparing Artemus Ward with Mark Twain, Bret Harte affirmed that the uniqueness of Mark Twain was "more thoroughly national and American than even the Yankee delineations of Lowell."[19] J.G. Holland in *Scribner's* magazine, however, criticized the lecture circuit and complained that ephemeral fame was valued over learning, virtue, and social accomplishment. The "literary buffoon" was honored by the crowd, he wrote, suggesting American humorists like Mark Twain. The crowd was pleased by a "showman," an "object of curiosity." The lyceum and its serious educational lectures had been replaced by this. He argued, "The lecture room must cease to be a showroom of fresh notorieties, at high prices." [20]

Twain later commented on the lecture circuit of that time: "Beecher, Gough, Nasby, and Anna Dickinson were the only lecturers who knew their own value and exacted it. In towns their fee was $200 and $250; in cities $400. The lyceum always got a profit out of these four . . . but generally lost it again on the house-emptiers." He wrote: "There were two women who should have been house emptiers—Olive Logan and Kate Field—but during a season or two they were not." Logan was an actress. Field's notoriety came from letters she sent to the *New York Tribune* about Dickens's readings in 1867. There was, says Twain, "a frenzy of enthusiasm about Dickens." Field telegraphed these letters, which was something of a novelty at the time. "By and by she went to the platform; but two or three years had elapsed her and her subject—Dickens—had now lost its freshness and its interest. [21]

Audiences crowded Twain's lectures. In 1871, he returned to the lecture circuit, managed by James Redpath's firm in Boston. The lectures began in Bethlehem, Pennsylvania, in October. On November 22, 1871, the *Brooklyn Daily Eagle* and the *Brooklyn Daily Union* both reviewed Twain's lecture on Artemus Ward at Henry Ward Beecher's Plymouth Church. The *Brooklyn Union* wrote of "an audience who from the first manifested that they had come with the determination of being amused." The *Brooklyn Daily Eagle* offered what are presumably snippets of conversation, although it is difficult to determine whether these are overheard, or bits of creative writing:

> "My, what a handsome young man to be a lecturer!"
> "He married over three millions of money, and lectures for fun."
> "So he ought, if he's a funny lecturer."
> "He isn't a bit funny now that he's married."
> "He's got a baby and that takes all the humor out of him." [22]

On the last day of 1871, while on lecture tour near Paris, Illinois, Twain wrote a letter to his wife Olivia concerning how, in a moment along the tour, he recalled his childhood:

> It was the West & boyhood brought back again, vividly. It was as if
> twenty-five years had fallen away from me like a garment & I was a lad
> of eleven again in my Missouri church of that ancient time. [23]

He had become a master of the calculated pause. Audiences would see a sparkle come to his eyes, a twitch breaking across his lips, and then they would wait for a punch line. Twain later acknowledged this aspect of his speaking repertoire:

When a man is reading from a book on the platform, he soon realizes that there is one powerful gun in his battery of artifice that he can't work with an effect proportionate to its caliber: that is the pause- that impressive silence, that eloquent silence which often achieves a desired effect where no combination of words howsoever felicitous could accomplish it.[24]

His humorous anecdotes from *Roughing It* were often told in a deadpan manner. "The humorous story is told gravely," Mark Twain said. "[T]he teller does his best to conceal the fact that he even dimly suspects there is anything funny about it."[25]

The *Overland Monthly* described Twain's stage presence and his rapport with his audience:

Mark Twain's method as a lecturer was distinctly unique and novel. His slow, deliberate drawl, the anxious and unique perturbed expression of the visage, the apparently pained effort with which he framed his sentences, and, above all, the surprise that spread over his face when the audience roared with delight or rapturously applauded the finer passages of his word-painting, were unlike anything of the kind they had ever known.[26]

Twain came to know some of his audience through these lectures. He later wrote, "An audience likes a speaker with the same weaknesses and the same virtues as they themselves have. If the lecturer's brow is too high and the brows of the audience are too low, look out. Or if a highbrow audience sees a lowbrow lecturer there's trouble."[27]

We have Twain's daughter Susy's account of observing one of his lectures at Vassar College in Poughkeepsie. Susy Clemens recalled:

It was the first time I had ever heard him read in my life, that is in public. When he came out onto the stage I remember the people behind me exclaimed "oh, how queer he is!" "isn't he funny!" I thought papa was very funny although I did not think him queer. He read "A Trying Situation" and "The Golden Arm," a ghost story that he heard down South when he was a little boy.[28]

Susy Clemens writes that she knew what was coming: a startling moment. She "resolved not to be startled" and then she watched the entire audience as "they jumped as one man."[29] This suggests that Susy Clemens may have been able to anticipate an audience's reactions like her father could. During his 1884-1885 lecture tour with George Washington Cable Twain indicated that he could read his audience's responses. Twain's attention to this suggests that, as a lecturer, he was ever conscious of audience response. A reporter from the *Baltimore American* directly asked him if he was able to gauge an audience:

Oh, yes. If you hear a rustle here or there, or see a particularly stolid face, you can tell that there is something wrong with yourself [...] Audiences have their peculiarities, you know. It is a great inspiration to find a particular individual respond to you as if you were in telegraphic communication with him. You are tempted to address yourself solely to him. I've tried that experiment. Sometimes it is dangerous. Laughter is very infectious, and when you see a man give one great big guffaw, you begin to laugh with him in spite of yourself.[30]

B. AUDIENCES FOR THE TWAIN-CABLE LECTURE TOUR

The subscription sales audience of *Huckleberry Finn* was primed by a lecture tour that Mark Twain organized with his tour manager James Pond in 1884. *Huckleberry Finn* was being readied for publication when Twain went on a speaking tour with George Washington Cable. The "Twins of Genius" tour, as it was called, went to eighty cities and they shared 103 lecture performances, each lasting about two hours. On November 5, 1884, they opened their lecture tour in New Haven, Connecticut. An excerpt from *Huckleberry Finn* appeared in the *Century* one week later. They concluded their tour in Washington, DC, on February 28, 1885. Mark Twain made some $16,000 on this tour.[31]

They were a peculiar team, Twain and Cable, and they were cast as antithetical. A deeply religious and socially conscious mulatto from Louisiana, Cable moved audiences with his stories of Creole life. Twain was cast as a humorist and his audience came to expect laughter. Cable's stand on slavery and postwar treatment of blacks was criticized in the South and Twain and Cable avoided lectures there because of Cable's controversial positions. Twain's lack of Christian commitment grated on Cable and Cable's sectarian religiosity grated on Twain. Critic Carrie Johnston contends that their pairing "effaced Twain's connection to the South," identified Cable as a regional writer, and consolidated Twain's national reputation.[32] Well aware that audience members and readers sometimes wrote to Twain, Cable had played a practical joke on him. Cable gathered 150 of Twain's friends to request autographs by mail. The letters were timed to arrive on April Fool's Day and not a single stamp or reply envelope was included.[33]

Aside from these prank letters, Twain received authentic letters from his audience about his lectures with Cable. William Smart was likely in the audience for one of the Twain-Cable lectures at Chickering Hall in New York on November 18, 1884. He wrote to him immediately afterward:

> I have just been hearing you read, and my pleasure was only marred by the regret that Scotchmen have so few chances of hearing you at any time. Now I do not know if you care anything about lecturing but if you ever did think of visiting my country I think you would have a very great success. Perhaps you are aware how widely your books are read and understood in Scotland. I know I am not alone in having read

every word you have ever published I think; and I know how keenly you are appreciated in that dull witted country.

Smart identified himself as a Glasgow merchant and said that he would gladly inquire into lecture possibilities for Twain in Scotland, a place where Twain never lectured. He concluded his letter:

> If all this is impertinence never mind. I only write because I feel that I know you: your works are so exactly yourself that I felt you were no stranger the moment you opened your mouth.[34]

Many years later, Linnie M. Bourne wrote a recollection of the Cable-Twain tour to Twain on November 3, 1907:

> Years ago when I was a slip of a girl, I made a funny slip of the tongue over your name. It was when you were giving a joint reading here with Geo. W. Cable. As I was hurrying along to your reading with my dear grand-daddy we were overtaken by a man friend who wanted to know where we were bound, all so fast I explained- "We're going to hear Cain and Able read."[35]

Twain appears to have had some effect upon George Washington Cable, who gave attention to Twain's humor and to "masking." Cable had a strong interest in reform and he was a secretary for an investigation of prisons and asylums in New Orleans. In his works, he sought to expose conditions affecting blacks and to raise concern for social equality. With his novel *The Grandissimes*, Cable engaged in what John Cleman and others view as political work, interrogating public society in Creole Louisiana.[36] Several years before Twain's *Pudd'nhead Wilson* explored racial matters, Cable's novel acknowledged that miscegenation was common in slavery and implied that no color line could be clearly drawn. In his social analysis, Cable concluded that the blacks he encountered were caught in an economic plight and a condition of illiteracy. Yet, he noted that many of them appeared to prefer status and fine clothes and "manners" to personal development, or pursuing issues of social justice.[37]

From February 5, 1884, to February 28, 1885, Twain traveled with Cable. *Huckleberry Finn* was not yet published but Twain read excerpts from his novel to about 500 people at each location. "Tom and Huck's Remarkable Achievement" in what is sometimes called the "Evasion" chapter was often what he chose to read. These public appearances made audiences aware of Twain's new novel and promoted its distribution. The second installment of *Huckleberry Finn* appeared in the *Galaxy* in January 1885 alongside George Washington Cable's essay "The Freedman's Case in Equity." Southern newspapers castigated the article and objected to Cable. The lecturers took their tour north and African American people came out to see them and shake Cable's hand. The occasion was an introduction for some of these people to Mark Twain.

When Twain was asked why the two writers were touring together, he said:

> Why have I got Cable with me? Well, I don't feel like taking the respon-
> sibility of giving the entire show. I want someone to help me [...] Then
> I want company, good company.[38]

They traveled widely. While in Rochester, New York, Cable took a copy of Thomas Malory's *Le Morte d'Arthur* from some shelves and handed it to Twain. The story of King Arthur and his Round Table stirred the writer's imagination. It suggested to him a story of time travel, of present meeting past, a social satire that would become *A Connecticut Yankee in King Arthur's Court*. Meanwhile, the Twain-Cable tour traveled across the landscape of the Midwest: to Chicago, Milwaukee, Madison, Minneapolis and St. Paul, then back to Chicago. Twain visited his family in Keokuk, Iowa. As a snowstorm swirled around the opera house there, Twain performed to an audience that one reporter said "almost fell from their seats." Soon the *Brooklyn Eagle* was writing (March 20, 1885): "You have heard of Mark Twain's new book, *Huckleberry Finn* [...]"[39] After the laughter, press, and income generated by the Twain-Cable tour, many people had.

As we will later see, Twain made longer journeys on his world lecture tour in 1895. He began this in the United States, assisted by his tour manager James Pond, and continued across western Canada. From there he sailed across the Pacific to Australia. The repeated press generated by the tour appears to have consolidated Twain's growing public visibility. On July 15, 1895, in Cleveland it was a hot ninety degrees. There were some 2,600 people in Twain's audience at the Music Hall and no air conditioning. In the midst of the audience, some 200 news boys were restless. Twain abbreviated his performance and quickly got out. "[I]t was a menagerie," he wrote to Henry Huddleson Rogers.[40] As he resumed his North American tour, he was to earn more than five hundred dollars per performance. On August 14, 1895, he commented in a letter to Samuel Moffett on having many "unknown friends" in America. "Lecturing is gymnastics, chest-expander, medicine, mind healer, blues destroyer, all in one," he wrote.[41]

Most of the friends of Mark Twain's lecture audiences remain unknown. We can surmise that Twain's lectures were a mind healer and blues destroyer for some people in his audience. Newspaper accounts suggest that the lectures were often a delightful experience. James Redpath stated his desires as a lecture promoter clearly: "We want more from a man or woman than books can give- the living voice, at least electric with enthusiasm and earnestness."[42] Twain provided this, making captivating contact with the people in his audience. "He [....] seeks to establish a sort of button-hole connection" said a reviewer.[43]

John D. Rhodes, a stenographer in Washington, DC, wrote to Twain that he regretted not hearing him lecture, but that he had made a great impact upon his life. In a tribute to Twain's seventieth birthday he wrote on December 14, 1905:

> Ever since I have been old enough to regret, I have regretted that you deserted the lecture platform before I was old enough, or was living in a place where I could hear you. After years of reflecting on your writings, I have decided to write you a letter, and tell you that my life has been made happier, and I have come to look at things in a sunnier light, than I would had I never been raised on a diet of Mark Twain.
>
> I have read all your books I have been able to get hold of, I believe all, and am boy enough yet to say I think the Adventures of Huckleberry Finn is my favorite, with Tom Sawyer a close second. I think every child in the land should have those books offered to it as soon as it begins to take pleasure in reading, and I am sure from my own experience that much happiness would result.[44]

A search for the letters, diaries, and autobiographies of audience members like John D. Rhodes may bring us closer to his contemporaries and give us a more complete understanding of the variety of audience responses to his lectures. Mr. Rhodes read as many of Twain's books as he could find. He wished that he had seen and heard Twain on the lecture platform. Happiness is what Twain brought him, he says, and he recommended his books for childhood readers.

NOTES

1. Ezra Pabody, Minneapolis, appears in the James K. Hosmer Collection, Minneapolis Public Library. The Minneapolis library also houses the Hoag Mark Twain Collection.

2. For this review see Charles Neider, Mark Twain's *Autobiography*, New York: Harper Perennial, 2000.

3. Henry Wonham, *Mark Twain and the Art of the Tall Tale*, New York: Oxford University Press, 1993. p. 291. See also Fred Lorch, *The Trouble Begins at Eight*. See especially pp. 237–43.

4. Henry Wonham, 290, 296.

5. Walter Ong, *Orality and Literacy: The Technology of the Word*. London and New York: Methuen, 1982, 148–49, 37–45.

6. Mark Twain observed Dickens on December 31, 1867, at Steinway Hall. His comments first appeared in the *Alta California* in January 1868. This comment also appears in the *Autobiography*, edited by Charles Neider, New York: Harper, 1959, p. 229.

7. *Autobiography*, ed. Albert Bigelow Paine, rpt. 2003, Part 2, p. 237. A variation on this appears in *Autobiography*, ed. Elinor Smith et. al. Berkeley: University of California Press (2010) p. 224.

8. Mark Twain, *How To Tell a Story*. Peter Messent points to Artemus Ward's techniques and quotes Twain. See Peter Messent, *The Short Works of Mark Twain: A Critical Study*, 2001, p. 28.

9. *New York World*, September 4, 1895. *Mark Twain, The Complete Interviews*. Ed. Gary Scharnhorst. Tuscaloosa: University of Alabama Press, 2006. p. 194.

10. Mark Twain's arrangements for publicity have been mentioned by Fred Lorch, Louis J. Budd, Ron Powers, and others.

11. Twain's material on Hawaii became part of *The Innocents Abroad*. See *Mark Twain's San Francisco*, ed. Bernard Taper, Heyday, 2003 and Fred W. Lorch, *The Trouble Begins at Eight*, Ames: Iowa State University Press, 1968.

12. Albert Bigelow Paine, *Autobiography*, Appendix D, p. 1601.

13. Albert Bigelow Paine, *Autobiography*, pp. 1602–03. *Brooklyn Eagle* (May 11, 1867): 3.

14. "How the Author Was Sold in Newark" (1869) in *Sketches, New and Old*, Uniform Edition, Vol. XIX New York: Harper and Brothers, 1903.

15. *Mark Twain and Mrs. Fairbanks*, p. 46; See Fred W. Lorch, *The Trouble Begins at Eight*, Ames: Iowa State University Press, 1968. p. 45.

16. Fred Lorch provides the first of these accounts: December 23, 1868, and Fort Wayne *Daily Gazette*, January 4, 1869, p. 46. One example of notes from individuals who responded to Twain's lectures is the Clyde and Edith Barcus Scrapbook, page 15, University of Nevada. Mark Twain lecture, Innocents Abroad. Piper's Opera House. Southern Nevada, Boomtown Years. See *The Trouble Begins at Eight*, Ames: Iowa State University Press, 1968.

17. The contrasting views of the *Indianapolis Journal* and the *Indianapolis Daily Sentinel* were both published on January 5, 1869.

18. *Chicago Tribune* (January 8, 1869). Fred W. Lorch speaks of "Jumping Frog" being published "to the delight of many readers." p. 44. We may ask who these delighted readers were. His letters to the *Alta California* and the *New York Tribune* had been printed. His humorous articles "went the rounds of the press" and, Lorch says, were "reaching many of the communities where he later had lecture engagements." For many, Mark Twain was already a familiar name: "In fall 1868, they knew the name Mark Twain and liked what he wrote." *The Trouble Begins at Eight*. Ames: Iowa State University, 1968. p. 44.

19. Bret Harte comments are cited in Mark Twain Letters, Vol. 2.

20. J.G. Holland, "Star Lecturing," *Scribner's* 8 (May 1874): 110.

21. A. B. Paine Vol. 2, p. 527. Kate Field was a popular lecturer and writer. Justin Kaplan writes that Twain's letters from abroad to the *Alta California* were "enormously popular" in the west and "surprised and delighted most of his readers." Yet, how can one know unless we have excavated this audience's responses? This was, as Kaplan points out, "an avid, newly lettered and newly leisured mass audience." It was one that "shaped the character of the books, magazines, newspapers and lecture programs of the Gilded Age," p. 57. This suggests the importance of finding the common audience, who affected these print and oral interactions.

22. *Brooklyn Daily Union* (November 22, 1871), *Brooklyn Daily Eagle* (November 22, 1871).

23. Mark Twain, Letter to Olivia Clemens, December 31, 1871. *Mark Twain Letters*, Vol. 4, University of California Press, p. 527.

24. *Autobiography*, Charles Neider, p. 238.

25. Mark Twain, *How to Tell a Story*.

26. *Overland Monthly* Vol. 33, Is. 196 (April 1899): 375–80. p. 380.

27. *Mark Twain and I*, Opie Read, p. 53.

28. Susy Clemens, *Papa: An Intimate Biography*, ed., Charles Neider. pp. 130–31.

29. Ibid.

30. Ron Powers, *Mark Twain: A Life*, p. 485.

31. *Keokuk Daily Gate City*. January 16, 1885. See Stephen Railton website, *Mark Twain and His Times*, also Ron Powers, *Mark Twain: A Life*, p. 499.

32. Carrie Johnston, "Mark Twain's Remarkable Achievement: Effacing the South for Northern Audiences," *Rocky Mountain Review* (2013): 67.

33. Fred Kaplan, *The Singular Mark Twain*, New York: Doubleday, 2002. p. 407

34. William Smart, Letter to Mark Twain, November 18, 1884, New York. MTP, University of California. Rasmussen, 106.

35. Linnie M. Bourne, Letter to Mark Twain, November 3, 1907. R. Kent Rasmussen points out that Linnie Bourne was probably about twenty-eight when she heard Twain and Cable in a Congregational Church in Washington, DC, on February 28, 1885. MTP, University of California. Rasmussen, 246.

36. John Cleman, *George Washington Cable Revisited*. Boston: Twayne, 1976. An African American audience followed Cable and was further introduced to Twain. Readers of the *North American Review* would later hear about Twain from Booker T. Washington: "In a word, he succeeded in literature as few men of any age have succeeded, because he stuck close to nature and to the common people, and in doing so he disregarded in large degree many of the ordinary rules of rhetoric which often serve merely to cramp and make writers unnatural and uninteresting," ctd. Fishkin 105.

37. John Cleman, *George Washington Cable Revisted*, p. 24.

38. *Baltimore American* (November 29, 1884).

39. *Brooklyn Eagle* (March 20, 1885).

40. Mark Twain, Letter to Henry Huddleston Rogers, July 16, 1895. MTP, University of California.

41. Mark Twain, Letter to Samuel Moffat, August 14, 1895. MTP, University of California.

42. Cherches dissertation, 235, ctd. by David Haven Blake, Walt Whitman p. 153.

43. Ron Powers, *Mark Twain: A Life*, p. 148.

44. John D. Rhodes, Letter to Mark Twain, December 14, 1905, Washington, DC. MTP, University of California. Rasmussen, 224–225.

FIVE

Childhood Reading

Soon after Mark Twain's first books appeared, his writing entered family circles and among his audiences there were children. Childhood readers comprised an important segment of Twain's readership. This segment of his audience beckons for investigation. Even when children could not yet read, they were listeners to their parents or to their siblings' readings of Mark Twain's anecdotes and stories. For example, one may not often think of *The Innocents Abroad* and *Roughing It* as childhood reading. However, these works were widely available to young people in a family where periodicals and books were read aloud. Critics have long sought to explain the immense popularity of *The Innocents Abroad*. Clearly, many readers found *The Innocents Abroad* funny. It echoed to them familiar matters of religion and society. Twain's readers have commented on how *The Innocents Abroad* and *Roughing It* affected them emotionally. The sentimentalism of the period registers in the reading of Thomas S. Hubert, who later became a minister in Warrenton, Georgia. Hubert was fifteen years old when he wrote to Twain on November 17, 1875:

> Excuse the liberty I take in writing to you but I must give way to my "whim" and write. I have read two of your works viz, "Innocents Abroad" and "Roughing It." I am pleased with both and often have cried while reading it. For instance, In the latter book when yourself & companions were lost in a snow storm and asked each other to meet you in Paradise, I could not refrain from giving vent to tears. In your quaint style of writing one moment I would be in tears while the next in laughter.[1]

Hubert's letter suggests a manner of reading in which he took aspects of Twain's narrative quite seriously. While some elements of Twain's narrative struck him as funny, others moved his sentiments. In this case, a scene that Twain had approached with tongue in cheek humor was read by a boy as a perilous dramatic moment. The notion of loss of life and the possibility of Paradise stirred Hubert's religious sensibilities and brought tears.

In Missouri, the Napton family of Elkhill Saline County wrote to Twain, December 4, 1877, about their brother Frank, an inspired reader of Mark Twain's books:

> Is there the slightest possibility of your writing and publishing any other books. "Innocents Abroad" "Roughing It" & "The Gilded Age" have about up-set our youngest brother Frank (the youngest of nine)- a youth of seventeen, now six feet two in his stocking feet, and like yourself, a "Missouri puke," "and to the manner born."
>
> If you contemplate issuing any more books like those above mentioned please let us know in due time in order that we may get him out of the way—send him to Patagonia—or some other region where access to them will be impossible. Some time since—the Judge—pater familias- gave him ten dollars to invest in books to suit his own fancy. At first he thought of buying an illustrated copy of Bunyons Pilgrims Progress, but on reflection, being religiously inclined, gave your works the preference. He has since read them forty times, and then re-read them backwards and cross-ways. He has literally read them to pieces. It would, or ought to, do your heart good to see them, — the books, He is so chuck-full of them, that no matter what may be under discussion in our family after supper controversies, — whether law, politics, literature, or divinity, the Holy land, the life of Christ, or the silver bill, — five minutes cannot elapse without his putting in, "Mark Twain says so & so &c &c,"—a delightful grin immediately enlightening his countenance. He is worse than old Claude Halcro, and his immortal John Dryden. To cap the climax he has begun writing a book of his own, and takes yours for his models. Can you wean him from his folly...[2]

The Naptons, who were the sons of state Supreme Court judge William Barclay Napton, added: "Seriously,—we all read your books almost as much as Frank." The letter provides a strong example of family reading. Twain's books were popular for all the brothers, although they were of different ages. The family of this notable judge obviously could well-afford to purchase books. In many cases, parents were the buyers of books for their children. However, here Frank Napton was given ten dollars to buy his own books and he chose to get books by Mark Twain.

This letter writer, who recognizes Twain as a humorist, brings an attempt at humor to his description of his little brother's reading. He would send his Twain-obsessed brother to Patagonia, the antipodes of the earth, so that he would be unable to gain access to another Mark Twain book. The boy incessantly quotes Twain and is modeling his own writing upon Twain.

The family of William Howard in Bethlehem, Pennsylvania, made their copy of *The Innocents Abroad* a significant household item. Twain was read aloud in the family circle and was appreciated by both father and son. In December 1885, William Howard wrote to Twain:

> "Mark Twain" is become with me as elsewhere, a household word from my wife down to the youngest of our five boys—Innocents Abroad is the best abused of our books— it threatens to go fast to the dogs in respect of ears, and has suffered not a little from the arbitrary rule of thumb—Last evening my wife read aloud to the family circle, your interesting contribution to the Dec. Century—Like your other writings it had the merit of gratifying our boy of ten as well as his father—apart from its genuine humor, we all agreed it would like pure wine, improve with time, because of its vivid representations of a phase in the growth of our civil war, not heretofore recorded in the chronicles.[3]

As the often thumbed material book endures successive readings, it becomes dog-eared; it "threatens to go fast to the dogs." The five Howard boys hear Twain's stories and essays read aloud in the family circle by Mrs. Howard, who is a subscriber to the *Century Magazine*. In this case, as R. Kent Rasmussen has pointed out, she was reading from "The Private History of a Campaign That Failed" in the December 1885 issue. This apparently motivated William Howard, a journalist and politician, to write to Twain.

Of course, the novels by Twain with the most impact upon young readers were *The Adventures of Tom Sawyer*, *The Adventures of Huckleberry Finn*, and *The Prince and the Pauper*. Laughter and play are at the center of the life of Tom Sawyer, one of the most visible fictional characters in American life. From nineteenth-century illustrations through twentieth-century film adaptations and Norman Rockwell images, Tom Sawyer has become one of the most prominent childhood characters in the world. On June 24, 1876, Mark Twain wrote to the board of directors of the American Publishing Company:

> Tom Sawyer is a new line of writing for me, & I would like to have every possible advantage in favor of that venture. When it issues, I would like to have a clear field & the whole energies of the Company put upon it.[4]

The energies of the company, however, were elsewhere. The American Publishing Company clearly had no idea that *The Adventures of Tom Sawyer* would become an American classic. Twain increasingly realized that Elisha Bliss was neither the prophetic voice nor the source of happiness his name might suggest. He was a calculating businessman. His pate was as bald as that of the American eagle and his mutton-chop sideburns swept up into a fierce mustache. Mark Twain would often complain about his publisher. He sought royalty contracts rather than a flat fee contract with the American Book Company. He liked the fact that the company was a subscription publisher, targeting a popular audience.

Mark Twain was interested in reaching a broad, popular audience. He later told his biographer A.B. Paine, "I have always hunted for bigger game—the masses."[5] By now displeased with the American Publishing Company, Twain thought to have James Osgood publish his next book. Sensing his imminent departure from his roster of authors, Elisha Bliss brought a contract out of his safe and placed it in front of Twain. It stipulated that Twain had to give his sketches to the American Publishing Company. *Sketches, New and Old* was issued as a subscription book by Bliss in July 1875. Following publication of *The Adventures of Tom Sawyer*, Twain continued to explore the possibility of publication with Osgood. His childhood memories and imagination were now focused upon the Mississippi River. Attention to the region of his own childhood would soon transform into a bold venture: the writing of *Huckleberry Finn*.

Letters to Twain, autobiographies, and oral commentaries show that boys often saw their own images in Twain's characters Tom Sawyer and Huckleberry Finn. "I have finished the story and didn't take the chap beyond boyhood," Twain wrote on July 5, 1875, to William Dean Howells. His friend encouraged Twain to continue *The Adventures of Tom Sawyer* for serialization in the *Atlantic* by having the character grow into adulthood. Twain rejected the idea of changing the book at all. He added that while Tom Sawyer was a young character, he had not intended his story as a children's book. "It is not a boy's book at all. It will only be read by adults. It is only written for adults."[6] Howells thought that *The Adventures of Tom Sawyer* would appeal to boys. Twain gradually came to see this also. In November 1875 he wrote, "Mrs. Clemens agrees with you that the book should issue as a book for boys, pure and simple- and so do I. It is surely the correct idea." In *The Adventures of Tom Sawyer*, Twain writes, "most of the adventures in this book really occurred; one or two were experiences of my own, the rest those of boys who were schoolmates of mine."[7]

Twain's hesitancy to identify his novel as one for children suggests that he resisted the children's literature genre, observes Sarah Wadsworth, who finds "disjunctions among audience, genre, and text." Yet, the emergence of distinct genres for boys and for girls was a fact of his time and this increasing gender-specific segmentation of the market was evident in the work of authors like Louisa May Alcott, Horatio Alger, and then Twain.[8] Publishers had begun to promote an expanding juvenile market. *Little Women* created narratives of female fulfillment that would help girls to "move beyond everyday circumstances," Barbara Sicherman observes.[9] Twain's text provided an adventurous narrative, ostensibly for boys, which may have served a similar function.

The Adventures of Tom Sawyer had begun to earn its earliest fans when Howells wrote: "Mr. Clemens, on the contrary, has taken the boy of the Southwest for the hero of his new book, and has presented him with a fidelity to circumstance which loses no charm by being realistic in the highest degree, and which gives incomparably the best picture of life in that region as yet known to fiction"[10] The region appears to have been heartily in agreement. Twain's book became a favorite in Missouri and images of boyhood in Hannibal and life on the Mississippi River were soon familiar worldwide.

The story of twelve-year-old David Watt Bowser is well-known. Bowser contacted Mark Twain by mail one day. It was the start of a correspondence between "Wattie" and Mark Twain that included more than ten letters. Wattie wrote:

> At school we were required to select some man among the living great ones (a live dog is better than a dead lion, you know), with whom we would exchange places, and I selected you. My reasons for so doing, you will see in my composition, if you do not throw both articles into the fire, before you have read even this far [...] A few of us boys thought it would be a "lark" to send our compositions to our favorites, and ask them if they would be willing to change with us, and if their fame, riches, honors, and glory made them perfectly happy—in fact to ask them if they would "Be a boy again."

David Watt Bowser had read *Tom Sawyer* and he asked Twain: "When you were a boy did you think you would be a great man, or were you like Tom Sawyer?" As Twain's writing about *Huckleberry Finn* and "Old Times on the Mississippi" had brought recollections, so too these letters must have. For there was an added surprise in the letter from "Wattie": His teacher's name was Laura M. Dake—the Laura Hawkins of Samuel Clemens's youth. To be a boy again? He pondered that. To "Wattie" he wrote on March 20, 1880:

> Would I live it over again under certain conditions? Certainly I would! The main conditions would be, that I should emerge from boyhood as a "cub pilot" on a Mississippi boat, & that I should by & by become a pilot, & remain one. The minor conditions would be these: Summer always; the magnolias at Rifle Point always in bloom, so that the dreamy twilight have the added charm of their perfume; the oleanders [...] always in bloom, likewise, the sugar cane always green [...]

"I like plucky heroes rather than martyrs, don't you?" Wattie wrote. "I am looking forward anxiously to the next book."[11]

That next book was the classic children's story *The Prince and the Pauper*, in which a prince and a pauper change places. Before 1880, James Osgood, who had been a senior partner in Ticknor and Fields, had assumed that company's catalogue. Twain signed a contract with James Osgood for his medieval story, *The Prince and the Pauper*. It would become his daughter Susy's favorite of his stories. Former president Rutherford B. Hayes remarked on the impact that *The Prince and the Pauper* had upon his extended family. On April 6, 1882, he wrote in a letter to Twain:

The children of all ages, of my numerous household, have enjoyed your new book so much that I must thank you on their and my own behalf. The child in his eighth year and the child in his sixtieth, and all between them in age and of both sexes were equally hearty in their applause and delight. The Prince and the Pauper is as entertaining as Robinson Crusoe to the Young Folks, and the older ones see in it a most effective presentation of the inhuman criminal laws, hardly yet wiped out, of English jurisprudence, and the only defence, or explanation rather, of the Puritan Codes of New England ancestor. I congratulate you on your great success in this admirable book." [12]

The child in his eighth year was the actor John Grant Mitchell, Jr., who starred in *The Man Who Came to Dinner* in 1939. In that same year he appeared in *The Grapes of Wrath* as the supervisor of the U.S. Department of Agriculture Camp. [13]

Amusing things came from the children who wrote to Twain. *Tom Sawyer* and *Huckleberry Finn* appealed personally to Herbert Shaw Philbrick of Liberty, Maine, the son of a machine shop owner. Twain's characters seem to be quite alive for this young reader, who wrote to him in July of 1888. He wishes to know about their present whereabouts and about Huckleberry Finn's future.

I like your book and you and Tom Sawyer and Jim. I think you are very plucky and know how to get out of scrapes awful well. I should like to know if you have ever heard any thing of the king and the duke since they were riding by (fence) rail, and the men that you and Jim left on the wreck. I wish you would write another book and tell us if Aunt Sally "civilized" you. How old are you? I am thirteen. [14]

Like *Tom Sawyer*, *The Adventures of Huckleberry Finn* was a book that drew many childhood associations from readers. Both novels offer nostalgia for adults, recalling their childhoods. One anonymous interviewee in Oregon told that state's oral history archive:

When I was a kid I fished down there. Old Joe used to live below the tunnel in a houseboat. I went fishing on Saturday with my friend Sam. We had old can poles and we used our mother's hair pins and curl[ed] them up to make pole eyes. We were real Huckleberry Finns. [15]

The experience of readers imagining themselves as Huckleberry Finns has been repeated many times over. Henry E. Barrett, clerk for the surrogate's court in Tioga County, New York, recalled how important these characters were in his boyhood. He expressed his gratitude to Twain in a letter on April 18, 1894.

It has struck me as wrong that I should go on and not say to you what I feel. From my boyhood, when I was kept from play by my interest in "Tom Sawyer" and "Huck Finn," till now, your books and stories have given me more genuine pleasure than those of any other author. I think so often of the many pleasant hours you have given me and have made up to me the lack sometimes of pleasant companions. [16]

This phenomenon of childhood fascination with Tom Sawyer and Huck Finn would continue into the next century. Gilbert Draper of Montreal, as a seven year old, wrote to Twain. Draper would become a journalist who composed songs and wrote mystery stories.

> I did like your books very much I did get Tom Sawyer and I like it very much, and so I got Huckleberry Finn. There were both very nice. I did like them better than any books I ever read. So I thought I would tell you how much I liked them. I been sick a long time. I cannot think of anything else to write so I will says goodbye. If you should answer my letter I would be very glad. [17]

Several of Twain's other novels also made an impact upon children in the final decades of the nineteenth century. *A Connecticut Yankee in King Arthur's Court* may not immediately come to mind as a novel that is read by children. However, one little boy in Minnesota, Dean B. Gregg, was evidently quite taken by the book. He imagined himself as Hank, the story's protagonist, when he was told Twain's story by his father. He turned scenes from the story into a game that he played, enlisting his parents as characters in his drama. Jesse A. Gregg of St. Paul wrote to Twain on November 24, 1889:

> I have a boy four years old and he is full of vim. He wanted me to tell him a story a few days ago and I told him about "A Connecticut Yankee in King Arthur's Court" taken from the Century. He "Caught on" at once and ever since he has been "Hank." The story has to be read and told to him several times a day. He got a piece of clothes line and made a Lasso and using me for a horse he Has a tournament every evening and I wish you could see him drag Sir Sagramour, Sir Gallahad and Sir Launcelot out of their saddles. Then Merlin (his mother) has to steal his Lasso and he gets his gun and shoots Sir Sagramour.
>
> Its kind of tough on me to trot up & down the lists for half an Hour at a time but then as ["]Hank" is the most beautiful boy you ever saw I don't mind it For the past two years it has been a fight of about an hour to get him to go to bed Now soon after Dinner he comes to his mother and says "Hank wants his Tights (his night pants) on, and after a Tournament he goes to bed with out a word, all because Hank does that way, and generally he used to object to saying his prayers. . . . [18]

Another generation of childhood readers, born in the late 1880s and in the 1890s, was also introduced to Twain's books. Shortly after the turn of the twentieth century, one schoolboy found the act of reading *Roughing It* during his school lessons to be a memorable escapade. In 1905, William H. Ridgway told Twain that *Roughing It* was his favorite book by him. On the day after Christmas, 1905, he sent a letter from Coatesville, Pennsylvania, noting that he had received a Christmas present of the Harper's edition of Twain's works. Ridgeway recalled sneaking glances at the book while he was in a classroom in school:

> The reason this particular volume is my favorite, is because 30 years ago when I was at school I smuggled it into the sacred precincts of the great study room of the Quaker College, where all was supposed to be Peace, Quiet, and Hard Study. With my Latin grammar before me I had "Roughing It" sliding in and out under the lifting cover of the desk. . . .[19]

That Twain's stories were helpful to many young, ailing children is clear from letters sent to him. From Montclair, New Jersey, Charles Whiting Baker, Jr., wrote to Twain on December 5, 1905, in honor of his seventieth birthday:

> Wheeler and I (he is my brother fourteen years old) read your stories lots. Wheeler is just getting over an operation for appendicitis, and so his nurse read your funny things to him, but it hurt him to laugh hard. I am ten years old, and I take music lessons. We have two turtles, two puppies, and one dog, two angora kittens, about twenty doves and twenty-four goldfish. Your stories are good to read when we are sick. Wheeler would cry out "read! read! read!" when he was sick. I think Wheeler is a good deal like Tom Sawyer, only he isn't into as much mischief, but he knows how to make me do his work for him allright.[20]

This letter writer died of an illness while at a military base during the First World War. He was honored at the First Congregational Church in Montclair, as one of a half-dozen young men from the parish that perished in the war.

In the last years of Twain's life, children continued to write to him. Edwin A.W. Bohl of Peoria wrote on January 2, 1909:

> I am 11 years old to-day and have read almost all of your books written for boys my age and have laughed and enjoyed and enjoyed them like anything. My Papa was reading in the evening paper about your Xmas gift of that elephant and I just thought as I had a typewriter given me for my birthday that I would write and tell you that I wish that it had been me instead of you that was given that elephant. I know that I would have just piles of fun with it.

He added that he had been given many books at Christmas and on his birthday: *The Isle of the Lake* by W. M. Goss, *Dan Monroe* by Stoddard, *The Boys Fortune Hunting in Egypt* by Alger, and *Two Little Savages* by Seton. Frances Hodgson Burnett, the English author of *The Secret Garden*, had corresponded with him.[21]

Mothers also wrote to Twain about their children's reading, or listening to his stories. Gertrude Weld Arnold of Nutley, New Jersey, on February 3, 1910, told Twain that her family had read *Tom Sawyer* and *Huckleberry Finn* aloud.

Although a stranger, I give myself the privilege of writing to you to tell you of what seemed to me an altogether charming remark which our young twelve year old son made in regard to your work. We had all been enjoying Tom Sawyer and Huckleberry Finn extremely and reading the books aloud during the winter, as well as your autobiography. The numbers of which we can hardly wait to come out.

I had been working over a list of books for children's reading, and as I often do, had asked Weld's opinion saying "Weld, how do you feel about Tom and Huck. Do you think it is as good for a boy to read about them as about King Arthur and his knights." He thought a moment- and then said, "Mother if you didn't put them in, I think it would be robbing a boy of something that was pretty good." Believe me- with gratitude for the delight your writings have given us all, Sincerely yours. Gertrude Weld Arnold.[22]

The mother of future editor William Allen White was concerned that her son "went stark mad over Mark Twain" because Twain was considered an atheist, Barbara Sicherman points out.[23] Perhaps, Mrs. White had only herself to blame because she gave her children books by Louisa May Alcott and Mark Twain. William Allen White began checking out books from the Eldorado City Library in Kansas, Sicherman observes, and he read dime novels as well as the quality literature on his father's book shelves, like Plutarch's *Lives*.[24]

Some twentieth-century readers thought that Mark Twain's fiction made a good gift for a boy. When University of California, Berkeley, chancellor Edward W. Strong was a child he received a set of Mark Twain's works for watching a bulldog.

He asked my father if his son could take care of the bulldog for most of the summer, and my father said surely I could [...] When Mr. Laing returned from his vacation he was very pleased that his bulldog had been groomed and was in good shape. He made a present of Mark Twain's published works, and the two volume Bigelow [Paine] biography. I still have the set.[25]

Tom Sawyer's combination of traits made him both memorable and identifiable. The character became a popular reference for comparisons with boys in a variety of situations. Social worker Lillian Wald, the founder of American community nursing, referred to one New York boy:

When one of the nurses found a small boy attending school while desquamating from scarlet fever, and, Tom Sawyerlike, pulling off the skin to startle his classmates, we exhibited him to the President of the Department of Health.[26]

The mischievous Tom Sawyer in this comment is considered counter-cultural. Here he is oppositional-defiant, performing his ghastly act of epidermal exfoliation for negative attention. For some of Twain's contemporaries in the 1870s and 1880s, this Tom Sawyer appeared to be a poor role model for young readers. Libraries and schools were slow to adopt him or his pal Huckleberry Finn, or to approve of the antics of these characters. By 1900, when Lillian Wald was writing, Tom Sawyer was familiar as a character that resisted convention and social controls. He and Huckleberry Finn practiced a kind of social rebellion that Wald could point to when referring to the recalcitrant boy in the nurse's care. [Sarah Wadsworth identifies Tom Sawyer as a character in the "bad boy" tradition that includes Horatio Alger's "Ragged Dick."[27]

In the later years of the twentieth century, an association with Tom Sawyer came to mind for several men who reflected back upon their childhoods. Jimmy Gentry of Tennessee, who served in the U.S. infantry at the Battle of the Bulge, recalled: "We'd get some boards and nails, and put tar in the cracks to keep it from breaking, and paddle up and down the river. We were Tom Sawyer all over again." Thomas T. Adams of New Jersey told an interviewer, "I remember the freshman English teacher once telling me, 'Do you think you're Tom Sawyer?' She told me that once, and I don't know whether it was a compliment or not." The students began calling the teacher "Madame Sawyer," he said. Michael Sweeney, who went into the military, recalled: "The radio was kind of a treat. So I read. I read everything and enjoyed everything. I guess I really liked all of it." Sweeney served in Vietnam from 1965–1969, becoming commander of a marine detachment at Fort Hancock and later an operations officer. He was a Lieutenant Colonel upon his retirement. While interviewing Sweeney, Richard Burks Verrone asked, "Do you remember any books that really had an influence on you, that you really enjoyed?" "I wouldn't call them necessarily influential," Sweeney said, "but certainly *Tom Sawyer* and *Huckleberry Finn*. I read a lot of outdoors stuff. I was involved in Scouts for years, Boy Scouts. So I liked outdoor books and adventure books and all that."[28] The self-identification of readers with Tom Sawyer is evident in these comments.

A. GIRL'S READING

The Adventures of Tom Sawyer is a book that has been cherished by female readers as often as it has been enjoyed by young male readers. While self-identification with their gender likely has played some role in girls' reading of the novel, the fragmentary evidence suggests that they have readily adopted the characters of the story. Considering *Huckleberry Finn*, Shelley Fisher Fishkin has asked if girls reading the novel identified with Huck Finn rather than the female characters in the story.[29] The evidence suggests that they did. One might likewise ask if girls identified with Tom in *The Adventures of Tom Sawyer*, even with the strong presence in that story of Becky Thatcher. The answer to this seems to be "yes." At the very least we can say that reading the point of view of a young male protagonist did not keep girls from enjoying the novel.

The reading habits of communities of young female readers may help us to better understand how girls and young women read *The Adventures of Tom Sawyer*. Barbara Sicherman has recognized that "girls developed their own reading cultures that provided refuge from the restrictions surrounding their lives."[30] Janice Radway's exploration of female networks of readers of romance novels has underscored the idea of self-creation and demonstrated the claims of women to independence in their reading.[31] Several other works on women's reading have suggested that reading can be empowering for young girls and that readers may constitute communities or a social order of relationships. Cathy Davidson's *Revolution of the Word* (1986) and Kate Flint's *The Woman Reader, 1837–1914* (1995) were among the studies that provided a basis for work in this area. Barbara Sicherman in *Well Read Lives* (2010) examined how girls moved from "an overprotected childhood marked by extreme gender stereotyping" toward identity and finding satisfactions in reading not available to them in other ways.[32] With books like Louisa May Alcott's *Little Women*, which she carefully explores, and *The Adventures of Tom Sawyer* and *The Adventures of Huckleberry Finn*, these readers found their way into what Sicherman calls "uncharted territory."[33]

Library records indicate that several female readers were fond of adventure stories, as Ronald Zboray has demonstrated. Martyn Lyons writes: "We know from reading surveys, for instance, that young girls frequently enjoy adventure stories that are generally classified as "boy's" literature." Lyons quotes Alice Henry from the 1870s: "The days when I used to pore over Captain Mayne Reid's boy's books, in a quiet way I was looking forward to travelling myself."[34] Such experiences as Alice Henry's suggest a desire among girls for adventure. That girls read romances while boy's read adventures appears less a truism when one looks at library circulation records of nineteenth-century readers. Those records show that boys occasionally read romances and girls often read adventure stories. Both boys and girls avidly read *The Adventures of Tom Sawyer*.

In a story that appeared a few years after the novel's publication, we hear of a girl reading this "boy's book":

> An Austin young lady said good night to her beau, at the front door, last night, and went into a room where her sister sat reading Mark Twain's book, *Tom Sawyer*. "What are you reading, sister?" she asked. "Tom Sawyer." "I don't care a cent if he did; I guess I've got a right to kiss Jim if I want to, and Tom better mind his own business." It was a new revelation to "Sister."[35]

Here a Texas girl's time spent on a date is contrasted with her sister, who spends time with a book. The sister, perhaps wishing for a date, hears the assertion that she (the Texas girl) can kiss Jim if she wants to, in effect making the story-character, Tom, the sister's date for the night. The Texas girl suggests that she sees Tom Sawyer as a trouble-maker, who had "better mind his own business." For this girl, resistance to Tom Sawyer might also serve as her way to break out of her family role in what Janice Radway has called a "minimal but legitimate form of protest."[36]

The niece of city editor Henry Dwight Spencer in Bloomington, Illinois, wanted to know who Tom Sawyer would become as an adult. Spencer wrote about his daughter to Twain on March 8, 1882. He also wrote thinking about whether Mark Twain might write moral fiction that would have an effect upon the future of his young readers:

> I plead no excuse for this letter, as probably, if the truth were told, nothing but a selfish motive might the cause of my writing. I have read most of your publications and I like a great many others, have been both instructed and entertained by them. I am uncle to nine nephews and nieces to whom Tom Sawyer is a real hero—a living character.
>
> Last evening, one of my nieces asked, "Uncle Harry, won't Mark Twain ever tell us what sort of man Tom Sawyer became. Won't he tell us if we ask?" I of course told her I did not know& she then said "Will you ask him?" I could not refuse & so here is the question [:] "Mr. Twain" What sort of man did Tom Sawyer become?

Spencer goes on to suggest a topic for a book that would instruct young men to pay their dues in the career of their choice and become persons of integrity. This would be unlike those, he says, "who are not willing to commence sweeping the stores as their fathers did, but insist on being cashiers &c without going through the drudgery of the trade. . . ."[37]

Prompted by his daughter, Spencer considers the future of many Tom Sawyers: the young men around him. He suggests that novels have the potential to affect lives and he encourages Twain to write an instructive moral fiction. Curiously, he says little at all about what little girls like his daughter who read about Tom Sawyer might become.

Jennie S. Walker of Flint, Michigan, was twelve when she wrote to Mark Twain on April 19, 1882:

> I have read your Tom Sawyer and am very much interested in it. Wont you please tell me whether Tom and Huck Finn had the initiation that night. If you have the time. We have all your works. Papa said he knew you once, his name is Gorge L. Walker. Tom must have had a hard time to keep still with the spirit of three boys in one, was Huck composed of two or three boys. If you have time please answer my letter as soon as you can. You must be a ever so nice because you writer such nice books.[38]

The initiation of Tom Sawyer's gang occurs in chapter two of *Huckleberry Finn*, which Twain had begun writing but did not publish until several years after this letter. One might ask whether Jennie Walker's letter raised the idea of an initiation. In Twain's preface to his book, he calls Tom Sawyer "a combination of the characteristics of three boys." So, Jennie Walker wonders if Huckleberry Finn might be a few boys rolled into one as well.

Nine-year-old Florence Dean Cope had the same interest as Jennie S. Walker. She was the daughter of William Dean Howells' first cousin Ione Cope and, much like the niece of Henry Dwight Spencer, she wanted to know how Tom Sawyer's life turned out as an adult. Florence Dean Cope wrote to Twain on October 28, 1883:

> I am a little girl nine years old. I have been reading Tom Sawyer quite a great deal and I think it is a very funny book and now I write to ask you to write a book of his manhood. I am great reader that is I read very much, and of course I delight in all kinds of books like that. We have two books that you wrote Tom Sawyer is one of them and The Prince and the Pauper is another. I delight in reading both of these books very much. I would be pleased if you would answer my letter. My address is Florence Cope, Corner Winner Ave, and Broad Street, Columbus, Ohio. I have a brother fourteen years old and a little sister eight. I will be ten years old the 24th of next month and my little sister was 8 a few days ago. All of our family would enjoy a book of Tom's manhood and whether he turned out a robber or not after all. I am in the fifth reader and enjoy those books immensely. I would not know how to thank you enough if you would write another as good as the one about Tom and all our family would be very glad. I think Tom is just perfect. I am getting very tired so I must stop here. [39]

Another young fan of *Tom Sawyer*, Fannie S. James of Eau Claire, Wisconsin, was a granddaughter of the prolific English writer G.P.R. James. This adventurous girl would one day become a journalist, a medical librarian, and a teacher. As an eleven-year-old, she simply wanted to play with Tom Sawyer and Huck Finn:

> I am a little girl living in Eau Claire, and admire "Huckleberry Finn" and "Tom Sawyer." Although I am a girl, I would like to play with them and get into such scrapes and would be delighted to find twelve thousand dollars. I didn't like them to take the dead cat, to the graveyard; for I love kitties and wouldn't have one killed for all the warts in Christendom. I have seen the pictures in your "Sketch Book," I looked at them before I went to bed, I didn't sleep very well or have very sweet dreams that night.
>
> I have read, and like, some parts of "Innocents Abroad," especialy where the gentlemen were at the hotel in France and tried to express their wishes in French to the waiter who only understood English. I intend to go to Europe and will go and see the great "Christifer Columbo" and mummies if possible. It must be fun to write as you do. My grandpa (G.P.R. James) was an author. [40]

In the nineteenth century, books were often like "companions." Authors were people who could be known like one's neighbors and social acquaintances. When a girl, or a young woman, opened a book, her reading practice generally engaged in what Barbara Hochman has recognized as "an interpretive convention that involved taking for granted the imaginative unity of author and text."[41] Mark Twain made "friends" of his readers observed Marie Jousaye, a reporter in Winnipeg. She wrote to the readers of the *Globe* about how meeting Mark Twain stirred her memories of her childhood reading:

> Like most everyone who has heard of or read of Mark Twain, I had formed a mental photograph of him. . . . this was the picture I had in my mind's eye as I stood in the parlor of the Manitoba, waiting, with my heart beating somewhat faster than usual, for this man whose genius and pen have so often had the power to stir my heart, arousing both laughter and tears. It is no stranger whom I about to greet, but a very old and dear friend, whose acquaintance I made years ago., when myself and a group of bare-footed boys and girls used to gather in the shade of a big woodpile and follow the exploits of Tom Sawyer and Huck Finn with hearts beating in unison with the young scapegraces in all their adventures. . . . My audience- mostly boys-listened in breathless silence, and when I had finished Ned drew a long breath and remarked tersely: "That man Twain was a boy himself once, and don't you forget it." And we all echoed the sentiment.[42]

From Hot Springs, Arkansas, Hebe G. Rector, who had been daughter-in-law of the Arkansas governor, Henry Massey Rector, wrote about her daughter Ernestine on May 17, 1891:

> My little daughter than whom you could have no warmer or ardent admirer, has for years been threatened with a malady that has deprived her of many such amusements & companions as she would have most enjoyed. Her best, most congenial friend during this time has been Tom Sawyer.
>
> She has entered him with heart & soul, into every experience of life. So often indeed has the boy been called upon to entertain her that in his present form he can no longer respond; it has occurred to me that possibly you would be willing to give her the pleasure of receiving, directly from you, an autograph copy of the work. I only ask what you alone can give. I will most gladly expect to meet the expense involved. Could you understand the circumstances of the child, I feel assured you would pardon my presumption in making this request. Our present copy of the book will be preserved a lasting testimony to the enjoyment which your wonderful portrayal of child's life has given our one family of children.[43]

Ernestine Rector was the only child born in the Arkansas governor's house until the Second World War. Subsequently, Chelsea Clinton was born there while Bill Clinton was the Arkansas governor, as were Governor Mike Huckabee's children when he was governor.

Samuel Clemens was the father of three girls. Notes in newspapers after the turn of the century indicated the attention that the author bestowed upon young girls. Letters continued to arrive to him from girls across the world. In a turn of the century newspaper this note appeared:

> A little New Zealand girl wrote recently to Mark Twain to ask if his name was Clemens. She knew better, she said, because Clemens was the man who sold patent medicine. She hoped not, for she liked the name of Mark. Why, Mark Antony was in the Bible. Her letter delighted the recipient. "As Marc Antony has got into the Bible," Mr. Clemens characteristically remarked in telling about it, "I am not without hopes myself.[44]

Gertrude Swain of Greeley, Nebraska wrote to Twain on October 7, 1902:

> I've been going to write to you for a long time, ever since I saw that piece in that paper about Huck Finn being a bad book. I am a little girl twelve years old. I have read Huck Finn about fifty times. Papa calls it my Bible. I think it is the best book ever written, and I don't think it would hurt any little boy or girl to read it. I think it would do them a lot of good. I don't think that preacher knew what he was talking about.
>
> I think the folks know it all by heart, I have told them so much about it, especially all of Jim's signs. Poor Huck, he did get into more trouble, and get out of it so slick.
>
> When I was down to Omaha, this Summer papa and I looked every book store in the whole city, it seemed to me, to find Tom Sawyer, but we couldn't find it, and I was just ready to cry when we got home. I supposed we could find it at the first store we went to; an then we didn't find it at all. I think Huck is just fine and I wish there was more like it.[45]

Margaret Potter Black, an author, the daughter of an Illinois steel baron, sent Christmas wishes in 1902, recalling her childhood reading:

> When I was four years old I spelled out "Tom Sawyer" to myself, defending my copy from all would-be readers until I had finished it. Since that first reading (and I should not dare say this unless it were truth) there has been no joy in my life that you have not made richer, no sorrow that your work has not show[n] me how to bear- best.[46]

In the *Saturday Review*, November 19, 1904, "A Mother" records the books that her sixteen-year-old daughter has been reading. These are some eighteen books, including Dickens's *A Christmas Carol*, *The Cricket on the Hearth*, and *A Tale of Two Cities* and Mark Twain's *Adventures of Tom Sawyer*. We know nothing about how this girl read these books. It appears that her reading accomplishment expanded her mother's pride and possibly the girl's knowledge. Perhaps more significantly, Twain may have given some of his young female readers like this a more expansive sense of America and the world. In his study of the *Intellectual Life of the British Working Class,* Jonathan Rose points to the example of Mary Lakeman, a fisherman's daughter in England. Lakeman read *Tom Sawyer, Huckleberry Finn,* and *The Last of the Mohicans.* Rose writes that "all created a romantic childhood vision" and a sense of unlimited freedom and open space.[47]

In a letter dated March 31, 1906, eleven-year-old Elizabeth Owen Knight of Rockville, Maryland, wrote:

> I know you will be surprised to hear from a little Maryland girl that you have never seen. I wish I could know you, for I have enjoyed your books so much and I want to write and tell you how much I have enjoyed them. I think it was so funny for those people of Boston to make a law that no children under a certain age should read your books, for I read them long ago and I think all children would enjoy them as much as I did if they could only read them.

She comments that a boy on their farm was given *The Adventures of Tom Sawyer* to read. However,

> one night he let his clothes out of the window and left in the night. The last we heard from him he was out in Ohio, and father says if he had lent him "Tom Sawyer abroad" to read he would not have stopped on this side of the ocean.[48]

Florence Benson, a fourteen-year-old in New York, shared her birthday with Mark Twain. On November 30, 1907, she wrote to the author:

> I have seen the New York Tribune this morning that to-day is your birthday—and it is mine too! I am writing to wish you many happy returns of the day and to tell you that I think Tom Sawyer is the nicest boy I have ever known.[49]

Across these many years, from its publication in the mid-1870s to the last years of Twain's life, perhaps some fictional freedom and open space was available to young readers of *The Adventures of Tom Sawyer.* Repeatedly, girls who wrote to Mark Twain told him how much they liked his book. We may ask what it is like for a girl to read a "boy's book" and question whether gender makes a difference in reading. There has been widespread recognition that women have had to negotiate various discourses about femininity and expectations and models of womanhood. Some feminist critics have questioned the range of messages that were being offered to a girl. Judith Fetterley, in 1977, asserted that women reading "men's texts [...] are forced to become characters in those texts."[50] This may be so. Yet, it appears that most female readers enjoyed *The Adventures of Tom Sawyer.* Likely, the novel, like Louisa May Alcott's *Little Women,* enabled girls to "move beyond everyday circumstances."[51]

Even though *Tom Sawyer* was assigned reading in some schools, oral history and survey responses suggest that Twain's novel was frequently voluntary reading for many girls. We may ask if they identified with the socially approved Becky Thatcher more than the recalcitrant Huckleberry Finn. Readers first meet Becky as she is seen on a front porch: a space between the home and the world, one that is something of a stage or a pedestal. Tom will have to cross borders into her world of wealth and privilege. Becky is interested in books, or she is at least curious and tenacious enough to discover Mr. Dobbins' anatomy book. Tom is not much of a reader. When Tom tries to read, his attention lags: "The harder Tom tried to fasten his mind on his book, the more his ideas wandered. So, at last, with a sigh and a yawn, he gave up."

The recollections of readers tell us that the story of Tom, Huck, and Becky was shared by children who listened to it or read it collectively in groups. Readers participated in the play and exchange of Twain's characters. Mabel Bates Back of Kentucky recalled reading *The Adventures of Tom Sawyer*. "And while we'd rest under the apple tree and we'd have story time [...] Read Tom Sawyer or something [...] they all read. Used to go in and there was books piled everywhere." [52] Mary Ellen Leftwich was an avid reader of Twain's *Adventures of Tom Sawyer*. Born in November 10, 1916, in Arkansas, she moved to a farm at Gunnison, Mississippi, where she first read Twain's novel. Leftwich liked the novel so much that she decided to share it with others. She recalled attending "chapel programs" weekly at the local high school with her elementary school friends. One day it was her turn to make a presentation for group reading. "I gave *Tom Sawyer*. It was too long for a chapel program. But anyway, I had the type students that could do it, and they loved doing it. And I just really enjoyed that." [53]

Mark Twain's *The Adventures of Tom Sawyer* was clearly memorable for these readers. Twain's novel appears to have held the attention of Leftwich's group in the Mississippi chapel. She actively sought out that community of readers to share the novel with. We can see that the recollection remained vivid for her many years later. Likewise, for Mabel Bates Back, among all the "books piled everywhere," *The Adventures of Tom Sawyer* stood out in her memory.

When these readers encountered *The Adventures of Tom Sawyer* they were practicing voluntary reading. Some were engaged in group reading experiences. Mary Leftwich read aloud to a group of young people and worked to provide them with something more than a condensed version despite time constraints. Mabel Bates Back recalled sitting under an apple tree as a child, where "all read" outside a room filled with "books piled everywhere." In these sites of literacy, there was participation in reading as a social practice. These girls are examples of what Barbara Sicherman has identified as girls who "created communities of learning, imagination, and emotional connection." [54] Like many other girls, as library records show, they read adventure stories and exhibited flexibility and variety in their reading interests.

Did these female readers read Tom Sawyer differently from young male readers? Can we find out? It is difficult to do so from such brief snippets of testimony. Perhaps we can characterize these readers. They are readers of a regional character. Some are rural, working class readers. They are not all white middle class women from relatively privileged circumstances. The mother, who spoke in 1904, was proud of her daughter's reading. The working class Englishwoman Mary Lakeman found her world view expanded by the book. Mabel Bates Back, a rural reader in Kentucky, said little about what she thought of the book. However, Mary Ellen Leftwich was enthusiastic about sharing it in the chapel program in Mississippi.

When *The Adventures of Tom Sawyer* first appeared, in 1875, the initial sales for the book were not as strong as those for *The Innocents Abroad* and *Roughing It*. However, the novel's resurgence in the twentieth century, in the elementary school curriculum and on the screen, has made it a perennial favorite. In 1930, the film *Tom Sawyer*, starring Jackie Coogan and directed by John Cromwell, catapulted the young boy back into wide public notice. By the time of the 1938 film by David O. Selznick, a film that Gary Scharnhorst has called a dress rehearsal for *Gone with the Wind*, Tom Sawyer was clearly alive and well.[55] Viewers received a nostalgic greeting as the film opened with intertitles: "Out of the heart of Mark Twain and into the heart of the world." The book and its characters, interpreted through film adaptation, became something fresh for this new generation. Tom became a heroic character in this film and the candid use of his point of view allowed Twain's satire to shine through.

The character and his creator, Mark Twain, received further popular recognition throughout the decade of the 1930s. Tom Sawyer had long had a special appeal for young readers and he had become an archetypal figure. But in the 1930s and 1940s, American culture appears to have been especially receptive to this image. In 1936, Norman Rockwell prints, like his illustration *Tom Sawyer (Whitewashing the Fence)*, appeared on the cover of the *Saturday Evening Post* and President Franklin Roosevelt dedicated the Mark Twain Bridge in Hannibal. Ten years later, in 1946, when Frank Capra filmed *It's a Wonderful Life*, Mark Twain was mentioned in the film. In the film, when George Bailey (James Stewart) is spared by divine intervention, it is a volume of *Tom Sawyer* that the angel Clarence holds in his hands. Of Mark Twain, he says, "You should see what he's writing now."[56]

What a work of fiction is for those who encounter it inevitably has much to do with the historical and social context of its reception. In the 1930s, the film director Frank Capra could count on his audience's familiarity with Mark Twain and his character Tom Sawyer. However, how this audience responded to Tom Sawyer was a little different from how readers of the 1870s responded. This is certainly true of Twain's female readers. The ways in which readers interacted with his fictional creation were influenced by social expectations surrounding their gender. Indeed, the very reading of *The Adventures of Tom Sawyer* was more discouraged among girls in the 1870s than it was in the 1930s. By then Henry Nash Smith could make the observation that *Tom Sawyer* "made Mark Twain's boyhood an international possession."[57] However, another observation could be made as well: the boyhood of Tom Sawyer had often been read by girls.

NOTES

1. Thomas Shivers Hubert Letter to Mark Twain, November 17, 1875, MTP, University of California. This letter appears in R. Kent Rasmussen, *Dear Mark Twain*, Berkeley: University of California, 2013. pp. 40–41.

2. The Napton Family Brothers' Letter to Mark Twain. The letter writers John, Harry, Charles, and Lewis Napton wrote about their brother Frank, who later was a city clerk in Polson, Montana, and then a rancher in Oregon. MTP, University of California. See Rasmussen, 52–53.

3. William Howard Letter to Mark Twain, December 9, 1885, from Bethlehem, Pennsylvania. MTP, University of California. See Rasmussen, 123–124.

4. Mark Twain, Letter, June 24, 1876. *Mark Twain and his Publishers*, Berkeley: University of California Press.

5. This comment is noted by Frederick Anderson in *Mark Twain: The Critical Heritage*, London: Routledge, 1971, p. 15.

6. Mark Twain, Letter to William Dean Howells, July 5, 1875, *Mark Twain Letters*, Vol. 6, University of California Press, p. 503.

7. Mark Twain, *The Adventures of Tom Sawyer*, i–iv.

8. Sarah Wadsworth, *In the Company of Books*, Amherst: University of Massachusetts Press, 2006. pp. 44–45.

9. Barbara Sicherman, *Well Read Lives*, Chapel Hill: University of North Carolina Press, 2010, 6.

10. William Dean Howells, *Atlantic*, May 1876, p. 105.

11. David Watt Bowser's exchange with Mark Twain, in 1880, appears in "Dear Master Wattie: The Mark Twain-David Watt Bowser Letters," ed. Pascal Covici, Jr., *Southwest Review* (Spring 1960): 106–108. Permission to publish was given to Covici by Bowder's niece, Mrs. E.C. Stradley of Dallas and Mark Twain Estate trustees. See Pascal Covici, Jr., p. 107 and the discussion in Ron Powers. *Mark Twain*, p. 440.

12. Rutherford B. Hayes Letter to Mark Twain, April 6, 1882. See Rasmussen, 89–90. R. Kent Rasmussen has pointed out that Hayes' diary indicates that attorney John Grant Mitchell's family was among Hayes's house guests. As Rasmussen notes, the former president was likely the child in his sixtieth year and future actor John Grant Mitchell, Jr. (1884–1957) was the eight year old. Mitchell would later appear in *The Man Who Came to Dinner* (1940) and in *The Grapes of Wrath* (1940), in which he portrays a kindly U.S. Department of Agriculture camp director who greets the Joad family.

13. R. Kent Rasmussen, *Dear Mark Twain*, p. 91. Hayes also read *A Connecticut Yankee in King Arthur's Court*, notes Rasmussen, and the former president remarked that the novel was "Instructive: not equal to 'Prince and Pauper.'"

14. Herbert Shaw Philbrick Letter to Mark Twain, July 31, 1888, Liberty, Maine. MTP, University of California. Rasmussen, 137–138.

15. Anonymous. Columbia Slough, Oregon Digital Oral History Archive.

16. Henry E. Barrett, Letter to Mark Twain. April 18, 1894, Tioga County, New York. MTP, University of California. Rasmussen, 167.

17. Gilbert Draper Letter to Mark Twain, from Montreal [1909]. MTP, University of California. Rasmussen, 259–260.

18. Jesse A. Gregg Letter to Mark Twain, St. Paul, Minnesota. November 29, 1889. MTP, University of California. Rasmussen, 142–143.

19. William Hance Ridgeway Letter to Mark Twain December 26, 1905 from Coatsville, Pennsylvania. MTP, University of California. Rasmussen, 226–227.

20. Charles Whiting Baker, Letter to Mark Twain, December 5, 1905, Montclair, New Jersey. MTP, University of California. Rasmussen, 223–224.

21. Edwin A.W. Bohl Letter to Mark Twain, January 2, 1909. Peoria, Illinois. MTP, University of California. Rasmussen, 262–263.

22. Gertrude Weld Arnold, Letter to Mark Twain, February 3, 1910. Nutley, New Jersey. MTP, University of California. Rasmussen, 251–252.

23. William Allen White is quoted by Barbara Sicherman in *Well Read Lives*, Chapel Hill: University of North Carolina Press, 2010, p. 49.

24. William Allen White is quoted by Barbara Sicherman in "Reading and Middle Class Identity in Victorian America, Cultural Consumption, Conspicuous and Otherwise," *Reading Acts: U.S. Readers' Interactions with Literature 1800–1900*, eds. Barbara Ryan and Amy M. Thomas. Knoxville: University of Tennessee Press, 2002. p. 145.

25. Edward W. Strong adds that as his reading became more proficient, he began reading stories to his younger brothers. Strong later became a professor of Philosophy and the University of California, Berkley, chancellor from 1961–1965. Bancroft Library. Oral History, "Freedom of Speech" Movement. University of California Berkeley.

26. Lillian Wald, *The House on Henry Street*. New York: Henry Holt, 1915. p. 48.

27. Sarah Wadsworth, *In the Company of Books: Literature and Its Classes in Nineteenth-Century America*, University of Massachusetts Press, 2006. pp. 80–81.

28. Jimmy Gentry, Oral History Interview, University of Tennessee, Knoxville. Center for the Study of War and Society; Thomas T. Adams, Oral History Interview, Rutgers University History Department Oral Archives of World War II. Interviewed on May 18, 1997; Michael Sweeney, Interviewed by Richard Burks Verrone, Texas Tech University Archive. Oral History.

29. Shelley Fisher Fishkin, 69. Kate Flint, in her "Afterword: Women Readers Revisited" for *Reading Women*, recalls "So my sense of who I wanted to be like was formed by Arthur Ransome's Swallows and Amazons books. . . . by the *Adventures of Tom Sawyer*, and by a series of stories by Anthony Breckenridge set in a boy's prep school." See Janet Badia and Jennifer Phegley, eds., *Reading Women: Literary Figures and Cultural Icons from the Victorian Age to the Present*. Toronto: University of Toronto Press, 2005. p. 290.

30. Barbara Sicherman, "Reading and Middle Class Identity in Victorian America, Cultural Consumption, Conspicuous and Otherwise," *Reading Acts: U.S. Readers' Interaction with Literature, 1800–1900*, ed. Barbara Ryan and Amy M. Thomas. Knoxville: University of Tennessee Press, 2002. 144.

31. Janice A. Radway, *Reading the Romance: Women, Patriarchy, and Popular Literature*. Chapel Hill: University of North Carolina Press, 1984, rpt. 1991.

32. Barbara Sicherman, *Well Read Lives*, Chapel Hill: University of North Carolina Press, 2010, 2.

33. Barbara Sicherman, *Well Read Lives*, 5.

34. Martyn Lyons, 371. This relational tendency has been discussed by Carol Gilligan, *In a Different Voice* (Cambridge: Harvard University Press, 1982), in which she also considers gender identity, moral development, and the inner-work of young women coming to terms with the silencing of their roles in society.

35. Fred Hart, *The Sazerac Lying Club: A Nevada Book*. San Francisco: S. Carson, Boston: Lee and Shephard. New York: C. T. Dillingham, 1878. p. 188.

36. Janice A. Radway, 222.

37. Henry Dwight Spencer Letter to Mark Twain, March 8, 1882. MTP, University of California. Rasmussen, 86–87.

38. Jennie S. Walker, Letter to Mark Twain, April 19, 1882. MTP, University of California. R. Kent Rasmussen notes that Jennie Walker's father, George Walker, was one of the founders of the Buick Motor Company.

39. Florence Dean Cope, Letter to Mark Twain, October 28, 1883. MTP, University of California. Rasmussen, 99.

40. Fannie S. James, Letter to Mark Twain, December 7, 1891. MTP, University of California. Rasmussen, 163.

41. Mary Kelley cites examples from letters, autobiographies, commonplace books, and diaries in *Reading Women/Women Reading*. Barbara Hochman discusses books and authors as companions. Hochman calls this "friendly reading" and points out that Louisa May Alcott was promoted as the reader's friend. Ronald Zboray and Mary Saracino Zboray offer evidence that interacting with an author was a pleasure of reading. See Barbara Hochman, pp. 12–13, 23, 29. Barbara Sicherman notes the blurring of boundaries between the author and her character. She indicates that this idea began to fade in the last decades of the nineteenth century, ctd. by Hochman, p. 29. The letters that poured in from children to Twain suggest that his young readers felt that they had a special relationship with him.

42. Gary Scharnhorst, ed., *Mark Twain: The Complete Interviews*, p. 168.

43. Hebe G. Rector, Letter to Mark Twain, May 17, 1891, Hot Springs, Arkansas. MTP, University of California. Rasmussen, 157–158.

44. The anecdote about the New Zealand girl appears in the *Roland Record*, March 6, 1901. Roland, Iowa.

45. Gertrude Swain, Letter to Mark Twain, October 7, 1902, Greeley, Nebraska. MTP, University of California. Rasmussen, 200–201.

46. Margaret Potter Black, Letter to Mark Twain, December 23, 1902, Chicago. MTP, University of California. Rasmussen, 207–208.

47. Jonathan Rose, *The Intellectual Life of the British Working Class*. New Haven: Yale University Press, p. 355. Also in Reader's Experience Database: Mary Lakeman (RED 4927). *Saturday Review*, November 19, 1904.

48. Elizabeth Owen Knight, Letter to Mark Twain, March 31, 1906, Rockville, Maryland. MTP, University of California. Rasmussen, 230.

49. Florence Benson, Letter to Mark Twain, November 30, 1907, Rasmussen, 247–248.

50. Judith Fetterley, "Reading about Reading: 'A Jury of Her Peers,' 'The Murders in the Rue Morgue,' and 'The Yellow Wallpaper'" in Elizabeth Flynn and Patrocinio P. Schweickhart, eds. *Gender and Reading: Essays on Readers, Texts and Contexts*. Baltimore: Johns Hopkins University Press, 1986. p. 159. Also, see Judith Fetterley, *The Resisting Reader: A Feminist Approach to American Fiction*, Bloomington: Indiana University Press, 1978. xx, xii.

51. Barbara Sicherman, *Well Read Lives*, Chapel Hill, University of North Carolina Press, 2010, 5–6.

52. Mabel Bates Back, Knott County Farmer, Kentucky Family Farm Oral History Collection. Interview, June 1991. Louie B. Nunn Center for Oral History. University of Kentucky Library, Lexington, Kentucky.

53. Mary Ellen Leftwich, University of Mississippi Oral History Project, Hattiesburg, Mississippi.

54. Barbara Sicherman, *Well Read Lives*, 3.

55. Gary Scharnhorst points out that in the 1930s *Tom Sawyer* was made into a film twice, including the production by David O. Selznick in 1938. Scharnhorst has suggested that it was a "virtual rehearsal" for *Gone with the Wind*. Slavery in each film is a backdrop. The main characters are not black, but black characters are present, although in comic or stereotypical roles. Shelley Fisher Fishkin comments on this in *Lighting Out*, pp. 92–93.

56. *It's a Wonderful Life*, dir. Frank Capra, 1946.

57. Henry Nash Smith comment noted by Shelley Fisher Fishkin, *Lighting Out*, p. 92.

SIX

Reading in Cultural Institutions

Cultural institutions like the school, the library, and the church have mediated reading across the years. An investigation of their records, when available, provides another level of analysis besides that of the individual reader. In these institutions are those who have positioned themselves as guardians of culture and who have admitted or resisted Mark Twain's work. Through studying them we may discover "the constraining effects of social structure," as Christine Pawley has observed in *Reading Places: Literacy, Democracy, and the Public Library in Cold War America* (2010) and we learn more about what Elizabeth Long (2003) has called "the social infrastructure of reading."[1] Institutions sponsored reading Twain, or they did not. Cooperative institutions acted as a form of "organized sociability" that brought communities together.[2] People, in particular social and cultural circumstances, engaged in interpersonal contact that shaped literacy and reading patterns. Childhood reading, in particular, was at the center of disputes in various communities about whether Mark Twain's writings should be offered to young readers or withheld from them. Educators and librarians were deeply involved in this work as cultural gatekeepers.

A. *TOM SAWYER* IN THE CLASSROOM

Mark Twain's *The Adventures of Tom Sawyer* entered childhood education early in the twentieth century. Critics continued to express moral concern: could young readers be persuaded by the novel to imitate the mischievous characteristics of Tom Sawyer? However, despite this, teachers gave Tom Sawyer a pass into the elementary school curriculum. *The Adventures of Tom Sawyer* was often read. The moral proscriptions of the nineteenth century appear to have lifted and the novel was increasingly recommended to students. In 1913–1914, in the *Elementary School Teacher*, one sees an Illinois survey that recommended *The Prince and the Pauper* and *Tom Sawyer*. In the *English Journal*, a periodical that frequently published articles based upon surveys of student reading, we see *Tom Sawyer* often mentioned. In January 1915, in "High School Reading" Franklin T. Baker of Teacher's College observes a changing definition of "light reading":

> We once had to read only Sunday books on Sunday. We got, therefore, more fun out of a surreptitious hour spent with Huck Finn and Tom Sawyer than we ever had with these gentlemen from the Mississippi on weekdays. They were light reading.

However, it is not Baker's memories of sabbatarian reading or transgressing it with Mark Twain that is his concern. Rather, he points to light reading as a form of play and enjoyment that required reading in school can diminish. For Baker, an English teacher's job is difficult because books like *Tom Sawyer* that ought to be "enjoyed" become assigned as a duty, "making work of play."[3] It is interesting that he makes use of a reference to Huck Finn and Tom Sawyer, who enjoy play but neither of whom enjoy school.

In October 1916, F.A. Scofield reported that in the "outside reading," or noncurricular reading, of students at the Eugene, Oregon, high school *Huckleberry Finn* was the top choice. Tom Sawyer followed *The Iron Woman* on this list, as the third most popular book. The students read a total of 354 books, with Twain's works a clear favorite among both boys and girls. The top nonfiction vocational book was *Vocations for Girls*, followed by several books on vocations in education.[4]

Despite its popularity in Oregon, *Huckleberry Finn* is conspicuously absent from the list compiled from the high school in Decatur, Illinois, in January 1917, suggesting, perhaps, some suppression of the book, or its difficulty for these readers. *Tom Sawyer* is the fifth most popular book on the list from students in Decatur. J.O. Engleman recorded the responses of 800 high school students and then 225 eighth grade students. He found that more than a quarter of them read no newspapers. Their favorite books were not classic literature but titles like *Eyes of the World*, *Girl of the Limberlost*, *Pollyanna*, and *Freckles*. The high school gave them points for outside reading and they were most interested in fiction and then in "stories of inventions." The principal concludes that to offer classic literature is "trying to do the impossible."[5] In the same year, in "Reading in the Rural Districts," May Dexter Henshall reports *Tom Sawyer* high on a list of the thirty most popular books of 400 read in a rural district in California. The study asked what the children were reading and observed that "they like the realistic stories, rather than the fairy tales."[6]

Among the most interesting of the studies of this time is one of the reading interests of the children of immigrants in Hibbing, Minnesota.

The high school there reported a high percentage of students whose families spoke European languages. These were children from the homes of iron mining workers. Many were from backgrounds that were Finnish, Swedish, Italian, Jewish, Austrian, Slovenian, and French. Sixteen different languages were represented among them. They were asked twenty-three questions about their reading on March 21, 1918 between nine and ten o'clock in the morning. Arthur Guy Empey's *Over the Top* was their favorite book and "*Tom Sawyer* was a close second," with twice as many boys as girls naming it.[7]

Surveys like these were conducted throughout the 1920s. In them, we continue to see the wide popularity of *Tom Sawyer* among American schoolchildren. In 1925, at Public School #171 in Manhattan, a junior high school in Harlem, "The consensus of preferences was for *The Man without a Country* (the first on the list presented) and *Tom Sawyer* and *The Spy*. Students were asked to "mark the three books you would like to read next."[8] The *Elementary School Journal* records that children at Capitol School in Lincoln, Nebraska, read *The Prince and the Pauper*. Marjorie W. in grade 7B presumably says: "A story of two boys alike but very unlike in station. Through an adventure the prince and the pauper change places and learn something of each other's lives. I enjoyed this book very much, and I believe any other boy or girl would too." Reid J. in grade 7A said, "Tom Sawyer was a mischievous boy. I recommend this because it is very funny and real."[9]

School systems continued to measure the voluntary reading that their students did outside school time. In the *Elementary School Journal* of 1928, we see a survey of "Voluntary Reading. Grades IV-VIII." The schools surveyed were in Bloomington, Decatur, and Normal, Illinois. Among the 46 most popular books was *Tom Sawyer*, read by 489 boys, 344 girls, for a total of 833 students. *Huckleberry Finn* was read by 340 boys, 207 girls, or 547 total students.[10] In 1930, the Queens Public Library lists *Tom Sawyer* in "Books for a Day's Work or the Evening's Entertainment." This was produced for a series called "The Enchanted Book World for Little People Everywhere." *Creative Youth* (1930), a study developed by progressive educator Hugh Mearns, shows girls reading *Tom Sawyer* and selections from Twain's *Autobiography*.[11] In 1935, an educator pointed to the use of *Huckleberry Finn* for didactic purposes "to cultivate social democracy and to substitute it for snobbishness." *Tom Sawyer* was used "to develop satisfaction in work as play."[12] The *Brooklyn Eagle* reported on May 15, 1941, under the title "Roland Rockets," an elementary school report. After reading *Robinson Crusoe* and "Ali Baba and the Forty Thieves" from *Arabian Nights*, the fifth grade reported: "Miss Taylor is reading to us the *Adventures of Tom Sawyer* by Samuel Clemons [*sic*]."[13]

The sale of Mark Twain's books reached across age and class as well as across national boundaries. Because the books were widely distributed and Twain retained his reputation as a humorist, most critics thought of

Twain principally as a writer for popular culture. Twain himself report-edly said that popular books were less like wine and more "like water," adding: "But everybody drinks water." However, Mark Twain's readers also included those who read both high culture texts and middle brow culture texts. Twain was referred to in books on the ancient Greeks. In a text on *The Iliad*, footnote #220 reads: "Dr. O.W. Holmes remarks that the humor of many persons consists largely in understatement. That this is very true of American humorists will be evident to any one who peruses a few pages of Mark Twain or Artemus Ward. W. J. M. Starkies' study of Aristophanes links Twain with the tradition of ancient comedy." Aristo-tle is quoted. "This is an instance of the jest (Greek follows) best illustrat-ed by Mark Twain's Tom Sawyer: the revelation of the two pirates. . . . So long as they remained in that business, their piracies should no longer be sullied with the name of stealing." [14]

While readers of all ages and classes were reading *The Adventures of Tom Sawyer*, Twain's story also became a hot property for the stage. When one adapter wrote to invite Twain to his version of *Tom Sawyer*, Twain wrote: "How kind of you to invite me to the funeral. I have seen Tom Sawyer's remains in all of the different kinds of dramatic shrouds there are." His letter pointed out that there had been numerous adapta-tions and, like them, that of his correspondent would "go out the back door on the first night."

> You are No. 1365. When 1364 sweeter and better people, including the author, have tried to dramatize Tom Sawyer and did not arrive, what sort of show do you suppose you stand? That is a book, sir, which cannot be dramatized. One might as well try to dramatize any other hymn. *Tom Sawyer* is simply a hymn put into prose from to give it a worldly air. [15]

He concluded, "I know you only mean me a kindness, dear 1365, but it is a most deadly mistake. Please do not name your Injun for me." He never mailed this.

B. *HUCK FINN* IN THE SCHOOLS

It has been argued that Twain's *Huckleberry Finn* is effective teaching material. Proponents of this view hold that the story may engage young reader identification. It can be used, some say, to educate young people on social and racial issues and matters of conscience. Gregory Jay has concluded that *Huckleberry Finn* cannot be "trusted to effect a predictable revolution in the beliefs of students." [16] If one is teaching the novel to encourage a social justice message, one reader may arrive at a different interpretation than that of another reader. Even so, *Huckleberry Finn* has been used for didactic purposes "to cultivate social democracy and to substitute it for snobbishness." *Tom Sawyer* was used "to develop satisfaction in work as play."[17] In the 1930s the progressive educator Hughes Mearns, an advocate of John Dewey's educational views, said: "We try to remember that thirty years and more ago the pedagogues of the period were classifying Huckleberry Finn decisively with Peck's Bad Boy [...]" Discussing elementary school reading, Mearns encouraged reading this novel.[18]

The popularity of Twain among students of all ages appeared early in the new century. A teacher from Waco, Texas, Dorothy Scarborough, told Twain in a letter of January 25, 1906, that he and his works were well-known in Texas. "I make a practice of reading every scrap from or about you," she wrote. "You have an unlimited number of friends down here, unknown to you, but to whom you are indeed well-known, in print if not in the flesh." These Texans who read Twain could be found in her own classroom at Baylor University, Scarborough said:

> The other day, in a class that is doing advanced work in composition with a view to journalism, I assigned as a subject for an impromptu theme an appreciation of some living writer. The themes were to be written in twenty minutes, then read aloud in class. When the papers were turned in, I found, by actual count, that exactly one-third of the members of the class had written to you.[19]

While students today are still introduced to Mark Twain's works in classrooms, American educators have recalled the difficulty of working with Twain's novel alongside public responses. Sarah Simmons, a school principal in Virginia recalled:

> A teacher in the school where I was principal wanted to use *Huckleberry Finn* as a novel for her sixth graders and, at that time, there was a very big outcry against using any Tom Sawyer's, or Mark Twain's books about Tom Sawyer, Huckleberry Finn, in the classroom because of the connotation for African-Americans.[20]

Other teachers recall being enthralled by the book at a young age. One of these readers, an interviewee for a Mississippi oral history project, wondered if contemporary students read, or if they have only become acquainted with *Huckleberry Finn* through television and film. Irene Ponder Napier, born December 21, 1917, in Mt. Olive, Mississippi, taught for twenty-one years, beginning in 1942 at the Sand Hill School in Beaumont, Mississippi. She received a B.S. in Education in 1951. She was an educator concerned with civil rights. She was asked by interviewers if the student today was any brighter than the student of yesteryear. Napier said:

> No, I don't think so. Well, when I was young and back when I first started teaching, children would read a lot. I know once in the fifth grade I would wait from day to day for Miss Phillips [to] read the story of *Huckleberry Finn*: she'd read a chapter a day. And you can start reading to children now and they don't want to hear that because they already saw that on television, don't you know?[21]

Twain's character, Huckleberry Finn, disliked school, church, and all forms of socialization that would "sivilize" him. His fierce departure from such social norms was likely one of the reasons why institutions in the late nineteenth century that were focused upon propriety censored the book in which he appeared. It appears that for Napier access to books and the desire to read is exactly what young people need.

Huckleberry Finn carries the "ongoing aftershocks of a book" that Barbara Hochman has spoken of in reference to Harriet Beecher Stowe's *Uncle Tom's Cabin.*[22] The issue of teaching or not teaching *The Adventures of Huckleberry Finn* has arisen in several school districts across the years since *Brown v. Board of Education* in 1957. Since this issue now revolves around Twain's treatment of race, this concern will be treated in the next chapter when we look at the reading of African Americans. Common readers, unlike critics of our time, appear to not have struggled greatly with the racial implications in the final section of *Huckleberry Finn*. Critics have offered the thought that Twain's ending suggests the re-enslavement of the slaves in the 1880s.[23] Early in the novel, as the imaginative and mischievous Tom Sawyer enters the story, the suggestion that he seeks to "tie up" Jim contributes a dark foreshadowing to the story. A common lamp becomes Aladdin's magical lamp. The story twists away and when Tom reenters, Jim will indeed be bound and Huck will be complicit in Tom's energetic and warped games. Ron Powers writes about the book's ending: "The hard-won stature that Jim has gained during the downriver voyage is discarded; suddenly he is a compliant darky, childishly enduring Tom Sawyer's manic torments. Similarly, Huck loses the moral consciousness that the river crises instilled in him." Stephen Railton sees slapstick in Jim's behavior. He says there are two Jims in the book. There is the suffering Jim who shows the cruelty of the society. There is the stock character of minstrel shows at the beginning and the end of the book. Powers suggests that blacks in the South developed protective mechanisms to deal with racial prejudice as a "survival strategy."[24] Twain's nineteenth-century common readers appear to have expressed no discomforts such as these about the book's ending. Repetition of the word 'nigger' in Twain's text tends to be of greater concern for the contemporary common reader than concerns about depictions of Jim in the book's first and final sections.

C. READERS IN LIBRARIES

From the time that Mark Twain's books first appeared libraries have purchased them. One of the initial questions that librarians had was how to catalog his books. On February 3, 1863, the name "Mark Twain" first appeared in the Virginia City *Territorial Enterprise*. Five years later, Mark Twain was still a new name to most readers. Some knew him as a humorist from the West. His family called him Sam and to friends he was Samuel Clemens. However, the world came to know him best by his pseudonym. Book readers have found this author listed under "C" for Clemens, as often as under "T" for Twain. When the nineteenth-century library specialist Charles Ami Cutter discussed how libraries listed authors with pseudonyms, he highlighted the problem of Mark Twain. He discussed how Dickens was no longer listed as Boz, except by the Dutch: "No one would think of looking under Boz now," Cutter said. Of Samuel Clemens, he wrote: "Mark Twain is in a transition state. The public mind is divided between Twain and Clemens. The tendency is always to use the real name; and that tendency will be much helped in the reading public if the real name is always preferred in catalogue."[25]

Today, in most public libraries, we see books shelved under the name Mark Twain. Readers always associate Samuel Clemens with the pen name he took when he went west to Nevada. Needing a means of earning a living, he became a writer for newspapers. He had been a Mississippi River boat pilot and derived his pen name from the way that riverboat crews measured the depth of the water. The leadsman would call out "mark twain" to affirm that the water was deep enough for the boat to continue on its way. The phrase "mark twain" meant "two fathoms deep." It was a familiar phrase in Samuel Clemens's world. A Civil War soldier writes:

> "February 13th we awoke in the morning to find our camp flooded with water from the river, everything drenched, and we were wading out to higher ground, and the boys were singing the nautical song as we marched out: "Mark Twain. Mark above water Twain, nine feet, no bottom."[26]

One of Twain's readers, Reverend Dewitt Miller of New York, inquired about the nom de plume for a book he was compiling on the subject:

> Will you have the goodness to send me as fully as you may be able the history of y'r pseudonym- "Mark Twain." How it was originated when you first used it, & in what connection on all these points I sh. Be exceedingly glad to be informed.[27]

Critics have made much of how the name suggests a duality, for "twain" means "two." There was Samuel Clemens, father and husband, financial speculator, and there was the writer, Mark Twain. There was Twain West: the man from Missouri who had gone to Nevada and California and absorbed southwestern humor. There was Mark Twain in the East: a man who married into a genteel family and was a writer living in Hartford, attempting to gain the respect of New England's literary elites. Mark Twain was a southern writer who lived in the north. Readers encountered him as both a newspaper writer and as a humorist. He was also a lecturer, a curly haired showman they laughed with, and this provided him with a source of money, especially when his finances experienced a serious downturn. The name Mark Twain is one that became familiar throughout the entire world.

D. CENSORSHIP OF *HUCKLEBERRY FINN*

Librarians have often assumed the role of cultural guardians, selecting for their collections what they have believed would be suitable books for their patrons. They exercised definitions of taste or appropriateness in their public policies and controlled access to books, at least within their own library systems. The censorship of *Huckleberry Finn* from public libraries and school curriculums has been one of the conspicuous aspects of that novel's reception. The action of library and school boards has had some impact upon the encounters that common readers have had with the book. Fay M. Blake once told an interviewer that she stealthily approached the censored book: "That was when there was a big fuss over *Huckleberry Finn*. You know, you take a long time to reach the book on the shelf, and you take it off slowly. In other words, you do some stalling action, but you don't speak out publicly."[28]

Blake's surreptitious approach to the book on the shelf was prompted by the controversy that surrounded Twain's novel. *Huckleberry Finn* was sold as a subscription book by canvassers, but sometimes it found its way into book stores. The novel also found its way into libraries. However, *Huckleberry Finn* found its way out of one library as soon as it came in. The Concord Public Library banned the book, announcing that it was not for children. Mark Twain had, of course, already said as much. While some people assumed that the appearance of young characters automatically meant a book for young readers, Twain asserted that he had written the novel for adults. To him, the action of the Concord Library was an act of stupidity. Yet, he also recognized that censorship in Concord meant heightened sales. People would hurry to buy and read the book to see what was so objectionable about it. The *St. Louis Post-Dispatch* saw this also: and wrote "The directors of the Concord Public Library have joined in the general scheme to advertise MARK TWAIN'S new book Huckleberry Finn."

Seeing the advantages of public controversy around his book, Twain wrote to Charles L. Webster on March 18, 1885:

> Dear Charley,
> The Committee of the Public Library in Concord, Mass. Have given us a rattling tiptop puff which will go into every paper in the country. They have expelled Huck from their library as "trash and suitable only for the slums." That will sell 25,000 copies for us sure.[29]

A reporter from the *St. Louis Globe Democrat* interviewed Concord Library board members about their censoring of *Huckleberry Finn*. One of the board members said:

> While I do not wish to state it as my opinion that the book is absolutely immoral in its tone. . . . it contains but very little humor, and that little is of a very coarse type [...] I regard it as the veriest trash [...]

Another board member responded:

> It deals with a series of adventures of a very low grade of morality [...] and all through its pages there is a systematic use of bad grammar and an employment of rough, coarse, inelegant expressions [...] The whole book is of a class that is more profitable for the slums than it is for respectable people, and it is trash of the veriest sort.[30]

Newspapers had differing opinions. The *Boston Advertiser* claimed that Twain's novel was filled with "coarseness and bad taste." Three thousand miles away, California editors thought otherwise. "There is no limit to his inventive genius," wrote the *San Francisco Chronicle*.[31] However, like the *Boston Advertiser*, several early critics complained that the book had coarse language. Its protagonist was antisocial. He rejected religion. He didn't like school. He didn't speak good grammar and he just couldn't spell correctly. Little was said about the novel's interrogation of racism. No one complained in print about the 211 uses of the n-word. In an age when Stephen Foster was writing songs for Minstrel Shows, no critics argued that Jim appeared too much like a stock minstrel show character in the novel's first pages. There were no literary critics questioning the book's ending. And none argued that Mark Twain was selling out to appease his reading audience.

Louisa May Alcott echoed the Concord Library's dismissal and criticized *The Adventures of Huckleberry Finn*: "If Mr. Clemens cannot think of something better to tell our pure minded lads and lasses, he had best stop writing for them."[32] Of course, Alcott may have sensed that her novel *Little Women* and its sequels were in competition with Twain's book. Twain explicitly observed that he was not writing the book for young readers. He could have pointed out to Alcott something that she already knew well: writers may write different books for different audiences. Alcott, years before, under a pen name A.M. Barnard, had written lurid Gothic tales that would certainly appear in no children's libraries. These included: "The Rival Prima Donnas" (1854), "Behind a Mask," and "The Abbot's Ghost." *The Skeleton in the Closet* and *The Mysterious Key* were published in 1867 as dime novel stories. None of them were destined for the nursery or appropriate for a child's bedtime story.

Libraries also had opinions about whether Twain's books were suitable as juvenile fiction. Asa Don Dickinson was a librarian at the Sheepshead Bay branch of the Brooklyn Public Library when he wrote to Twain on November 19, 1905. He had read *Huckleberry Finn* aloud to the blind people with whom he worked and he had a dream that one day there would be "a national library for the blind." Twain's novels, *Tom Sawyer* and *Huckleberry Finn*, apparently stirred some controversy at the Brooklyn Library.

> I happened to be present the other day at a meeting of the children's librarians. In the course of the meeting it was stated that copies of Tom Sawyer and Huckleberry Finn were to be found in some of the children's rooms of the system. The Superintendent of the Children's Department, a conscientious and enthusiastic young woman- was greatly shocked to hear this and at once ordered that they be transferred to the adults' department. Upon this I shamefacedly confessed to having read *Huckleberry Finn* aloud to my defenseless blind people, without regard to their age, color, or previous condition of servitude. I also told them of Brander Matthews opinion of the book, and stated the fact that I know it almost at heart, having got more pleasure from it than from any other book I have ever read, and reading is the greatest pleasure I have in life.

Twain replied:

> I am greatly troubled by what you say. I wrote Tom Sawyer and Huckleberry Finn for adults exclusively and it always distresses me when I find that boys and girls have been allowed access to them."

He then suggests that if an unexpurgated Bible is in the children's library then it too should be removed, with Solomon, David, Satan, and the rest of the sacred brotherhood.

Dickinson, the librarian, replied in another letter: "Your letter rec'd. I am surprised to hear that you think Huck and Tom would have an unwholesome effect on boys and girls." Clearly Dickinson was referring to himself when he next wrote:

> I know of one boy who made the acquaintance of Huck in 1884, at the age of eight, and who has known him intimately ever since, and I can assure you he is not an atom the worse for the 20 years companionship [...] Huckleberry Finn was the first book I selected to read for my blind (for selfish reasons, I'm afraid) and the amount of innocent enjoyment it gave them, has never been equaled by anything I have since read.

By March, Asa Dickinson was at the Bay Ridge branch in Brooklyn.

> At the January meeting it was also decided not to place Huck and Tom in the children's rooms with "Little Nellie's Silver Mine" and "Dotty Dimple at Home." But the books have not been "restricted" in any sense whatever. They are placed on open shelves among the adult fiction, and any child is free to read adult fiction if he chooses.[33]

An April 4, 1885, letter from William Evarts Parkhurst, the editor of the *Courant* in Clinton, Massachusetts, provided some confirmation that

Twain was accurate in his view that the Concord Library ban on his book would increase sales.

> Presuming on a brief acquaintance with you, formed on the occasion of your visit to our town some fifteen year ago, I made you a copy of my paper, by wh. you will see that our Library directors have decided to keep your sale of ["]Huckleberry Finn" by refusing it a place in our library. I can assure you, that the anxiety to see and read "Huckleber-ry" is on the increase here; the adults are daily inquiring where "Finn" can be had, and even he children are crying for "Huckleberries"; the only way by wh. We can preserve some of our young lads in the facts of moral rectitude is a promise to give them a copy of Mark Twain's rejected "H.F."- Both as an incentive and an opiate the promise of a copy of this work is a marked success.[34]

With some exceptions, there was not a great deal of library censorship of these Twain novels. Recognizing this, Bernadette Lear, a library schol-ar, has pointed out that *Huckleberry Finn* and *Tom Sawyer* were in the Scranton Public Library, which "owned most of Twain's works." Howev-er, in a similar community in Wilkes Barre, librarian Hannah Packard James evidently excluded these novels from the collection. Lear notes Robert M. Rodney's study of which Twain books were most popular by decade and the Charles Compson library study of Twain's books in St. Louis. She reminds us that tracing the role of librarians in creating liter-ary canons provides us with another measure of a novel's impact besides that of the assessments of critics.[35]

The uniform edition of Mark Twain's works was purchased by many libraries in the United States and abroad, making Twain's works further available to people of all classes. Many libraries had gradually collected Twain's works across the years. L. Fred Silvers wrote on July 16, 1902, to Twain that the Central Baptist Church of Elizabeth, New Jersey, had purchased his book on Joan of Arc and subsequently obtained "a Com-plete set of your works." "Not uniformly bound, purchased at various times, but all there," he wrote. He added that "this collection represents my personal tastes, so we have full sets of Dickens, Scott, Bulwer, Coop-er, Conan Doyle, Reade et als besides any new novels thought worthy of circulation." Twain wrote back, recalling the Concord Library ban: "I think your selection of authors is a healthy advance upon the old-time S.S. [Sunday school] library menu."[36]

Some libraries appear to have continued to control access to Twain's works, as a matter of policy. In Syracuse, John A. Lockwood was puzzled by the Carnegie Library's rule limiting borrowing volumes of fiction. After all, he was taking out Twain's travelogue, *A Tramp Abroad*, and surely that wasn't fiction, although Twain had created some embellish-ments. On November 15, 1906, Lockwood wrote to Twain:

Having occasion to try to improve my mind, I called recently at the Carnegg library in this city and asked for "A Tramp Abroad." The young woman who presides over the distribution of the book at said library said- "You already have one book of fiction, you cant take out two." But I argued, you surely dont call A Tramp Abroad "fiction; it is travel, or history, rather." "It's fiction," she remarked decisively. I hope you will tell Mr. Carnegee that if he allows your works on travel to be called fiction you will take them out of his libraries altogether.[37]

E. CHURCHES AND RELIGIOUS READERS

The churches represent another institutional structure that affected the reading of Twain's works. Beginning with *The Innocents Abroad*, Twain met with both favorable and critical comments from ministers, priests, editors of religious publications, and church members. The passengers on Twain's infamous *Quaker City* journey were churchgoing members of a variety of religious congregations. In these religious circles, Twain's satire stirred controversy. Readers from various Christian denominations lined up on all sides to applaud or denounce Twain's commentary. Some found humor in Twain's *The Innocents Abroad* and others frowned upon it. In *God's Word through Preaching* (1875), John Hall wrote: "Each man must determine how much is to be given to study, only let him not call it study when he is lying on the sofa, laughing over 'The Innocents Abroad.'"[38] Among some readers, that positive view of *The Innocents Abroad* held up through the end of the century. In the last years of the century, readers were reminded that *Innocents Abroad* was still to be recommended. The *Salt Lake Herald* commented: "One preacher from Boston told Mark that he was going to have that book introduced into every Sunday school in New England, and he was satisfied it gave a better description of the Holy Land than any other book ever written."[39]

The Catholic Columbian Reading Union observed that Bishop Spalding and Archbishop Kain had a different view: "Archbishop Kain especially condemned the cheap novels that incite the young mind by presenting lurid pictures of criminal life. In his address before the Sunset Club of Chicago, Bishop Spalding mentioned two books destructive of faith and of the best culture, *Innocents Abroad* and *Peck's Bad Boys*."[40] It is not mentioned how Twain's book could possibly be damaging to faith, or why it was associated by the bishop with *Peck's Bad Boys*. These Catholic sources rejected the book.

The *Quaker City* voyage was promoted as a pilgrimage. It was presented as a spiritual journey to revered shrines of the Holy Land. The idea of life-pilgrimage was centered in the Bible and was more a heart's journey toward significance than the pilgrimage to a place. The primary meaning of pilgrimage within Christian thought was concerned with the journey of individual believers through this world to heaven. Such a pilgrimage concerned the larger reality of one's life. Of course, Twain didn't see the *Quaker City* journey this way at all. He tended to see some of his fellow passengers as naïve and deluded. They held to the prevailing view of the Middle Ages, that one was simply lodged here on the earth. Life was ephemeral; this was all a passage.[41] For Twain, however, the *Quaker City* voyage was all simply tourism.

The Innocents Abroad was hardly the only book of Twain's to cast a spell upon religiously oriented readers. *The Prince and the Pauper* appears to have a curious hold over the Reverend Edward O. Sharpe of Watseka, Illinois. Sharpe suggested the book's staying power in his own life. He had begun his ministry in Iowa in 1883. Two years later, while in Illinois, on November 6, 1885, he wrote to Mark Twain, obviously affected by Twain's novel. Yet, it is difficult to know to what degree he was being facetious as he wrote about its strange power over him:

> I have some—what against you! Your books have always been of lively interest to me, and whenever I have read one, have laid it aside with a sigh of relief—because it comes out right. The last volume to receive my attention was Prince and the Pauper and there is trouble right here. I cannot let go of it and it won't stay read. Some how or other, that miserable Tom Canty keeps following me and scratching my imagination until I am forced to go with him again through his troubles. I know it is all a—true story, but it bothers me worse than some little things I have told. (I am a minister.)
>
>   Can you not devise some remedy for my trouble. Tell me how to get loose, or I may try to become a king myself just to get into no end of trouble. I am a humble servant of the vineyard, as it were, and I do not think you ought to so unsettle me. At any rate I demand a recipe that will recover me. . . . [42]

The next year, in 1886, Twain was hoping that a contract with the Vatican for a biography of Pope Leo XIII would add luster and lucre to the publishing firm that he had started. Instead, it was a publishing calamity. Whatever international audience Twain imagined for the book did not appear. The U.S. domestic audience did not respond particularly well to the book either. Some critics have pointed out that many Catholic immigrants to America were not yet literate. Twain later wrote: "We did not consider how often Catholics could not read, how often, when they could, they did not wish to read [...]"[43]

The Columbian Reading Union of Paulist Fathers would serve as one correction to this lack of reading by encouraging book distribution among Catholic immigrants. However, the commentators in its periodical, the *Catholic World*, were often not favorable to Twain, whose secular jibes they regarded as disarmingly agnostic. In 1890, the publication responded to *A Connecticut Yankee in King Arthur's Court* by scoffing at Twain's "ignorance in regard to the church, to which he seems to credit all the evils of the world in early times.[44] In an unsigned diatribe against

Twain's novel, the *Catholic World* recalled *The Innocents Abroad*: "A correspondent sends us this notice of a writer who has done all in his power to make ludicrous many objects and places venerated for their historical associations." The writer then turned to review Twain's most recent novel:

> Mark Twain's Yankee at the Court of King Arthur is full of that peculiar humor for which the author is notorious. He casts about liberally the creations of his deep ignorance in regard to the church, to which he seems to credit all the evils of the world in early times. In his mind the chief agencies of civilization are soap, steam, gunpowder, and electricity. He has all the irreverence of the worshipper of the almighty dollar and all the bitterness and hatred of the church which led the Puritans to those savage attacks on our art, music, and the requirements of civilization which the church founded and fostered. The book will not do much to elevate his reputation as a humorist, while it shows him to be more ignorant of history than one could have believed. [45]

The *Catholic World* appears to have been perhaps overly sensitive to the novel. It often referred to Twain as a "reckless scoffer at things held sacred." In Hank Morgan's journey to the year 513, the Catholic Church, viewed as a feudal institution, is one of Twain's primary targets. Twain had followed some of the contemporary commentary about the Catholic Church's resistance to science. He looked at the essays of Robert G. Ingersoll, a Republican, agnostic lawyer who defended science against clergy. The anti-Catholic atmosphere in America, fueled by unease about increasing immigration from Europe, remained strong at this time. Papal cautions against modernity seemed regressive to some critics. John W. Draper wrote *History of the Conflict between Religion and Science*. Henry C. Lea, Philadelphia publisher, wrote his anti-Catholic church diatribes in his *History of the Inquisition of the Middle Ages*. Twain read these documents. Soon after the publication of Twain's novel, Pope Leo XIII, the pope whose biography Twain had published, issued the encyclical *Rerum Novarum* (1891), defending the rights of laborers and initiating the Catholic social justice tradition.

Twain, of course, could not see the seeds of Vatican II in the work of Leo XIII. Predicting a different future, before he wrote *Connecticut Yankee*, Twain wrote in his notebook: "For a play. America in 1985. The Pope here & an inquisition. The age of darkness back again." [46] Of course, the pope in 1985 was John Paul II, a pope who was conservative in doctrine and in sexual matters but ecumenical and globally engaged: an inquisition in 1985 was hardly likely. Twain fed on the fears of his own age. As Louis Budd points out, "As the Roman Catholic Church entered a period of militant growth after 1870, newspapers and magazines quivered with forebodings that parochial schools were undermining the public system. This eventually swelled to new thunderheads of prejudice [...]" [47] Mark

Twain apparently took this to heart. "Look at the movement for parochial schools," he wrote. "Let me educate your children & I will determine your ultimate form of gvnmt."[48] Twain's suspicion of the Catholic Church was also encouraged when his brother, Orion Clemens, joined the American Protective Association.

Consequently, there were ever tensions between Twain's writings and the Catholic audience's response to them. Indeed, these were particularly vociferous after *Connecticut Yankee*. Some readers, like the Catholic moralist Louise Sandrock, rejected this book and cautioned her readers about allowing his *Adventures of Tom Sawyer* and *Huckleberry Finn* to fall into children's hands. "The vulgarities and bigotries of Mark Twain and Bill Nye should never be put in juvenile hands," wrote Sandrock in the *Catholic World* in 1890.[49] Opposition of this sort appears consistent with concerns voiced early in the nineteenth century about the alleged power of fiction to corrupt young minds. Twain's censors appear to have been a moral minority. Agnes Reppelier, writing in the *Catholic World* in 1882, preferred the humor of "holy men" to that of Mark Twain. She wrote: "Yet, because men of the Mark Twain type have a jeer ever ready for things they fail to understand, we need not suppose that there is no proper field for that sense of fun which was manifestly given us for some good purpose." By 1905 she had lightened up considerably on Mark Twain. Speaking at his seventieth birthday celebration, Reppelier said:

> There is no corner of England or the United States where Mark Twain's name fails to awaken some response. There is not a remote book-store in Great Britain . . . where I have not found American literature represented by *Innocents Abroad* and *Huckleberry Finn*. . . . I have found one or two names which are open sesames to the foreign intelligence: Chicago and Mark Twain. . . .[50]

Reppelier's comments suggest that we need to consider *when* in life a reader recorded a response to Twain. Attitudes can change over time in the same reader. The obscure twenty-eight-year-old from Philadelphia who wrote in a sectarian Catholic publication in 1882 is not altogether the same as the fifty-year-old essayist who was widely recognized for her books and publications in the *Atlantic*. These comments also remind us that where a reader places her attention is an important factor in the evaluation of a text. A reader might have a racial, ethnic, or regional orientation, or be focused upon a text's moral implications, as were Louise Sandrock and the young Agnes Reppelier. *Tom Sawyer* and *Huckleberry Finn* were magnets for that kind of righteous reading.

However, other Catholic readers were emotionally moved by Twain. Fr. J.P. Tower of Hyattsville, Maryland, was deeply touched by Twain's account of his daughter Susy's death in his *Autobiography*, which had begun to appear in periodical installments. He included it as part of his sermon in St. Jerome's Church in October 1906.[51] Twain, for his own part, held a broader concern with critiquing powerful institutions. Justin Kaplan has pointed out in his 1970 introduction to Twain's novel: "Mark Twain responded to events and currents in the world around him."[52] Twain was concerned with democracy and institutional reform.

NOTES

1. Elizabeth Long is cited by Christine Pawley, *Reading Places: Literacy, Democracy and the Public Library*. Amherst: University of Massachusetts Press, 2012. p. 9.

2. Christine Pawley, *Reading Places: Literacy, Democracy and the Public Library in Cold War America*. Amherst: University of Massachusetts Press, 2010. pp. 13–14.

3. Franklin T. Baker, "High School Reading," *English Journal* (1916).

4. F.A. Scofield, "Outside Reading," *English Journal* (October 1916).

5. J.O. Engleman (Superintendent of Schools, Decatur, Illinois), "Outside Reading," *English Journal* (January 1917): 20–27.

6. May Dexter Henshall, "Reading in the Rural Districts," *English Journal* (1915): 190–91.

7. Hibbing, Minnesota, *English Journal* (1918): 474–487.

8. Sarah Wadsworth points to changes in the construction of childhood and the popular construction of the child as audience. In chapter three, she investigates "the presumed expectations and requirements of juvenile readers, and Mark Twain's own ambivalence about that audience. . . . " p. 13. *In the Company of Books: Literature and Its "Classes" in Nineteenth-Century America*. Amherst: University of Massachusetts Press, 2006, p. 13, 17.

9. *Literature in the Elementary School Classroom*. University of Chicago Press, 1913–1914, p. 161. rpt. 1925, p. 705. Claire McPhee, "An Experiment in Reading in the Seventh and Eighth Grades," *Elementary School Journal*. p. 532.

10. "Voluntary Reading," *Elementary School Journal*. University of Chicago Press, 1928, rpt. 1931, p. 15.

11. *The Library Door*, Vol. 1. No. 3 (December 1930); Hugh Mearns. *Creative Youth*. Garden City: Doubleday, Doran, 1930.

12. *Elementary School Journal* (1935) p. 11. Elementary School Journal, Voluntary Reading. Grades IV–VIII. University of Chicago Press (1928) rpt. 1931: 15.

13. "Roland Rockets," *Brooklyn Eagle*, May 15, 1941.

14. *The Iliad of Homer*, Book I–VI, Introduction, Robert A. Keep. Boston: J. Allyn, 1887; W.J.M. Starkies, *The Archarians of Aristophanes*. London: Macmillan, 1909. Note #164 p. 177.

15. Mark Twain, *Autobiography*, ed. Charles Neider, pp. 170–71.

16. Gregory Jay, *American Literature and Culture Wars*, Cornell University Press, 1997, p. 139. Also see Gregory Jay, *America the Scrivener*, Cornell University Press, 1990.

17. *Elementary School Journal* (1916): 11.

18. Hughes Mearns, "Unsupervised Reading," *Creative Youth: How a School Can Set Free the Creative Spirit*. Garden City: Doubleday, Doran. 1930. p. 105.

19. Dorothy Scarborough, Letter to Mark Twain, January 25, 1906, Waco, Texas. MTP, University of California. Rasmussen, 227–228.

20. Sarah Simmons, March 22, 2000, Virginia Polytechnic Oral History Interviews. MTP.

21. Irene Ponder Napier, University of Southern Mississippi, Civil Rights Documentation Project, Oral History and Cultural Heritage.

22. Barbara Hochman, *Uncle Tom's Cabin and the Reading Revolution*, University of Massachusetts Press, 2012. p. 6.

23. Shelley Fisher Fishkin, *Was Huck Black?* Oxford University Press, 1993. p. 97.

24. Ron Powers, *Mark Twain: A Life*. New York: The Free Press, 2006. p. 495.

25. Charles Ami Cutter, *Rules For a Dictionary Catalogue*. Washington, DC: U.S. Government Printing Office, 1891, p. 18.

26. Civil War soldier A.J. Robinson served in Company E of the 33rd Wisconsin Volunteer Infantry. See A.J. Robinson, *Memorandum and Anecdotes of the Civil War, In Remembrance of the Boys Who Fought to Maintain One Flag, One Country and One People, 1860–1865*, Chapter VII, Vicksburg Campaign. Privately Printed, 1910.

27. Reverend Dewitt Miller, Letter to Mark Twain. MTP, University of California. See Rasmussen, 61.

28. Faye M. Blake, University of California, Bancroft Library, Regional Oral History.

29. Mark Twain Letters, Letter to Charles L. Webster, March 18, 1885. MTP, University of California.

30. *St. Louis Globe Democrat* (March 17, 1885). Quoted in *Introduction to Huckleberry Finn*, Fischer and Salamo, p. 763.

31. The *Boston Advertiser* cited the novel's "irreverence," as Justin Kaplan notes in *Mr. Clemens and Mr. Twain*, New York: Simon and Schuster, 1966. p. 268. The *San Francisco Chronicle* applauded Twain as one of its West Coast heroes, suggesting a cultural as well as a geographical distance between West Coast and New England audiences. See *Mark Twain: Contemporary Reviews*, ed. Louis J. Budd, Cambridge: Cambridge University Press, 1999. p. 270.

32. Louisa May Alcott is quoted by Justin Kaplan in *Mr. Clemens and Mr. Twain*, p. 268. See also James D. Hart, *The Popular Book: A History of America's Literary Taste*, 1950, rpt. Berkeley: University of California Press, 1961. p. 150.

33. Asa Don Dickinson wished this letter to be confidential. Now it is public and this letter has been previously published. Dickinson's attention to blind persons encouraged the American Library Association to start the Committee on Service to the Blind and they named him its director. In 1915, he spent time in India. As librarian for the University of Punjab in Lahore, he introduced methods that became important for the modern library system in India and Pakistan. Dickinson was a friend of Russell Doubleday and edited Doubleday, Page and Company books, beginning in from 1912. For the company, he compiled his Best Books series, which always included Mark Twain's *Huckleberry Finn*. He became Brooklyn College's chief librarian.

34. William Evarts Parkhurst, Letter to Mark Twain, Clinton, Massachusetts. MTP, University of California. Rasmussen, 112.

35. Bernadette Lear, "Were Tom and Huck on the Shelf?" *Nineteenth-Century Literature* 64 (September 2000): 213–214.

36. L. Fred Silvers, Letter to Mark Twain, July 16, 1902. Elizabeth, New Jersey. MTP, University of California. Rasmussen, 199–200.

37. John Lockwood, Letter to Mark Twain, November 15, 1906. Syracuse, New York. MTP, University of California. Rasmussen, 235–236.

38. John Hall, *God's Word through Preaching*, 1875, p. 269.

39. "Mark Twain in His Youth," *Salt Lake Herald* (June 5, 1896) p. 16; reprinted as "Mark Twain's Beginnings" in *St. Paul Globe* (January 13, 1901) p. 22.

40. Columbian Reading Union, *Catholic World*, p. 574.

41. In Greek, strangers and pilgrims are *xenoi kai parepidemoi*. In the Latin Vulgate, this is *peregrine et hospites*. Both phrases suggest a temporary residence on earth, a passing through. The word *Peregrinus* referred to a traveler from a foreign place. Martin Luther, translating into German, wrote *"Gaste und Fremdlinge,"* which is "visiting strangers." The Revised Standard Version of the Bible in 1946 uses the terms "strangers and exiles." The New English Bible of 1961 reads: "strangers or passing travelers." The New Revised Standard Version of the Bible, in 1989, refers to "strangers and foreigners." Some early Christians considered their lives as exiles from heaven and believed that their journey was to return to God.

42. Edward O. Sharpe, Letter to Mark Twain, Watseka, Illinois. MTP, University of California.

43. Mark Twain, *Autobiography.*

44. *Catholic World*. Vol. 51, Issue 302 (May 1890): 275.

45. *Catholic World*, Vol. 59, Is. 353 (August 1894): 715.

46. Ibid.

47. *Mark Twain's Notebooks and Journals*. Ed. Frederick Anderson, Lin Salamo, Michael B. Frank. Berkeley: University of California Press, 1980.

48. Louis J. Budd, p. 117. Budd notes Catholic hostility toward the Knights of Labor. Father Mc Glynn was supportive. The Pope excommunicated him. One wonders if this excommunication was not inconsistent with Pope Leo XIII's *Rerum Novarum*, an encyclical in support of labor.

49. Louise Sandrock, "Another Word on Children's Reading," *Catholic World*, Vol. 51, Is. 305 (August 1890): 679.

50. Agnes Repplier, *Catholic World*, Vol. 36 (1882): 127. In the following years, she would write frequently for the *Atlantic*, including "A Plea for Humor" (1891). In 1890, she recalled: "I am inclined to think the most melancholy experience of my boarding-school life was to read utterly unreadable books." *Catholic World*, Vol. 51, Is. 304 (July 1890): 550–58. Repplier's comments on Twain were published in *Harper's Weekly* (December 23, 1905).

51. J.P. Tower, Letter to Mark Twain, October 1906, Hyattsville, Maryland. Rasmussen 232–233.

52. Justin Kaplan, *Mr. Clemens and Mr. Twain*, New York: Simon and Schuster, 1966. p. 11.

SEVEN

The Variety of Readers

Gender, Race, Ethnicity

The great variety of readers of Mark Twain across gender, race, and region requires further exploration. This chapter gathers the responses of women, immigrant readers, and African American readers. We then look at the response to Twain within specific geographical contexts in the United States. In late nineteenth-century America, reading expanded across the middle class. Increasing numbers of people in the working class were gaining access to reading materials and were reading for self-improvement or entertainment. One the American critics most friendly to Twain's work, Brander Matthews, in 1902, saw "multiple publics."[1] Immigrants were reading books in English and in their native languages. African American reading circles and women's "clubs" were reading Twain's stories aloud. Some writers experienced uncertainty about reception in the 1880s and 1890s, Barbara Hochman has observed. Whereas readers had once viewed themselves in a "friendly" relationship with the author and the book, as companions, the audience was now more varied, or "increasingly fragmented and unknowable."[2] This chapter explores some sectors of Twain's audience during those years.

A. WOMEN'S READING

Many critics have commented on Mark Twain's female reading audience. It has been suggested that the influence of his wife Olivia and that of Mrs. Mary Fairbanks affected his tone and approach in his early works. The argument was first advanced by Van Wyck Brooks in 1920, who charged that these women close to Twain censored his work. As a result of their genteel editing and influence, the argument goes, Twain tended to rein himself in, so that his rough-edged western tales would not seem too scandalous to the ladies of the northeast. However, it is equally possible that Olivia Langdon Clemens very much inspired Twain's writing. Shelley Fisher Fishkin points out that Twain wrote within a domestic "angel of the house" harmony.[3] Other critics suggest that the sensibility of his female audience was to be an ongoing concern for Mark Twain. Laura Skandera-Trombley suggests that Twain "relied on female audiences for his greatest works of fiction."[4]

Women readers became part of Twain's audience amid several emerging trends in reading in the late nineteenth century: the growth of the middle class, the rise of diversity in the population through immigration, and a gradual movement of women into the public sphere, via teaching, nursing, reform, editing, and writing. Reading offered women a path to constructing self-image and identity in a society in which opportunities for self-development were limited, Barbara Sicherman has pointed out.[5] Critics of women's reading like Sicherman, Mary Kelley, and others hold that young women were able to imagine via fiction ways out of gender and class limitations. The image of a woman reading—an image of "tranquility, retreat, and serenity"—could be potentially subversive and dangerous, in conflict with convention, observe Janet Badia and Jennifer Phegley. They argue for a consideration of the woman reader "for her significance as a cultural phenomenon."[6]

Women's reading often occurred in groups and the interpretive community appears to have supported young women's reading. Barbara Sicherman observes that "reading remained . . . a social and collective as well as individual endeavor, one firmly rooted in relationships."[7] Ronald and Mary Saracino Zboray have demonstrated that books helped to connect families in relationships with reading as a shared activity. Through family exchanges, books connected generations of female readers.[8] They also contributed to shaping an individual's subjectivity. Women's reading groups encouraged what Mary Kelley refers to as "a trajectory that led from solitary reading to making meanings in collaboration with other readers."[9] Reading circles were often outside institutional boundaries, although some were sponsored by churches or by female academies. Some were held in homes, others at community centers. Collaboration and mutual improvement was often part of the agenda, as Kelley has pointed out.[10] Books in the libraries of these groups were often selected by members of the group and "marked the rapid expansion of the world of print."[11] As we shall see, the women's reading circle in Pontiac, Michigan, and the library that emerged from this collective is a good example of how this trend persisted at the end of the nineteenth century.

We may wonder what role gender and regional location played in a woman's reading of Mark Twain's works. Local interpretive communities, such as reading groups or family groups, played a part in her response. In her influential study *Reading the Romance* (1984), Janice Radway spoke of our "taking readers seriously" and showed how one might make use of oral history interviews in analyzing audiences.[12] Radway affirmed that what readers feel is quite important and that reading romances was a valuable compensatory literature, a temporary escape for some women from the roles of housewife and mother. Reading could also be a mild form of self-assertion against the limitations of domesticity. The interpretive community of women romance readers confirmed the value of reading.

When Alvora Miller wrote to Mark Twain, February 7, 1898, she recalled how she was restrained from reading his works within her family. She immediately wrote of "the limited number of your works which I have been permitted to enjoy."[13] She says to Twain that despite dissuasion from her family, she is "going to thank you heartily for the solid comfort I have taken in *Innocents Abroad* (and some of your shorter sketches)."[14] She has read the book, misplaced it, and read it again twice after twenty years. Rasmussen adds a note that Miller "was widowed a few years after writing this letter." We may wonder not only about her losing and finding the book again but also about the freedom she found to read both Stowe's *Uncle Tom's Cabin* and Twain's *The Innocents Abroad* successive times.

We have seen how a common reader like Louise Rutherford was criticized for reading Mark Twain because her family called her reading practice not "sensible." We have seen two Cape Cod sisters who were so uneasy about presenting their work to publishers that they admitted they "never went to a big city." In addition, we have looked at a woman in California as a subscription agent selling Twain's books and women in Middletown, New York, buying Twain's books. Common readers like Mabel Bates Back, Mary Ellen Leftwich, Faye B. Blake, and author Margaret Potter Black have reflected back upon the importance of Twain's stories in their childhoods.

We may add to this several female voices in R. Kent Rasmussen's collection of letters: Susan Matilda (Tilla) Bradshaw Swales of Detroit, on July 18, 1885, recalls that she had previously written Twain after reading *The Innocents Abroad*. She thanks him for his recent article "On Training Children" in the *Christian Union*. After having "given the boys no end of valuable hints on how to become bad boys," she says, it was gratifying to see that Twain has finally given parents a few ideas for control of their children. She goes on to applaud his tribute to his wife Livy and adds: "Long after Tom Sawyer and Huckleberry Finn are forgotten these eloquent and beautiful words will be quoted. . . . "[15] We also find Lillian Beardsley's plea in 1906 to Twain to not write any more sad stories like "A Horse's Tale" and a letter of the same year from folklorist Dorothy Scarborough at Baylor University in Waco, Texas, who later compiled one of the definitive studies of Negro folk songs. "You have an unlimited number of friends down here, but to whom you are indeed well-known," she tells Twain.[16] This small sample indicates that women from many different backgrounds were readers upon whom Twain made a distinct impression.

Certainly, Annie Adams Fields can best be situated as a patron of Twain, rather than as a common reader. Like Mrs. Mary Fairbanks, of Cleveland, she may be said to be representative of an affluent northern readership and the forms of propriety that Twain had to adjust to. When Mark Twain left his Hartford based publisher, he exchanged the rights for publication of his books to the prestigious Boston firm, Ticknor and Fields that had recently undergone reorganization and had become Osgood and Company. In the process of this transition, Mark Twain had met Annie Adams Fields, the wife of the publisher James Fields. She soon became an avid reader of Twain's work and a prolific author in her own right. In her autobiography, Mrs. Fields recalled a diary she had kept in the 1870s. In it she wrote: "Bayard Taylor and his wife left for New York. Mr. Parton dined out and we had a quiet evening [...] Parton thinks it would be possible to make the 'Atlantic Monthly' far more popular. He suggests a writer named Mark Twain be engaged, and more articles connected with life than with literature."[17]

That was the first time she heard of the writer, Mark Twain. In an editorial note to Mrs. Fields' biography we read:

> Of all the young Lochinvars of the pen who came out of the West while Mrs. Fields was keeping her diary, Bret Harte and Mark Twain were the daring and dauntless gallants who most captured the imagination and have the longest held it. To each of them she devoted a number of pages of her diary.[18]

Annie Adams Fields became an enthusiastic reader of Mark Twain soon afterward. She also became a friend to the Clemens family. In one diary note, Mrs. Fields records "Mrs. Clemens quite ill." She says that while Twain's past lecture in Boston was highly successful, in a recent one he "barely covered his expenses" and then spent the evening in conversation, drinking ale.[19]

The final words in Annie Fields' diary, from January 25, 1913, refer to Mark Twain:

> The days go cheerfully. I have just read Mark Twain's life, the life of a man who had greatness in him. I am now reading *Joan of Arc*. I hope to wait as cheerfully as she did for the trumpet call and as usefully, but I am ready.[20]

Elizabeth Paschal O'Connor, an author whose life was clearly affected by the example of her father, was unhappy with Mark Twain. As a child, she was introduced to the novels of Sir Walter Scott, which were among her father's dearest possessions. Consequently, she rejected Twain's criticisms of Sir Walter Scott. With *Life on the Mississippi*, Twain began his well-known critique of Scott's impact upon the American South. In volume two, he mocks a little castle at Baton Rouge as a product of Scott's romances:

> Sir Walter Scott is probably responsible for the Capitol building; for it is not conceivable that this little sham castle would ever have been built if he had not run the people mad, a couple of generations ago, with his medieval romances. The South has not yet recovered from the debilitating influence of his books. Admiration of his fantastic heroes and their grotesque chivalry doings and romantic juvenilities still survives here [...][21]

Twain speaks of "traces of its inflated language and other windy humbuggeries" and points back to the Capitol building, speaking of "ungenuine" materials and "this architectural falsehood." He attributes to Walter Scott the pseudo-English style of southern newspaper writers. All this pretentious gallantry and "grace" is the fault of Walter Scott's historical romances.

Elizabeth O'Connor, like her father, believed in honor, gentility, and the courtly love tradition. Twain asserts that the courtly love tradition has been inscribed upon the South to ill-effect. He writes of the Southern reporter:

> The trouble with the Southern reporter is — Women. They unsettle him; they throw him off his balance. He is plain, and sensible, and satisfactory, until a woman heaves in sight. Then he goes all to pieces; his mind totters, he becomes flowery and idiotic.

The trouble is, he says, "Women, supplemented by Walter Scott and his knights and beauty and chivalry, and so on." He points out that the "Maundy" Tuesday before Ash Wednesday signals Mardi Gras in New Orleans:

> Mardi Gras is of course a relic of the French and Spanish occupation; but I judge that the religious feature has been pretty well knocked out of it now. Sir Walter has got the advantage of the gentlemen of the cowl and rosary, and he will stay. His medieval business supplemented by the monsters and oddities, and the pleasant creatures from fairy land, is finer to look at than the poor fantastic inventions and performances of the reveling rabble of the priest's day, and serves quite as well., perhaps, to emphasize the day and admonish men that the grace-line between the worldly season and the holy one is reached.[22]

Twain concludes that Sir Walter Scott's fake medievalism has prevented progress. It is "Sir Walter disease." The South has been set backward. It is a crime greater than slavery.

> Then comes Sir Walter Scott with his enchantment, and by his single might checks this wave of progress, and even turns it back; sets the

world in love with dreams and phantoms, with decayed and swinish forms of religion; with decayed and degraded systems of government; with the silliness and emptiness, sham grandeurs, sham gauds, and sham chivalries of a brainless and worthless long-vanished society. He did measureless harm; more real and lasting harm, perhaps than any other individual that ever wrote. . . .

It was Sir Walter that made every gentleman in the South a major, or a Colonel, or a General, or a Judge, before the war; and it was he, also, that made these gentlemen value these bogus decorations. For it is he that created rank and caste down there, and also reverence for rank and caste, and pride and pleasure in them. Enough is said of slavery, without fathering upon it these creations and contributions of Sir Walter. Sir Walter had so large a hand in making Southern character, as it existed before the war. [23]

Elizabeth Paschal O'Connor did not like this at all. In *My Beloved South*, she critiqued Mark Twain's own claim to "southernness": Mark Twain said of himself that he was a "de-Southernized Southerner." O'Connor, who was known as "Betty," devoted a chapter of her autobiography, *I, Myself* (1911), to a response to Mark Twain's criticisms of Sir Walter Scott. Chapter 22 is titled "Sir Walter Scott's Responsibility for the Civil War." Across two pages she quotes Twain. [24] Mrs. O'Connor comments: "Unfortunately, in this assertion Mark Twain can be bolstered up by evidence, for nowhere in the world was Sir Walter Scott as much loved and widely read as in the South." Upon acknowledging this, she writes: "But what did he teach? Loyalty and self-sacrifice, a sense of loyalty to your kinsfolk, courage and valour in battle, open-handed hospitality and a sense of responsibility towards those dependent on you. Isn't that just as good a teaching as 'practical common sense,' progressive ideas, and progressive works?" [25] She immediately proceeds to criticize New Yorkers' bad manners.

As a young woman, Betty Paschal had become familiar with New York, where she became a journalist. Originally from Texas, with family connections in Virginia, she moved north to become a writer and reader for the *New York World*. There she married T.P. O'Connor. As one reads her autobiography, it soon becomes clear why she vociferously responded to Mark Twain's critique of Sir Walter Scott: her father was a devoted reader of the Scottish novelist. Chapter two of Mrs. O'Connor's autobiography begins: "I think the person of all others whom I have loved the most in my life was my father." She views her father as chivalrous: "He could more readily put himself in the place of other people than any man I have ever seen." [26] It appears that her father had to go to prison for a time and that he brought along Sir Walter Scott's fiction with him: "He was reading 'The Bride of Lammermoor' perhaps for the fiftieth time. He had taken it from the table in his office and slipped it under his jacket while being arrested [...] It is for this reason I feel as if Walter Scott were a kinsman of mine." [27]

Betty O'Connor was a well-read, self-proclaimed "romantic," who read both Walter Scott and Mark Twain. She notes a childhood interest in "Sleeping Beauty," while she was living in Austin, Texas. She says that in her childhood she "preferred Arabian Nights" and she upholds the value of fidelity with reference to Hawthorne's *The Scarlet Letter*. In Texas, she says, "If a man compromised the wife or daughter of another man, he knew the consequence beforehand. He paid for it with his life." She would write in the introduction to *My Beloved South*: "Each day the memory of the South becomes more and more a cherished dream." [28]

Mrs. O'Connor became acquainted with Mark Twain's writing while she lived in New York. She had received assistance from Mrs. Vanderbilt. Mr. Hulbert, an editor, had advised her to read a dozen books on the field of journalism. Like Twain, she was in sympathy with African Americans who were finding their way in American life after the Civil War. As a child, following her mother's death, she had been raised by a black nanny and an Irish nurse. She liked wearing "a long blue cloak lined with red" and she took a liking to Uncle Remus in Joel Chandler Harris's story. She wrote to Harris in the 1880s. [29]

Twain, however, maintained his dislike of the traits that he equated with reactionary feudalism. He did not approve of Mrs. O'Connor's "feudal" South. He rejected what he regarded as antiquated institutions and tried to have hope in the prospects of America "to counter his pessimistic determinism." [30] Science and technology were the forces of the present and superstition and tradition were forces of the past. For Twain, the Walter Scott influence on the South kept it a backward society. He scoffed at the Southern inclination to make buildings look like castles. In Baton Rouge, he wrote, "Walter Scott is probably responsible for the capitol building, for it is not conceivable that this little sham castle would ever have been built if he had not run the people mad, a couple of generations ago, with his medieval romances." [31]

Unlike Mrs. O'Connor, a nineteenth-century writer, the issue was not romanticism and chivalry for the Southern author Margaret Walker. For Walker, the most striking and disturbing issue in reading Twain was race. At the Mississippi Arts Festival in Jackson in 1971, she recalled reading Mark Twain's stories as a child: "I came across the word nigger and I put the book down," she said. [32] The issue of race troubled her but she proceeded to read Twain and she later was interested in the writing of William Faulkner, she said. Clearly race and region were more important factors than gender in her reading of Mark Twain.

B. IMMIGRANTS TO AMERICA

Twain wrote during an age of increasing emigration from Europe. Among the immigrants arriving in America who read Twain were people who identified themselves religiously as Catholics, Protestants, or Jews. These individuals might be considered with respect to their national, religious, and ethnic backgrounds. In April 1875, Ladislaus W. Madarasz of Poughkeepsie, New York, wrote to ask Twain if he would let him use the name of Colonel Sellers for his "assumed name" while in Europe. Madarasz was a Hungarian immigrant, who could speak German, a "Mexican" dialect of Spanish, and Hungarian, and could read French.[33]

Another Hungarian, Joseph Dick, told Twain that while he could not thank Dickens for his work, he could indeed thank Twain.

> As a mark of my gratitude I wish to tell you that both, my father, who is in the wilds of Hungary and who read your sketches in German, and myself, consider your best work "The Experience of the McWilliams family with membranous Croup." My father, who had had similar experiences, shrieked with delight on reading it. . . . [34]

For some immigrants Mark Twain's West mixed and mingled with their impressions of America. *Roughing It* and *The Adventures of Huckleberry Finn* provided images of America for some of these readers. For example, there was Edward Rune Myrbeck from Stockholm, Sweden, a tradesman who recalled how his expectations of America were shaped by his reading. "I thought I was going to see Indians. I thought I'd see, I read about Mark Twain, Mark Twain's books. I thought I was going to see a lot of those people. I uh, I had never seen a Negro in my life. I was excited about seeing a Negro and there were lots of things you were excited about."[35]

Across the years other immigrants to the United States attested to the importance of Twain's books to them. An anonymous correspondent wrote to Twain on October 26, 1905:

> I crossed over to this country more than twelve years ago, with an Italian boy of sixteen, who had walked from Rome to Paris, where we met. His delight and my delight too, was to read together a French translation of Huckleberry Finn. Our knowledge of America was confined to "Huck Finn," and on arriving in Boston Harbor, the boy said to me "Qui est ce George Vashington don't on parle tant?" I told him the little I knew. To-day the boy is a well educated man speaking three languages, the Father of two gifted children and earning $25 weekly in a N.Y. engraving house. A thorough American in the sense of the Americanism Mark twain stands for- freedom from tradition, independent judgment, humor & wholesomeness. Little Huck started us. . . . [36]

Chris Healey from Ireland informed Twain that many of his own images of America were derived from reading his books. Twain's works had come to his aid during a time of illness, he said. He wrote the follow-ing fanciful letter from a Salvation Army Working Men's Hotel shortly after arriving in New York City:

> An Irish admirer of yours who has travelled 4000 miles mainly to see you, may I request the privilege of calling on you to pay my respects. Indeed I might claim this as a right. Here is the proof: Twenty four years ago a little Irish boy lay dying in a Liverpool hospital. The nurse spoke to him very kindly—a bad sign—& asked if there was anything he would like, which was even worse. In hospitals politeness is saved only for those who will soon be beyond the need of it. He wearily asked for a book to read, & they gave him "Babylon" by Grant Allen. There was a quaint American interest in the book which made the boy discov-er America for the first time. Before that it had been only a place on the map. Then he became interested, threw the first book away, & de-manded one about America- & they gave him Huckleberry Finn. He read it, & laughed, & laughed, & laughed, until he fell into the first sound sleep he had had for a fortnight. When he awoke twenty-six years later—it was only hours, but it seemed years since he had read the book- he hollered for it again& got it, & had some breakfast, the first for a week. The nurse was rude to him but he didn't mind—he had Huckleberry under his pillow. This is why he didn't pay much atten-tion to the doctor's remark that it was miraculous recovery, & Nature still had a fat purseful of miracles left. The boy only grinned, & he knew better: it was Mark Twain. Since then he has passed through the gallery of Tom Sawyer's friends, has travelled all over the world with various Innocents & Tramps & occasionally tramped with himself as the chief Innocent.[37]

Jewish American response to Twain was prompted by Twain's essay "Concerning the Jews." The essay emerged after a Jewish lawyer who read Twain's March 1898 "Stirring Times in Austria" raised a question for him: "why in your judgment the Jews have been and are even now in these days of supposed intelligence, the butt of baseless, vicious animos-ities [...] Can American Jews do anything to correct (this)?"[38] Upon read-ing "Concerning the Jews," Simon Wolf, the founder of the Jewish American Historical Society, sent Twain his book *The American Jew as Patriot, Soldier and Citizen.* Twain responded with "The Jew as Soldier," an essay asserting Jewish dedication and valor. Some critics, like Rabbi M.S. Levy, have detected in Twain's initial essay strains of what they believe are stereotypes, or anti-Semitic prejudice. Others have applauded the two essays as calls for acknowledgment of Jewish cultural contribu-tions and for the overall recognition of human dignity.[39]

Stanford E. Moses was one of these correspondents to Twain who wrote favorably about his article on February 10, 1907. He was a naval officer on board the S.S. *Georgia* docked at the Boston Navy Yard. He told Twain that in his essay he had "come nearer the mark than anyone else":

Twenty-five years ago my brothers and I used to read Tom Sawyer aloud; the listeners correcting, from memory, any slip of the tongue on the part of the reader. I have read "Ferguson" at Gibraltar; the "son of far away Moses," at Smyrna, and have followed the Equator with you. My wife and I have read Tom Sawyer and Huckleberry Finn,— and Joan of Arc;—and our small boy is waiting impatiently until he is old enough to hear Tom Sawyer read aloud and understand it. Crossing the Mississippi I see little bridges and cities, but catch a glimpse of the river at the steamboat wharves.

I have known you for so long, and you have brought into my life so much happiness and mirth, unmixed with bitterness, that I hope I may thank you for it all without seeming to intrude. "Concerning the Jews," you have come nearer to the mark than anyone else: I am a Jew, and know. But in Tom Sawyer and Joan of Arc, the heart of a boy and the heart of a girl, you have taught me what no one else has me. You have shown me the way to help children—and men—in the daily walks of life; you have made me judge their actions more charitably, more understandingly; and you have taught me the power of kindliness and sincerity.[40]

C. AFRICAN AMERICAN READERS

On a cold Monday evening in February, 1886, Miss Julie Moore walked up the steps to the residence of Mrs. George E. Knight at 22 Butler Street in Brooklyn. She was scheduled to do a reading from Mark Twain for the Literary and Sinking Fund Society of the St. Augustine Protestant Episcopal Mission. The announcement of her reading had appeared in the *New York Freeman*. The reading was being given "in the interest of the mission." Along with Miss Moore, there would be a chorus, an essay by Mr. Tunnel, and a humorous reading by Mrs. McWilliams. Refreshments were served.[41]

This gathering of African Americans in Brooklyn occurred one year after the publication of Mark Twain's novel *Huckleberry Finn*. In March 1885, the novel was banned by the Concord Public Library for the alleged impropriety of its characters. However, not a word was uttered at the time about the racial content of the book that has become such an issue for school boards since the 1950s. There is no mention of any concern about *Huckleberry Finn* among the African American readers in Brooklyn. To the contrary, they evidently liked Mark Twain's stories.

The members of the Literary and Sinking Fund Society of the St. Augustine Protestant Episcopal Mission were members of the first Episcopal church for African Americans in the city of Brooklyn. The formation of their reading circle had swiftly followed the appearance of the Brooklyn Literary Union of Siloam Presbyterian Church and the Concord Baptist Literary Circle. T. Thomas Fortune's newspaper, the *New York Freeman*, reported regularly on these events and sometimes published papers from the meetings.

Huckleberry Finn may have had some appeal for this reading circle as one of the first novels to make use of the vernacular speech of African American characters. Shelley Fisher Fishkin has pointed out, "Twain allowed African American voices to play a major role in the creation of his art."[42] The "multicultural polyphony" that Fishkin has heard in Twain's art was likely also heard by these readers in Brooklyn, as they read Twain's fiction aloud. Louis Budd observed that "today it is standard academic wisdom that Twain's central, precedent-setting achievement is Huck's language."[43]

Across the years, *Huckleberry Finn* has been read by people of every racial, ethnic, regional, and occupational background in America. The book can be read by children and young adults, by middle-aged people and elderly people, James Cox once pointed out, "and each time it will be a different book."[44] For those who read it for enjoyment, it is likely a different book from the book read by students who are assigned it in school settings, or the book that it is for critics who examine it. Late in 1880, Mark Twain wrote the "Notice" that he attached to *Huckleberry Finn*: "Persons attempting to find a Motive in this narrative will be prosecuted; persons attempting to find a Moral in it will be banished; persons attempting to find a Plot in it will be shot."[45] However, this is the book by Mark Twain that has been scrutinized by critics more than any other. It also has long been, in popular terms, Twain's most notorious work and, for some, his most memorable.

Several passages from Twain's *The Innocents Abroad* made a lasting impression on readers. They recalled Twain's references to seasickness in chapter three of *The Innocents Abroad*. Jeremiah Williams reports that when his father, John Williams, left Buffalo by boat a strong wind blew up on the lake: "Many of the sailors, as well as nearly all the passengers, were frightfully stomach-sick, or, as Mark Twain expressed himself in describing a similar scene, 'They all had the 'oh, my.'"[46] The "oh, my" emerges like a running joke each time the narrator of *The Innocents Abroad* greets someone with the phrase: "It's a lovely day." We read: "He put his hand on his stomach and said, 'Oh, my' and then staggered away and fell over the coop of a skylight." The narrator says: "I stayed there and was bombarded with old gentlemen for an hour, perhaps, and all I got out of any of them was 'Oh, my!'"

W.S. Brooks, an African American Methodist, also recalled this passage in *The Innocents Abroad*. He wrote that he was "reared a traveler" who began his work life by running errands. He writes of a railway journey from Chicago to New York and a steamship passage to Liverpool on the *Majestic* that began on February 27, 1895:

Sea sickness? I'll not undertake to describe it, I'm not equal to the task. I doubt if any man is. The nearest to a description that I remember to have heard is given in the experience of one of America's greatest descriptive writers, Mark Twain: "At first I was in terror, for I feared I should die...."[47]

The appearance of *The Adventures of Huckleberry Finn* was given advance notice by a lecture tour that Mark Twain shared with George Washington Cable. Cable's racially mixed background and polemics enabled the authors to draw the attendance of many African Americans on this tour. Twain's books and stories in periodicals were already reaching this audience of African American readers.

Mark Twain was by this time quite visible in black newspapers: The *Cleveland Gazette*, December 26, 1885, carried a biography and a large drawing of him. This was followed by an article titled "Doings of the Race." The newspaper carried an announcement from the *Chicago Conservator*: "The *Cleveland Gazette* is one of the best colored papers out, and under the present management will lose nothing as the editor is a good fellow and a racy writer." In the *Cleveland Gazette*, Twain became recommended reading. In "Our Girls, Their Reading," in the *Cleveland Gazette* (July 14, 1888), one is told that books can not only add to a girl's education but can keep her from falling into lovesickness:

> Keep up with the news of the day. No girl who interests herself in study, [of] practical politics, is apt to fall so far into gushing love sickness [...] Safeguards are what girls need at all times, and such reading will supply one. Read some good book, hearty wholesome fun, if you do not feel equal to any great effort. Mark Twain and Frank Stockton's humor have been a boon to us in this day of sensation and sentiment.[48]

News about Mark Twain often appeared in the *Washington Bee*, a black newspaper in the nation's capital. "Our New York Letter," Eleanor Kirk from Brooklyn (February 25, 1887) appears in the *Washington Bee*, March 5, 1887:

> Mark Twain's speech at the stationers and publishers dinner has had the effect of stirring up considerable discussion in reference to the cramming process of our public schools. He made several side splitting quotations from the manuscript copy of a little book, entitled English as she is taught, compiled by Miss Caroline B. Le Rau. Nobody knows better than America's chief humorist that nothing in the world could be funnier than the example he cited; and being a kind hearted man, and anxious for the welfare of the race, he realizes equally that nothing can be sadder.[49]

Soon the *Cleveland Gazette* (March 20, 1887) printed news of Twain's subsequent article: "Mark Twain appears in this number in a new role—that of a humorous critic of the methods of popular education, in an article 'English as She is Taught.'"

Eleanor Kirk's next word from Brooklyn appeared on March 22, 1887, in the *Washington Bee*:

> Mark Twain says the school system is idiotic and the little book "English as she is Taught," soon to be issued by Cassell and Cassell "has a wholesome mission of the calling of public attention to that humiliating fact." In the April *Century* will be found an article by this great fun producer, in which copious extracts have been made from the book. This paper is side splitting but the author of "Mrs. Beecher Criticized" is in earnest. She writes: "Go Mr. Mark Twain, and don't forget to advocate the addition of women to the school boards and the selection of those who are not like some we have heard of, afraid to go home from a meeting at nine o'clock at night."[50]

More often, Twain is portrayed less as a reformer than as an entertainer for one's leisure time. The *Leader* in Washington, DC, created a picture of Mark Twain: "Mark Twain passes a great part of his time in his library where he sits in a comfortable armchair, his feet tilted up on the window sill and a thick halo of tobacco smoke encircling his forehead." It is hard to imagine how Twain got many words onto the page in that pose. Yet, it may reflect the African American reader's desire for leisure. One may kick up one's feet, open the pages of the *Leader,* and read about Mark Twain.[51] Readers of that Washington newspaper in 1887 could kick up their feet and open Mark Twain's *The Adventures of Huckleberry Finn*. Or they might turn to another of the great publishing feats of the time: Mark Twain's recent publishing venture—two hefty volumes of the *Memoirs of Ulysses S. Grant*. After this, Twain would journey again back in time with his imaginative social critique, *A Connecticut Yankee in King Arthur's Court*.

When Mark Twain's *Pudd'nhead Wilson* appeared in England in spring 1894, it was called a "vigorous indictment of the old social order of the south." The problem, however, was that that "old" social order was not extinct. It had reared its ugly head again and racism persisted. We can see some of the notions of the time in the comments of Dr. John Fulenwider Miller (1834–1905), the Superintendent of Eastern Hospital in Goldsboro, North Carolina. Dr. Miller cited Twain's sketch on Adam in his speech before the Southern Medico-Psychological Association in Asheville on September 16, 1896. He made no mention at all of the racial concerns in *Pudd'nhead Wilson*:

> That inimitable American wit and humorist, Mark Twain, says that Adam is a very much neglected man; that he deserves a monument and that he would subscribe liberally for the purpose; that the world is indebted to him more than to any other man, for he gave us both hell and heaven. The faithful negroes of the South deserve a monument also for their loyalty to their owners and fidelity to duty under the most trying circumstances during the years of the late civil war.[52]

After this commendation of African American loyalty, the doctor, who was evidently a latter day apologist for slavery, suggested that there was more strain upon African Americans after emancipation. In his experience, he said, "many intelligent people of observation and full acquaintance of the negro have stated to me that they never saw a crazy or consumptive negro of unmixed blood until these latter years."[53] The doctor said, "I observe that the States of Louisiana, Mississippi, and South Carolina have more negroes than whites." The doctor claimed that he had "been thoroughly reconstructed and readjusted to the changed political relations of the negro." He had no complaint or prejudice, he claimed. Then he attempted to document increased insanity by statistics of people in asylums. Miller asserted that "demands were made upon the negro which his intellectual parts were unable to discharge." He added, "In his former condition none of these things disturbed his mind."[54] The specious conclusion is that African Americans could not deal intellectually with the novel condition of freedom and as slaves they were far more content and sane. Twain clearly did not get through to men like Dr. John Fulenwider Miller.

Little is said by library directors or school boards these days about *Pudd'nhead Wilson*, which is not often read in school curriculums. *Huckleberry Finn*, which has firmly entered the canon of American literature, is another story. Racial sensitivity surrounding *Huckleberry Finn* has increased since the time of *Brown v. Board of Education* in 1954. One reason for this is that a contemporary reader hears and sees the text differently than the nineteenth-century reader. Reviews of the novel in 1885–1886 did not mention racial relations in the novel. Justin Kaplan points out: "Not until twenty years after its first publication did a reviewer refer to it, in passing, as an "antislavery tract." One may ask whether this was a form of avoidance, or a difference in perception from that of some of our contemporaries. The reception of Twain's book went through transformations as it entered the twentieth century. Booker T. Washington played a principal role in changing perceptions of *Huckleberry Finn* by featuring the novel as an "American engagement with race."[55]

In 1957, the New York City Board of Education decided that *Huckleberry Finn* ought not to be taught in elementary schools and in junior high schools. Twain's novel could, however, be taught on the high school level. In that same year, the NAACP, on the heels of *Brown v. Board of Education*, called the novel racist. The 211 uses of the word "nigger" in this novel were called despicable and damaging. The NAACP rightly observed that sensitivity had emerged in relation to an abusive and derogatory term. Twain's defenders pointed out that the word was in common use in antebellum Missouri and that its use did not reflect the author's intentions. Indeed, he had most often put use of the word in the mouths of the most ignorant and uninformed characters in his novel. The word emerges from Huck in his initial naivete and it is spoken by his dissolute father and by other roughs. Twain, some argued, was presenting a satirical comment on the speaker. However, critics of the novel wouldn't have any of that. *Huckleberry Finn* was banned in Virginia in 1982. It was censored in Illinois in 1984. It was set aside in Connecticut—once Twain's home state—in 1995. The novel was challenged in school districts and courts in Arizona, California, New Jersey, and Oklahoma. Alan Gribben, recognizing that much of this had to do with one unfortunate word, got the "white-out" and erased the n-word in his version of the text. The novel deserves to be read in the schools Professor Gribben has argued. Mark Twain ought not to be changed, his critics have argued back. They assert that everything is present in his novel for a reason.[56]

Perhaps most significantly, Jim, the runaway slave, is given a "voice" and is drawn with full humanity in this novel. *Huckleberry Finn* represents both the first time that a common boy was the narrator of an American novel and also one of the first occasions of a black individual as a central protagonist of an American novel. Jim is, overall, a more complex character than the comic-minstrel show Jim, who some critics recognize at times in the novel's pages. This is also the view of Robert Hirst, curator of the Mark Twain Papers, who, as Ron Powers recognizes, points out that Jim stands up for himself, rejecting Huck's racist treatment of him. Of all nineteenth-century novelists, it is Mark Twain who focused a novel on postwar racism by looking back at its prewar qualities.[57] Jim represents America attempting to escape from the long calamity of slavery. The character of Jim grows throughout this novel. He draws reader attention and sympathy and indeed he has a surer standard of values than Huck, who gradually develops in conscience.

Huckleberry Finn also has been viewed as a declaration of independence from the genteel tradition. In writing *Huckleberry Finn*, Twain was critiquing conventions, while reflecting upon slavery and the years after the Civil War. He had come from Missouri, with no strong feelings about slavery. He had gone west and left behind the Civil War. He became absorbed in issues of the West, rather than those of abolition and emancipation. As a journalist, he focused on local matters. In *Roughing It*, there is barely a reference to the war. It appears that it is only after his settling at Nook Farm near Hartford, alongside the Stowe family and other abolitionists, that his perspective shifted. By the time he began writing *Huckleberry Finn*, the legacy of slavery had become a concern for him.

The negative assessments of Twain's work are contradicted by the popularity of the book through time, as David E.E. Sloane and others have pointed out.[58] Assertions by some readers that Twain's book inscribes racism are contradicted by Twain's financial assistance to young African Americans and the advancement of their careers through his generosity. Twain's philanthropic gestures toward young blacks are well known. He put A.W. Jones, a black theology student, through school at Lincoln University. He supported black churches with funds.[59] He sponsored Charles Ethan Porter, a black painter, to study in Paris. Porter, who had been born in Hartford, became a still-life painter. Twain set forth a plea for the Tuskegeee Institute with Joseph H. Choate at a Carnegie Hall fundraiser. Choate asserted that future African American lawyers and doctors were being assisted. Choate said, "If I were to present the next speaker as Samuel L. Clemens, some would ask, 'Who is he?' but when I present him as Mark Twain [...]" Applause erupted in the auditorium.[60] When Twain took the stage, he said:

> The negro in many ways has proved his worth and loyalty to this country. What he now asks is that through such institutions as Hampton, Fisk, and Tuskegee he shall be given the chance to render high and intelligent service to our country in the future. I have faith that such an opportunity will be given him.[61]

While in his youth, Samuel Clemens heard stories from Missouri blacks. The rhythms and images of those stories stayed with him. He often sang spirituals and other black folk songs. The Clemens household was assisted by a staff that included a cook and housekeeper, Maryann Cord, and George Griffin, their butler. John Lewis saved his sister in-law from certain death by grabbing and slowing down a disastrous run-away cart and he became a lifelong friend. John T. Lewis wrote to his friend Mark Twain on April 11, 1880. "Mr. Samuel Clemens, honored Sir I received a copy of your splendid work of 'Tramp Abroad' whitch I suppose to be a gift from your ever bountiful hand for which I will say that I except it as a grate treasure from noble generous heart and hand."[62] Twain would never forget how Lewis saved Ida Langdon by stopping her horse and buggy from crashing off a cliff August 23, 1877. The new, gray horse pulling the cart was startled and began to run. Livy yelled out, "Ida is driving too fast. Her horse is running away!" Lewis hurried his own wagon out in front of the one Ida was riding in, which was rapidly picking up speed. He grabbed the horse's reins and harness in his big hands and slowed the racing horse and vehicle. Lewis had a lasting friendship with Twain and he is buried near the family plot at the cemetery in Elmira. Twain scholars have always known of his many private jabs and jibes against racism. Careful readers of *Huckleberry Finn* also recognize the antiracism satire of the novel.[63]

D. REGIONAL READING

In this next section, we will briefly investigate three regional areas of the United States: Missouri, small-town Michigan, and Brooklyn, New York. Finally, we will look at responses to Twain among Western readers at the end of the nineteenth century and in the early part of the twentieth century. It is evident from their responses that Twain's images of the west provide a kind of nostalgia for these Western readers.

1. Missouri

Missouri claims Mark Twain as its own. Central to this claim are his residence in Hannibal and the exploits of his characters Huckleberry Finn and Tom Sawyer along the Mississippi River. As a result, Twain is memorialized in Missouri and continues to attract much interest from Missouri readers. When categorizing readers according to region, it is necessary to consider the variety of readers in any given locale. These readers are unique individuals and gender, class, ethnicity, race, occupation, religious orientation and other factors play a role in their lives.

The name of Mark Twain is indissolubly linked with images of the longest river in America. The Mississippi River is a spectacle: a broad, muddy river that absorbs the sun and carries life from its origins to the Gulf at New Orleans. In placing his characters upon the river, Mark Twain set them traveling in search of freedom. He beckoned toward the unconstrained ideal of boyhood imagination and toward an uneasy freedom for citizens of African American ancestry. Mark Twain's recollections of life along the river began when he agreed to write a series of magazine installments, titled "Old Times." He kept this project to seven pieces because he was focused on a larger project: a Mississippi River book. When Twain had started writing *The Adventures of Tom Sawyer* in 1872 he had found in his childhood in Hannibal rich material for this short novel. However, he began to reach beyond that novel to larger projects. He decided to explore his past and the future of the country with a travel journey on the Mississippi River that became *Life on the Mississippi*.

In 1875, when Edward King, an American Publishing Company author, begins to describe the Mississippi River and the Missouri River, he suggests that he will tell a story of Mark Twain as an apprentice steamboat pilot. He writes, "One sees, on a journey down the Mississippi, where Mark found many of his queerest and seemingly impossible types"[64] However, Mark Twain suddenly disappears from this tale and is never mentioned or seen again. It would be up to Twain himself to describe those "seemingly impossible types" in the works that would follow: *Life on the Mississippi* and *Huckleberry Finn*.

During this time, William Dean Howells, the editor of the *Atlantic*, requested from Twain the sketches on the Mississippi that would be printed in the magazine. In response to Twain's essay in the *Atlantic Monthly*, Thomas B.A. David, a telegraph operator in Wheeling, West Virginia, wrote on April 29, 1875:

I am very indebted to you, in round numbers I should say about $50,000, and I wish I could pay you—It all comes of "Old times on the Mississippi"—I had traveled some of the western waters, and the same propensity that always lifted me to the top of the stage coach, carried me to the Pilot house; and I have been renewing my youth in your papers—It will be no compliment to you to say that your reproduction of those scenes and characters is simply wonderful, but it may be when I tell you that I am laboring hard to convince my wife that it is not pure and unadulterated fiction—Woing her was easy work in comparison.[65]

Mark Twain's audience would often see this restless traveler in person. His own family in Missouri, however, did not see him often. Three days after Twain sent his letter to Bliss the Clemens family began a journey west to Missouri. They took a train to the shores of Lake Erie and then a steamer from Erie, Pennsylvania, across the Great Lakes. A steamboat brought them from St. Paul, Minnesota, from where they went downriver to the Clemens family in Keokuk, Iowa. July 4th ceremonies in Rand Park featured a thin man in a tall white hat, Orion Clemens, reading aloud from the Declaration of Independence. Mark Twain shared the platform with his brother, also speaking to the crowd.[66] The event was the only public appearance by the brothers together.

A few years later Twain made a trip on the Mississippi with his publisher, James Osgood, who anticipated a lucrative future with Twain. In April 1881, they set out on their journey on the Mississippi with secretary Roswell Phelps, boarding the *Gold Dust* in St. Louis on April 20. From Cairo, the area Dickens had satirized in *Martin Chuzzlewit* back in 1844, they continued south toward New Orleans, where they concluded their trip on April 28.

The trip provided Twain with contact with his past. It was also a testament to change. Towns had built up along the river. Others, like the islands around Cairo that he remembered, had disappeared. He wrote, "The river is so thoroughly changed that I can't bring it to mind even when the changes have been pointed out to me. It is like a man pointing out to me a place in the sky where a cloud has been."[67]

It was fascinating to see the day steal gradually upon this vast silent world; & when the edge of the shorn sun pushed itself above the line of forest, the marvels of shifting light & shade & color & dappled reflections, that followed, were bewitching to see . . . & the remote, shadowy, vanishing distances, away down the glittering highway under the horizon! And the riot of singing birds!- it was all worth getting up for, I tell you.[68]

Mark Twain's journey on the Mississippi attracted news articles:

On the steamer *Gold Dust*, Mark Twain spoke with the pilot who had heard rumors of him. He asked the pilot if he knew Sam Clemens. "What! Mark Twain?" said the other. "Yes, that's what they call him," was the rejoinder. "Well, I should say I did. Sam left here 'bout twenty years ago, an' has been writin' books ever since. He's better at that 'an he was steerin', for he wasn't much of a pilot." [69]

He arrived at his boyhood home, Hannibal, on a Sunday morning. There he saw a changed town, now of fifteen thousand people. It was a place where railroad lines converged. "Many of the people I once knew in Hannibal are now in heaven. Some, I trust, are in the other place." [70] He left the town on the *Minneapolis* on May 17, for a journey north up the river. It was the first time he had ever gone in that direction and he went alone.

"I have been writing a series of articles in the *Atlantic Monthly* on subjects connected with the Mississippi," Twain told a reporter there.

> "The new book will treat of your early life on the river?"
> "Yes, altogether of that subject."
> "When will it be finished?"
> "In about nine months."
> "And what will you call it?"
> "Oh, that is the last thing to be thought about. I never write as title until I finish a book, and then I frequently don't know what to call it. I usually write out anywhere from a half dozen to a dozen and a half titles, and the publisher casts his experienced eye over them and guides me largely in the selection. That's what I did in the case of *Roughing It.*, and, in fact, it has always been my practice." [71]

Once he was home again in Elmira, memories filled the writer's mind as he sat in his room atop the hill at Quarry Farm. From there and his rooms in Hartford, he began to write *Life on the Mississippi.*

> I never had such a fight over a book in my life before [...] I started Osgood to editing it before I had finished writing it. As a consequence, large areas of it are condemned here and there and yonder, and I have the burden of these unfilled gaps harassing me and the thought of the broken continuity of the work [...] [72]

Life on the Mississippi pulls together sixty rambling chapters. It incorporates Twain's articles "Old Times on the Mississippi" for the *Atlantic* in its first 216 pages. Three new chapters precede these seven articles, which are broken into two chapters each. The third chapter is the "raft" chapter he had written for *Huckleberry Finn*. Critics have suggested that the second half of *Life on the Mississippi* is different from the first. As a single volume, *Life on the Mississippi* was published on May 17, 1883. Critical praise for Twain's book was considerable. Yet, compared with sales of his earlier books, the sales for this one initially were not as strong. The Osgood Company sales of *Life on the Mississippi* in summer 1883 held at about 30,000 copies. Twain's *Innocents Abroad*, *Roughing It*, and *A Tramp Abroad* all exceeded sales of 100,000 copies. It has been said that James Osgood was not well-prepared for subscription publishing. In the view of Ron Powers, literary critics had yet to formulate ways to measure Twain's "innovations and complexities."[73] The book was recognized as something other than a "funny book."

Readers of Twain's book on the Mississippi may have seen in it the contrast of realism and romanticism, or adult learning with idealistic youth. One may notice how Twain contrasts the more cynical learning of the seasoned pilot with the naïve wonder of the young novice. Nature is everywhere present in Twain's book. In speaking of the river, he compares reading nature to the manner that one initiated in sacred mysteries would read a holy book. He writes: "The face of the water, in time, became a wonderful book- a book that was a dead language to the uneducated passenger, but which told its mind to me without reserve, delivering its most cherished secrets as if it uttered them with a voice."[74] Reading this, one is taken by Twain's sense of youthful wonder at the river. The figures and patterns of his writing reflect this open-eyed enchantment. Suddenly, the passage shifts in tone and style. The rational observation of what he has learned about the river enters. The immediacy of childlike wonder vanishes. He recognizes that the river can become perilous: "but the grimmest and most dead-earnest of reading matter."[75] The acquisition of rational knowledge affects his experience and his "reading" of that experience. "Now when I had mastered the language of this water. . . . I had made a valuable acquisition. But I had lost something too." He recognizes that "all the grace, the beauty, the poetry, had gone out of the majestic river!"[76]

This passage recognizes that age and education bring different ways of seeing the world. However, Twain does not merely concede this world to sober rationality alone. He implicitly affirms the value of wonder and imagination. Readers, likewise, have had various experiences of Twain's books, upon reading them at different stages of life. The *Adventures of Tom Sawyer* or the *Adventures of Huckleberry Finn* that one has read as a child may be rediscovered by the adult reader. The reader may find that, like the river, a novel like *Huckleberry Finn* has unexpected, treacherous depths.

In *Life on the Mississippi*, Twain describes changes along the river that suggest the passage of time. Twain's name is attached to descriptions by people who also reflected on changes to the region. An Illinois writer recalls how the first capital of Illinois, Kaskaskia, in Randolph County, was affected:

> The city of Kaskaskia was doomed to a sad and tragic fate. In one of those fantastic freaks of the Mississippi River, which the great and fame-crowned Mark Twain so charmingly and graphically describes in his classic book The Father of the Waters, the restless and wayward stream sought a new bed and course for itself and the ancient city of Kaskaskia [...] Thousands of acres of the richest and most desirable land in Illinois were swept into innocuous desuetude by this fierce

cataclysm and their soul washed into the Gulf of Mexico, and old Kaskaskia, including the State house with it.[77]

The town, which survives on the west side of the river, reflects the kind of change that Twain knew had been wrought upon the Mississippi across the years.

Some readers of *Life on the Mississippi* recognized Mark Twain as a serious writer, perhaps for the first time. The year 1883 brought reviews from England on *Life on the Mississippi*. In "The Reader" in the *Graphic* (September 1, 1883) we see the comment that

> Mark Twain, in the earlier chapters of his new book *Life on the Mississippi* gives such an admirable specimen of his powers as a serious writer of history, that one is almost tempted to wish that, for this occasion only, he would lay aside altogether his funny style, or at least subordinate it to the purposes of serious literary work. But the old Adam cannot long be subdued.

The suggestion is made that humor is just too tempting and "almost before the reader is aware that he has changed from the graphic to the grotesque, he is deep in sketches of life and character in all of which the great river forms the background."[78]

With this review comes a request for severity of subject and style. The critic sees literary quality in Twain's work and wishes that he would shed the role of humorist. Whereas Twain's popular audience at this time continued to gravitate toward his humor, this critic wishes for a different balance between his seriousness and his humor. The *British Quarterly Review* in July 1883 remarked: "Mr. Mark Twain conveys a great deal of instruction about the Mississippi and the life on it; but it is so entangled in his own particular vein of fun that it is not too much to say that the book is unreliable." This reviewer does not like Twain's "[e]xtravagances, perversions, inversions […]" or his quips about the faults of religion. "For young people the book will be a treasure, both letterpress and pictures will suit them […]" but adults will have a more "qualified" response.[79]

The first two hundred fifty pages of *Life on the Mississippi* was viewed by Lafcadio Hearn as a book that would have "historical value." To that point, Hearn asserted, it was "the most solid book that Mark Twain has written […]"[80] Johannes Jensen echoed this sense of historical value. "The description Mark Twain gives us of the Mississippi has the ring of a classic, it is permeated by knowledge and it is imperishable in its Herodotian sense of the place and the people that inspired the memory."[81]

The Prince and the Pauper, a medieval fairy tale, stands in contrast with *Life on the Mississippi*, a work of realism. The books show Mark Twain's imaginative range: his ability to segue from a fable and moral tale to a clear-eyed river journey. One book travels to a mythical past with two youths, while the other ventures up a seemingly mythical river, yet one as real and treacherous as any other under the sun. Soon Mark Twain would bring together two characters on the river, a troubled and clever boy and a resourceful slave with a gift for seeing or dreaming into the future. They would become a community of two on a little raft and, through their encounters, Twain would critique privilege, pretense, racial division, and the medievalism that held America back from progress. The interracial friendship of Huckleberry Finn and Jim would touch the imagination of readers and take them across the changing currents of race in America for more than a century.

J.C. Fuller of Cincinnati wrote to Twain on August 10, 1885, that, no matter what people around him said, he firmly believed that things like the Grangerford and Shepherdson feud in *Huckleberry Finn* reflected real issues in the American South:

> I have been compelled on more than one occasion to listen to objections from readers of the adventures of "Huckleberry Finn" to the sketch of the Grangerford and Shepherdson family feud. The mildest form of criticism concludes usually with the statement that to assume the existence of such a state of things in any part of the country is "unnatural, unreasonable ridiculous and absurd." While replying, in some heat I must confess, that this scene though sketched in your matchless style is in as far as the facts go but a leaf from the daily record of our days and times I have been asked with triumphant scorn to produce the data for my assertion which you will readily understand are not always at hand. The enclosed clipping from the Cincinnati Enquirer for Aug. 10th reveals a case exactly in point and is only one of the many brought to the notice of the intelligent newspaper reader every year. If it lies in your power either as writer or publisher to bring this knowledge to the attention of the lunkheads who disbelieve in the reality of the southern vendetta, I pray you do so, and confer an everlasting favor upon Yours truly, J.C. Fuller.[82]

2. Reading in Michigan

Women who created reading circles and women's clubs in Michigan took charge of the social betterment of their communities. These women "took their clubs seriously," as Barbara Sicherman has recognized.[83] They were concerned with issues like education and raising children, like Tilla Bradshaw Swales of Detroit, who wrote to Twain on July 18, 1885, about reading *The Innocents Abroad*. She reminded Twain of an earlier note she had written to him. Swales's letter was prompted by Twain's July 16 essay "On Training Children" in the *Christian Union*, which he wrote in response to "What Ought He to Have Done?" in the magazine's June 11 issue. Swales wrote: "About fifteen years ago I was impelled by my great delight in "Innocents Abroad" to write to you, which won for me in reply a little note, still kept among my chief treasures.[84]

The lasting popularity of Twain's *The Innocents Abroad* in Michigan is shown by the numerous published references to the book in the last decade of the century. In an Oakland County park in Michigan, August 24, 1892, John M. Norton rose to address the crowd assembled there. Noting how poor the roads between Detroit and Pontiac, Michigan, were in the 1830s, Norton recalled a trip he made via Mt. Clemens. This name apparently brought Mark Twain to mind, and he began to discuss the people he knew who operated the Detroit and Pontiac Railroad:

> As a fun maker the old Detroit and Pontiac Railroad Company probably surpassed any comic minstrels ever organized. Its directors were inveterate practical jokers and fun lovers, and if Mark Twain would write the true antics of these INNOCENTS at home, stating only facts, the work would eclipse all the fiction of his "Innocents Abroad."[85]

At that picnic were some of the "literary" women of Pontiac. They had begun a "Ladies Round Table" in the same year that Mark Twain's *A Connecticut Yankee in King Arthur's Court* appeared. Agnes Cudworth was the librarian of the Ladies Library of Pontiac that year. The Library Association was still using the Old Methodist Church, although a new building was planned for 1893. The women raised funds with baby shows, fairs, and banquets. In July 1882, the library opened in a second floor room of the gazette building. Mrs. Stout prepared a catalogue, listing the library's books, including a copy of Mark Twain's *The Innocents Abroad*. It was the Stout family endowment that enabled the women to place the new library in a brick building on Williams Street. By 1907 there would be 2,500 books on the shelves, including much of Mark Twain. Five years later, the endowment fund was listed at $2,000. Women had been instrumental in developing the library and many other services in Pontiac. As Martha Baldwin wrote, "Its hospital, library, literary clubs and temperance union are virtually her sole creations"[86]

The Annual Report of the Michigan State Board of Library Commissioners reported in 1900 that the Ladies Library Association was the chief library in Pontiac. There were small libraries at the high school and at the Eastern Michigan Asylum. However, among the 2,000 volumes in the Ladies Library collection were several Twain titles and the library had issued more than 5,000 books during the past year. Thanks to the gift from the Stouts, the women owned the building. The library was open daily from two to five and seven to nine. No doubt, that kept Agnes Cudworth busy.[87]

Mark Twain's *The Innocents Abroad* and his humorous stories were familiar to another group of readers in Kalamazoo, Michigan, 148 miles away. The Ladies Library Association there met on November 18, 1895, for a talk on "American Humorists" by Miss Harriet E. Thomas. Soon afterward, Frank Mayo performed in a New Year's Day production of *Pudd'nhead Wilson*. Nearby in Kalamazoo, the Frederick Douglass Club had a literary circle in which African American readers talked about Twain and other authors. The members were involved with social programs begun by Caroline Bartlett, a Unitarian minister who worked with the African American community. It appears that Bartlett introduced the group to Mark Twain's writing. One of the memorable moments of her career as a reporter had been an interview with Mark Twain in 1885. She was the daughter of a steamboat captain and claimed the knowledge of a riverboat pilot. Upon quizzing her, Twain consented to an interview.[88]

3. Reading Circles in Brooklyn

One of the unique features of Mark Twain's reputation was that it was sustained in America to high degree even while he was away in Europe and other parts of the world. Twain's notoriety in the United States never lagged in the mid to late 1890s. Newspapers continually circulated reports about him. Editions of his books were printed and circulated. Periodicals carried his stories and essays. In America, theater groups like the New York Telegraph Operators Dramatic and Literary Club met to present stage adaptations of his works. Readers continued to meet in literary society groups to hear Twain's works read and to discuss them.

An audience that was familiar with the Bible also became familiar with *The Innocents Abroad* and *Roughing It*. For example, Dr. Harry Plympton wrote from 291 Halsey Street in Brooklyn, asking Twain why a footnote in chapter twenty of *Roughing It* referred to chapter thirteen in the Book of Daniel.[89] Clearly, Twain's wry observations about religion interested him.

In a December 21, 1882, letter from William Bock of 304 President Street, Brooklyn, Bock claims that he named his son "Samuel Clements Bock." As Kent Rasmussen points out, a father would likely have made sure to name his son appropriately after the writer by spelling his name correctly. The letter is suspect, particularly because no one can identify either Mr. Bock or his son.[90] Yet, someone went to the trouble of writing this letter and making this claim.

Brooklyn readers had found genuine enjoyment in Twain's writing during the past few years. Public readers and speakers had often read Twain's humorous stories aloud to groups who assembled at area churches for recreation and entertainment. At the end of January 1897, a new reading circle was begun in Brooklyn with Mark Twain as its first subject. The *Brooklyn Eagle* announced: "Literary Symposium in the Midwood Club, Flatbush, News from the Suburbs: A literary movement has been started in the Midwood Club [...] The next literary meeting will be held on Wednesday evening this week. The topic is Mark Twain and His Writings."[91]

The Midwood Literary Club of Flatbush meeting of Wednesday January 27, 1897, was held in the women's parlor of the clubhouse. "The principal topic of the evening was 'Mark Twain and His Writings' we are told. A paper on that author's literary career was read by Mr. A.C. Fraser.

A review of 'Personal Recollections of Joan of Arc' by Mr. Harold Lasher came next and was followed by a paper on Joan of Arc as a historical character read by Mrs. Charles Fuller. Then ensued a general discussion of the subject."[92]

An article on this "Midwood's Literary Circle" appeared in the *Brooklyn Eagle* on Friday, June 18, 1897: "A beginning was made with Mark Twain and the following authors were discussed on successive evenings in the order named: Oliver Wendell Holmes, Washington Irving, Edgar Allan Poe, Henry Wadsworth Longfellow, John Greenleaf Whittier, and Nathaniel Hawthorne.[93] The entertainment was in the nature of an experiment at first, but it soon aroused interest." The people who attended this meeting appear to have been middle class to upper middle class. They included business owners. The club was active in social service ventures. For example, some 3,000 people attended the Midwood Club benefit for the Home for Consumptives in June 1895. Philip Ford was on the gate committee with A.B. Tremain and J.W. Haviland. William Kinn Keese, Edward De Selding, Morrison Hoyt, and William Beardsley all officiated. Each of them was in attendance in January 1897 for the Mark Twain readings. Also there was E.W. Mersereau, a business owner and bicycling enthusiast, whose wife Ada attempted suicide in November 1899. Mersereau closed the doors of his American Can Company in 1901.

In February of the next year, the Empire Literary Club, across town, featured selections by Mark Twain: "Much amusement was caused by Theodore Budde, who read Mark Twain's 'New England Weather.'" The event took place in the home of Mr. and Mrs. A.S. Travis at 219 53rd Street in Brooklyn and Miss H.T. Travis played the piano. Violinist T. Rausch joined her for "Romanzo" by Spohr. The focus of this club was on "American authors." Mr. and Mrs. George T. Little of Quincy Street became members that night. William Barnes and W.N. Ackley of the St. Andrews P.E. Church were also actively involved in the proceedings. Mrs. John L. Parrish read a poem by Whittier.[94]

Hazard Lasher, who was involved with the Midwood Club, was a patron contributor to the Flatbush Library. He had stock in the Stuyvesant Press. He liked to play billiards and he was a player on team two of Midwood's Whist League. He became the club's secretary and art and library chair in 1902. Edward De Selding of 267 Fulton Street was once the owner of the Long Island Book Store, a book and stationery store. It was a place, said the store's ad, "where everything pertaining to that business may be had." DeSelding soon entered copublishing and he developed his career as businessman.[95] Both Hazard Lasher and Edward De Selding were regular readers of Twain.

Mark Twain was a favorite author of Midwood member Keese. When Keese presented "The Penalty of Humor" to the Long Island Historical Society he spoke of Mark Twain. Beginning with comments on Benjamin Franklin and Sidney Smith, Mr. Keese then told of a visit by Charles

Dudley Warner to Brooklyn. He said that "the entire audience expecting to be kept in roars of laughter, were regaled with a serious discourse." He compared this with Twain, a *Brooklyn Eagle* reporter noted: "Mark Twain, too, suffers, the speaker said, from the possession of humor. Nobody is willing to take him seriously, even in his great historical work on 'Jeane d'Arc, the Maid of Domremy.'"[96] Keese, who lived on Ocean Avenue opposite Prospect Park, became the Midwood Club's president in 1896. He commemorated that by writing a poem titled "A Song of Friendship." His poems were later published by the Dunlap Society. In "The Siamese Twins and Other Poems," the title poem suggests his acquaintance with Twain's *Pudd'nhead Wilson*, a story instigated by the thought of Siamese twins.[97]

Mark Twain had taken up residence in New York when Harrie Victor Schleren, at the Brooklyn Polytechnic Preparatory School, provided an oration on "The Characters of Mark Twain." On Friday morning February 8, 1901, he addressed teachers and fellow students in a program for "speech hour."[98] Harrie was the son of a recent former mayor, Charles A. Schleren, a millionaire businessman and philanthropist. Harrie Schleren later won second prize in poetry by writing on "Cary, Browning, Tennyson and the Rossettis." He was one of thirty one graduates of the Polytechnic Preparatory in June 1901 and heard the commencement address "The Circle of Life" by Dr. John Coleman Adams. The *New York Tribune* noted that Harrie Schleren later married Miss Alice Unckles at St. Andrew's Church in Meridian, Connecticut. They then lived at 13th Street and Argyle Road in Flatbush: a residence that was decorated white and green on their wedding day. Alice Schleren later wore a pale green broadcloth gown to a Brooklyn society house concert event at 206 Clinton Avenue.

Brooklyn residents not only could hear Mark Twain selection at the local social club. Mark Twain books were also a contest prize at a fair at the "Royal Arcamum." In the *Brooklyn Eagle*, one may read: "The Cortelyou Club have given a full set of Mark Twain's works, magnificently bound" for this contest. They were given to the person receiving the largest amount of votes.[99] Twain's books, by this time, were also well-represented at the Brooklyn Library and its branches. At a time when subscription publishing was fading, a Twain book could be sold in Brooklyn bookstores, given as a gift, or offered as a prize. Sometimes, as in these reading circles, it was simply read aloud for amusement and entertainment. Mark Twain still could get a good laugh.

There were also readers in Brooklyn who felt a connection with the author and who found solace in his works. Frederick A. Wright suggested that he could see Twain in his fiction. On September 19, 1908, he wrote from Brooklyn:

I have waited for a long time to thank you for the pleasure which your books have given me, but have hesitated for fear that even thanks ought not to intrude on the privacy of a public character. But now I am making the venture. Having known Huck Finn twenty two years, and Tom and Sid and Mary and Aunt Polly still longer, I feel as if these friends might give me an introduction especially so since the thing that I have most enjoyed in your books is the glimpse of yourself between the lines. So I have known you, though you have not known me.

Wright believed that Twain had created lasting childhood characters. He added that his wife had a keen perspective on his reading habits:

My wife . . . says that I read Mark Twain the way old ladies read the Bible (I am a clergy man)—a chapter before going to bed. Those boys and girls in your novels seem to me the most remarkable thing in American literature, and for me they have proved altogether the most enjoyable thing in American literature. I do not believe that any other literature has any representations of child life which are so universal and yet so concrete. I have a boy of my own now, and I am just having the fun of introducing them to him- these children that never grow up- "whose mortal years immortal youth became—"[100]

Wright, like several other readers who wrote to Twain, commented on the healing effects of Twain's work for him: "Once, after overworry, I staved off a breakdown by loafing around and reading your 'Following the Equator.'"[101]

4. Western Readers, 1880–1910

Readers from the American West after 1880 were primarily dealing with nostalgia when they referred to Twain's images of the West. The stories that Twain told echoed those that a few readers had heard from their own relatives who had lived in the West. For example, Susan Dabney Smedes, who had been born in Mississippi and had lived in the West, sat down at 1303 John Street to write a letter to her father:

You will be seventy-eight tomorrow, dating this reminds me of it [...] I was interrupted and lost the mail, and have read over your letter again, with renewed interest. It is very full, and strictly conforms to the description of Mark Twain in his last book, "Roughing It," which I have just read; which is remarkable, as you were rushing along by rail, whereas he took it by stage, horseback, and footback.[102]

For this reader, the nostalgia of her father's stories of the West remains vivid. She connects what she has read in her father's letter to her with what she has recently read in Mark Twain's book. Her father got it right, she affirms. She marks the time, her father's birthday, and affirms that his view from the train parallels the images that Twain, on stagecoach, horseback, and foot, has provided in *Roughing It*.

A different group of western readers were Native American Indians. P.M. Barker told Mark Twain on January 17, 1891, that *Roughing It* and his anecdotes in *Roughing It* were read by an officer of the Hudson Bay Company to Cree Indians in western Canada. Perhaps the stories provided some perspective for them on oddities within the white settler's world. [103]

One Native American reader simply recalled Twain's description of the moon. No doubt this Native American Indian reader was especially attentive to the natural world. The *Indian Advocate* of Sacred Heart, Oklahoma, has a distinct focus on nature. On March 1, 1906, we read there: "In 'Innocents Abroad' Mark Twain draws special notice to the point on the voyage across the Atlantic they observed the full moon located in just the same spot in the heavens at the same hour every night." [104]

Responses by readers to Twain's images of the West continued into the twentieth century. Some historians have claimed that pioneers' memories of the Gold Rush were affected by the writings of Mark Twain and Bret Harte. [105] These pioneer memories may have entered Bancroft's *History of California* (1884–1890), through his agents' collection of "Dictations" from pioneers. Twain's popular reputation was equally strong. Harry C. Peterson of the California State Library claimed that in May 1922, when "pilgrims" from the Historical Landmarks Committee traveled to Angel's Camp, they slept "in the very barroom in which Mark Twain heard the story of The Jumping Frog of Calaveras." [106] The *Overland Monthly* reported in 1929 that at Angel's Camp, a jumping frog contest was held. The images of frogs were placed in windows, painted on handkerchiefs, scarves, shawls, and children's capes. There was discussion of hosting a Mark Twain Memorial and Pageant. [107]

Roughing It was familiar to the Society of California Pioneers. Indeed, Twain's book is open for allusions to all types of "gold diggers." Among these is a female character in William Thomson's romance for *Overland Monthly*, who cross-dresses as a male to enter miner society. When Pauline's appearance is transformed by her change from rough clothing to a dress, she is stunning, a "sturdy digger":

> So striking was the change produced in Pauline by the resumption of her own apparel [...] and here ensued a scene utterly beggaring my powers of description. A Dickens or a Mark Twain could hardly do it justice. The sturdy diggers literally went wild with delight. Theirs were natures deeply moved by a romance so touching and unique, and no one could better appropriate the life-drama now played before their eyes. [108]

Mark Twain's audience often remembered him for his Western experience. Twentieth-century readers, in particular, appear to have looked back on a writer they associated with Missouri and with the Mississippi River. *Roughing It* and Twain's Western phase was recalled in 1903 in the

Sumpter Miner (Wednesday, September 9, 1903). The paper portrayed Twain out west in "Twain as a Miner."[109] Mrs. L.A. Sherman of Hastings, Nebraska (October 1938), likewise, associated Twain with the West. She had been born in Hannibal in 1861, one of twelve children. She was interested in pioneer experiences and wrote poetry. She recalls where Mark Twain's home was in Hannibal. Then she writes:

> I wish I could go west/Out where the old mountains are
> I think that would be best/ I have never been so far.[110]

Like many of Mark Twain's readers, the daydreaming Mrs. Sherman wishes to travel, for she has "never been so far." Twain provides these readers with the opportunity for imaginative travel. He reminds other readers of their Western homes. For example, one may wonder if attorney Carey McWilliams, the son of a state senator, is recalling his reading of *Roughing It* when he describes the town he lived in as something out of Mark Twain:

> So we lived on a ranch in the spring, summer, and fall, and then usually went to Denver in the winter when my father was in the state senate. It was in a way an ideal kind of an environment to grow up in. And the town itself was- Mark Twain would have appreciated the town. There were some cowhands in the area who would race their horses up and down Main Street on Sunday mornings, shooting off revolvers, disturbing the pious.[111]

This may reflect McWilliams's reading of the Western landscape of *Roughing It*, or Twain's satires on "the pious" in *The Innocents Abroad*, or both. He recognizes Mark Twain's appreciation of Western qualities and idiosyncratic details. However, he also notes how raucous, playful behavior, like that of Twain's coterie on the *Quaker City* in *The Innocents Abroad*, could get under the skin of the staid, conventional, and "pious" members of his own community.

Readers in the American West were particularly responsive to the book. Lew Griswold laughed at Twain's stories and was taken by his descriptions and scenes of California, with which he was familiar:

> Sir. I have just been reading Your "Roughing It," And I have laught until the tears run down my cheeks at your confounded Oddities and lies. Beemis'es adventures with his Buffalo bull, fir-instance And Jim Blaines story of the old ram Oh! Get out, its enough to make a monkey laugh. . . . Your description of California Life and cenes are good. I am an old California tramp myself and can appreciate the "eternal fitness of things" to a nicety. . . . [112]

Western fans of *Roughing It* also included young readers who picked up Twain's book decades after it was published. One of these readers was Marion Thurston Tibbitts of Denver, who wrote on April 1, 1905:

I am a High School girl and I write to thank you for the hilarious joy your books afford me. . . . They are a never ending source of pleasure to me and I want you to know that I am one more in the vast multitude who appreciate your books and if you have a wee spare moment please write me a little note that I can keep among my treasures.[113]

In his last year of life, Twain received a letter from Granville I. Chittenden, a lawyer from Denver, Colorado, noting the impact that *Roughing It* had made upon him. Reading the book again, he claims that he attempted to resist Twain's humor and could not.

When you took up your pen again several years ago old memories were awakened in my heart. I had read "Roughing It" in my early youth. I planned now to have a little fun of my own. I said to myself, I will read it again and, if possible, I will neither smile nor laugh. But I had scarcely read a chapter when, in spite of myself, I began to shake with laughter and I found the same pleasure and entertainment through all its pages as in the olden time.[114]

The American West continued to claim Twain as one of their own. In 1907, he was invited to a pioneers' reunion in Nevada and declined. He sounds a bit like Joseph Conrad in "Youth" in his response to Robert Fulton of Reno, Nevada:

Those were the days!—those old ones. They will come no more. Youth will come no more. They were so full to the brim with the wine of life. There have been no others like them. It chokes me up to think of them. Would you like me to come out there and cry? It would not beseem my white head.[115]

NOTES

1. Brander Matthews's comment is cited by Barbara Hochman, *Getting at the Author: Books and Reading in the Age of American Realism.* Amherst: University of Massachusetts Press, 2001. p. 22.

2. Barbara Hochman, *Getting at the Author,* p. 35.

3. Shelley Fisher Fishkin, p. 54.

4. Laura Skandera Trombley, *In the Company of Women,* Philadelphia: University of Pennsylvania, 1999, p. 197.

5. Barbara Sicherman, *Well Read Lives,* Chapel Hill: University of North Carolina Press, 2010, p. 67.

6. Janet Badia and Jennifer Phegley, Introduction to *Reading Women: Literary Figures and Cultural Icons in the Victorian Age to the Present* (Toronto: University of Toronto Press, 2005) pp. 6, 13. The "Reading Women" on Pomegranate's Stationary strike a pose of unaffected gentility, yet this suggests that one can be immersed in the possibilities for enlightenment and self-transformation that reading provides.

7. Barbara Sicherman, "Reading and Ambition, M. Carey Thomas and Female Heroism" *American Quarterly,* Vol. 45, No. 1 (March 1993): 79.

8. Ronald J. Zboray and Mary Saracino Zboray, "Have You Read . . . ?: Real Readers and Their Responses in Antebellum Boston and Its Region," *Nineteenth-Century Literature,* Vol. 52, No. 2 (September 1997): 142.

9. Mary Kelley, *Learning to Stand and Speak,* Chapel Hill: University of North Carolina Press, pp. 176, 181.

10. Mary Kelley, p. 112.

11. Mary Kelley, p. 117.

12. Janice A. Radway, *Reading the Romance: Women, Patriarchy, and Popular Literature.* Chapel Hill: University of North Carolina Press, 1991.

13. Alvara Miller Letter to Mark Twain, MTP, University of California. R. Kent Rasmussen, *Dear Mark Twain* pp. 170–171.

14. Ibid.

15. Tilla Swales Bradshaw Letter to Mark Twain, July 18, 1885. See Rasmussen, p. 115.

16. Lillian Beardsley Letter to Mark Twain; Dorothy Scarborough Letter to Mark Twain, MTP, University of California. See Rasmussen, *Dear Mark Twain* 231, 227.

17. Mrs. Annie Adams Fields, Diary, 143. Among her many works, Annie Fields wrote a book on Charles Dudley Warner, Twain's cowriter for *The Gilded Age* (*Charles Dudley Warner,* Philadelphia: N.W. Ayer and Son, 1904). She wrote that they ventured on "what is always a more or less unsatisfactory scheme, writing a book together. . . . [W]ith all its ingenuities and cleverness, the book can hardly be called a literary success (*Charles Dudley Warner,* 38–39). The Annie Fields diaries are unpublished and are at the Houghton Library, Harvard University.

18. Annie Adams Fields, Diary, Houghton Library, Harvard University, pp. 280–81.

19. Annie Adams Fields, Diary, Houghton Library, Harvard University, pp. 280–81, 289.

20. Annie Adams Fields, Diary, Houghton Library, Harvard University. January 25, 1913. p. 302.

21. Mark Twain, *Life on the Mississippi,* pp. 83–85.

22. Ibid.

23. Ibid.

24. Elizabeth Paschal O'Connor. *I, Myself.* New York: Brentanos, 1911. pp. 329–31.

25. Ibid, p. 331.

26. Ibid, p. 29.

27. Ibid, p. 24.

28. Elizabeth Paschal O'Connor's reference to "Sleeping Beauty" appears on pp. 43–44; *My Beloved South.* New York: G.P. Putnam's, Knickerbocker Press, 1914. Introduction, pp. 2–3.

29. Elizabeth Paschal O'Connor, *My Beloved South,* pp. 126–27. See Sherwood Cummings, *Mark Twain and Science: Adventures of a Mind.* Baton Rouge: Louisiana State University Press, 1988. p. 124. Also see Mark Twain, *Life on the Mississippi.*

30. Mark Twain, *Life on the Mississippi,* pp. 308–10.

31. Ibid.

32. Margaret Walker, "The Southern Write and Race," *Southern Writers,* p. 32.

33. Ladislaus Madarasz, Letter to Mark Twain, April 2, 1875, MTP, University of California, Rasmussen, 33–34.

34. Joseph Dick, Letter to Mark Twain. November 9, 1905. MTP, University of California. Rasmussen, 221.

35. Edward Rune Myrbeck in North American Immigrant Letters.

36. Anonymous, Letter to Mark Twain, October 26, 1905. MTP, University of California. Rasmussen, 219.

37. Chris Healey, Letter to Mark Twain. October 19, 1906. MTP, University of California. Rasmussen, 234-35.

38. Simon Wolf Letter to Mark Twain, "Concerning the Jews," *Harper's* (March 1898).

39. M.S. Levy, Milton Steinberg, and Herman Bernstein are among the individuals who have responded to Twain. Playwright Jerome Bayer also discusses Twain. Their papers are housed at the Jewish Center for History, New York.

40. Stanford E. Moses, Letter to Mark Twain, February 10, 1907. Boston, Massachusetts. MTP, University of California.

41. "Brooklyn Notes," *Freeman*, February 27, 1886.

42. Shelley Fisher Fishkin, *Was Huck Black?: Mark Twain and African American Voices*, Oxford University Press, 1995.

43. Louis Budd is cited in *Huck Finn among the Critics*, ed. M. Thomas Inge. Frederick, MD: University Publications, pp. 81–92.

44. James M. Cox, *Mark Twain: The Fate of Humor*, Princeton University Press, 1966. p. 224.

45. Mark Twain, Introduction to *Huckleberry Finn*.

46. Chas. C. Chapman & Company, *History of Washtenaw County*, Chicago: Charles C. Chapman, 1881, p. 670.

47. W.S. Brooks, "What a Black Man Saw," *Methodist Episcopal Church Review*, Vol. 17., No. 4 (April 1901): 298. Brooks' essay is featured at the Ohio Historical Society, African American Experience, 1850–1920.

48. *Cleveland Gazette*, July 14, 1888.

49. Eleanor Kirk, *Washington Bee* (February 25, 1887), *Washington Bee* (March 5, 1887). Eleanor Kirk was the pen name of Ellen Maria Easterbrook, also known as Mrs. Nellie Ames. She wrote *Up Broadway and Its Sequel*, New York: Carleton, 1870, *Henry Ward Beecher as Humorist*, 1887, and *Beecher Book of Days*, which includes days for notable people, including Mark Twain on November 3.

50. Eleanor Kirk, Ibid, response to "English as She is Taught," *Cleveland Gazette*, (March 20, 1887). There were several letters from correspondents to Mark Twain regarding "English as She is Taught." In *Dear Mark Twain*, R. Kent Rasmussen has collected some of these letters. See Caroline Coit, Letter to Mark Twain, June 19, 1887, Glenville, Ohio. Rasmussen, 132. W. DeLancey Howe, June 16, 1889, Cambridge, Massachusetts. Rasmussen, 140–141.

51. Eleanor Kirk, *Washington Bee* (March 22, 1887). "Prominent People," *Leader* (December 14, 1883): 3. The comment on Twain is followed by a mention of House Speaker Reed, "the largest man in the House. He weighs as much as Ex-President Cleveland and is taller."

52. John Fulenwider Miller, "The Effects of Emancipation upon the Mental and Physical Health of the Negro of the South." p. 2 Documenting the American South, University of North Carolina Chapel Hill.

53. Ibid, p. 5.

54. Ibid.

55. Justin Kaplan, *Mr. Clemens and Mr. Twain*, New York: Simon and Schuster, 1966. Booker T. Washington, "Tributes to Mark Twain," *North American Review* (1910): 829.

56. Alan Gribben's version of *The Adventures of Huckleberry Finn* is published by New South Books (2011).

57. Robert Hirst is quoted by Ron Powers in *Mark Twain: A Life*, New York: The Free Press, 2006. p. 497.

58. David E.E. Sloane, "Huck's Helplessness: A Reader's Response to Stupefied Humanity," in ed. James Leonard, *Making Mark Twain Work in the Classroom*. Durham: Duke University Press, p. 140. In this essay the questions focus upon what the reader feels and why he or she feels that way.

59. An example of this is found in the letter of Thomas A. Davis AME Zion Church who wrote for financial assistance from Twain: "It is well-known among colored people throughout the country that you have always spoken a word of kindness for them." February 6, 1880, Harry Ransom Center, University of Texas.

60. Mark Twain, *Autobiography*, Berkeley: University of California, 2010. p. 305.

61. Mark Twain, *Autobiography*, Berkeley, University of California, 2010. p. 309.

62. John Lewis Letter to Mark Twain, April, 11, 1880. MTP. University of California, Bancroft Library.

63. A subtle recognition of Twain's attention to justice for African Americans appears in the 2012 film *The Help*, which is based upon Catherine Stockett's novel. In one frame of the film, several of his books appear on a bookshelf in the home.

64. Edward King, *The Great South: A Record of Journeys in Louisiana*. Hartford: American Publishing Company, 1875.

65. Thomas B.A. David Letter to Mark Twain, April 29, 1875, Rasmussen, 38–39. See also William Dean Howells, Letter to Mark Twain, April 29, 1875.

66. Mark Twain Letter, June 24, 1876. Phillip Ashley Fanning observes that this July 4, 1876, event in Keokuk is likely the only time that Orion and Samuel Clemens shared a public platform. See *Mark Twain and Orion Clemens* (2003).

67. Mark Twain Letter to Olivia Clemens, April 21, 1882. *The Love Letters of Mark Twain*, p. 207.

68. *Life on the Mississippi*, Chapter 22, Oxford Mark Twain, 249, 466.

69. "A Day with Mark Twain," *Rollingpen's Humorous Illustrated Annual*, May 1882.

70. *St. Louis Post-Dispatch* (May 12, 1882): 2.

71. Ibid.

72. Mark Twain, Letter to W.D. Howells, November 4, 1882. *Mark Twain-Howells Letters*, Vol. 1, p. 418.

73. Ron Powers, *Mark Twain: A Life*. New York: The Free Press, 2006.

74. Mark Twain, *Life on the Mississippi*, p. 82.

75. Ibid, p. 64.

76. Ibid, p. 83–85.

77. "Transactions of the Illinois State Society for the Year 1916," *Publications of the Illnois State Historical Library* Vol. 22. Springfield: Illinois Historical Society. p. 37.

78. "The Reader," *Graphic* (London) 28 (September 1, 1883): 231.

79. We may ask if this volume appealed to children in England but less so to more judicious adult readers, or if this is just the subjective perspective of this reviewer. "Belles Lettres, Poetry, and Fiction," *British Quarterly Review* 78 (July 1883): 226–27.

80. Lafcadio Hearn is quoted in *Anthology*, ed. Shelley Fisher Fishkin, p. 42.

81. Johannes Jensen is quoted in *Anthology*, ed. Shelley Fisher Fishkin, p. 120.

82. J.C. Fuller Letter to Mark Twain, August 10, 1885, Cincinnati, Ohio, MTP, University of California. R. Kent Rasmussen, *Dear Mark Twain*, 119.

83. Barbara Sichenor, *Well-Read Lives*. Chapel Hill: University of North Carolina Press, 2010.

84. Tilla Bradshaw Swales Letter to Mark Twain, R. Kent Rasmussen, *Dear Mark Twain*, pp. 115–116.

85. "A Picture of Memory: Settlement in Oakland County," Speech at Supervisor's Picnic, Oakland County, August 24, 1892, *Michigan Pioneer Collections*, p. 22. Lansing: Robert Smith and Company, 1894. p. 407.

86. Martha Baldwin, "What Women Did for Oakland County," pp. 261, 266. In Pontiac, a Women's Literary Club emerged from a Chautauqua group in 1884. In 1888–1889, a Ladies Round Table group was formed, with a name that is strikingly reminiscent of *A Connecticut Yankee in King Arthur's Court*. It lasted one year. Mrs. Lewis of Detroit, visiting friends in Pontiac, was instrumental in starting the Women's Literary Club reading group that followed. They began to meet at the home of Lillian D. Avery beginning in October 1892, two months after the crowd had assembled for John M. Norton's speech at the Supervisor's Picnic in the park. The social dimensions of women's clubs are emphasized by both Mary Kelley in *Learning to Stand and Speak* (2006) and Barbara Sicherman in *Well Read Lives* (2010).

87. Martha Baldwin, p. 267. Annual Report, p. 29.

88. In Lillian Avery's report, she lists 3,000 volumes, p. 37. It is not clear that they had quite that many yet. See the *Annual Report of the Michigan State Library Commissioners*, Lansing: Robert Smith Printing, 1900. Librarian Agnes Cudworth passed away in her home in Pontiac, December 30, 1934. The responses of the *Kalamazoo Telegraph* and the *Kalamazoo Gazette* after December 11, 1871, are recorded in *Mark Twain Letters*, Vol.

4, ed. Victor Fischer and Michael B. Frank, p. 515. Also see MTP Edition of Narrative to James Redpath, December 11, 1871.

89. Harry Plympton, Letter to Mark Twain, Brooklyn, New York. November 27, 1887. MTP, University of California. R. Kent Rasmussen points out that Twain's mother owned a Bible with a apocryphal chapters and that verse 13 of chapter 12 may be relevant. See Rasmussen, 135.

90. William Bock, Letter to Mark Twain, December 21, 1882, Brooklyn, New York. MTP, University of California. See Rasmussen, 97–98.

91. *Brooklyn Eagle* (January 25, 1897) p. 4. Mark Twain activities included the New York Telegraph Operators Dramatic and Literary Club production of *Tom Sawyer* was at the New Central Opera House at East 67th Street in New York. The *Brooklyn Eagle* reported that the show was "presented by a cast of competent amateurs in which several Brooklynites are numbered." *Brooklyn Eagle* (April 7, 1893) p. 4.

92. *Brooklyn Eagle* (Thursday, January 28, 1897): 4.

93. *Brooklyn Eagle* (Friday, June 18, 1897): 5.

94. *Brooklyn Eagle* (February 13, 1898): 3. Seven years earlier a Christmas tree in Theodore Budde's residence at 151 53rd Street had caught fire. *Brooklyn Eagle* (December 29, 1891): 2.

95. An article notes Harold Lasher serving in this position, *Brooklyn Eagle* (Sunday, October 19, 1902): 5. An article indicates Mr. De Selding's background, *Brooklyn Eagle* (Tuesday, March 16, 1869). A report of July 1, 1892 notes that, while on vacation, De Selding was robbed of jewelry by two eleven year old boys, Thomas Maloy and James Joyce, who ran off to Coney Island and soon were apprehended. *Brooklyn Eagle* (July 1, 1892): 2. He was also a collector and owned a letter by James Madison within his collection, *Brooklyn Eagle* (June 9, 1896): 6. While each of these men read Twain, we know nothing of their reading practices.

96. *Brooklyn Eagle* (Tuesday, January 25, 1898): 13.

97. William Keese's efforts as a poet are noted in the *Brooklyn Eagle* (Tuesday, March 24, 1896): 11. His book of poetry is mentioned in the *Brooklyn Eagle* (May 24, 1902): 7.

98. "Schools," *Brooklyn Eagle* (Sunday, February 10, 1901): 42. In the same *Brooklyn Eagle* edition we read: "The humor of Mark Twain's treatment of serious subjects begins to be appreciated." *Brooklyn Eagle* (February 10, 1901): 18. Harry's graduation is listed, *Brooklyn Eagle* (June 8, 1901): 18.

99. "Royal Arcanum," *Brooklyn Eagle* (Saturday, September 13, 1902).

100. Frederick A. Wright, Letter to Mark Twain, September 19, 1908. Brooklyn. MTP, University of California. Rasmussen, 256–257.

101. Ibid.

102. Susan Dabney Smedes, *Memorials of a Southern Planter*, Baltimore: Cushings and Bailey, 1888, p. 273. Letter of June 1, 1886.

103. P.M. Barker Letter to Mark Twain. MTP, University of California. Rasmussen, 153.

104. *Indian Advocate*, Sacred Heart, Oklahoma (March 1, 1906): 77.

105. David Glassberg, *Sense of History: The Place of the Past in American Life*, Amherst: University of Massachusetts Press, 2001, p. 173.

106. David Glassberg, p. 188; Harry C. Peterson, "Ghost Towns on '49 Tour: Historic Spots to Live Again in Story," *Call* (May 15, 1922).

107. David Glassberg, 191; Cyril Clemens, "A Visit to Mark Twain Country," *Overland and Out West Monthly*, 7 (April 1929): 116–17, 127; *Overland and Out West Monthly* (May 1929): 145–150.

108. "Romance of the Gold Fields," William Thomson, Vol. 34, Is. 203, *Overland and Out West Monthly* (November 1899): 408.

109. Willard B. Farwell. "The Society of California Pioneers, Part II," *Overland and Out West Monthly*, Vol. 29, Is. 171 (March 1897): 292–302.

110. Mrs. L.A. Sherman, Hastings, Nebraska, Federal Writer's Project, October 1938. Library of Congress.

111. Cary McWilliams, *Honorable in All Things*. California Digital Library. Online Archive. Japanese American Relocation Archive.

112. Lew Griswold, Letter to Mark Twain. February 6, 1875. Lew Griswold asks for Twain's autograph and photograph, so "that I have the Picture and likeness of the funniest man and the D__Dest liar in the World." *Baltimore American* (November 29, 1884). MTP, University of California. Rasmussen, 29–31.

113. Marion Thurston Tibbitts, Letter to Mark Twain, April 1, 1905. MTP, University of California. Rasmussen, 217.

114. Granville I. Chittenden, Letter to Mark Twain, February 3, 1910. MTP, University of California. Rasmussen, 267–268.

115. *The Selected Letters of Mark Twain*, Charles Neider, p. 294.

EIGHT

The Global Audience

Mark Twain spent many years of his life living overseas in Europe. With the restless energy of a world traveler, he cultivated an international following. For a correspondent wishing to communicate with him, one of the dilemmas was how to reach Mark Twain with a letter. From Australia, one letter writer addressed a letter to "Mark Twain, God knows where." A young girl from France had another idea, as Twain noted: "This morning's mail brought another of these novelties. It comes from France—from a young girl—and it is addressed:

> Mark Twain
> c/o President Roosevelt
> The White House
> Washington, America"[1]

The wide circulation of Mark Twain's books throughout the world and newspaper comments about "the American humorist" contributed to the familiarity readers had with Twain in Europe and throughout the English-speaking world. So too did his physical presence as he lectured worldwide. From the 1870s into the twentieth century, Mark Twain became an author whose work was recognized and read internationally. Twain's books crossed national boundaries and so did the Clemens family as they went to Europe in the late 1870s. Here we will begin with a look at Mark Twain's reception in England in those years and afterward. This will be followed by a look at his reception on the European continent and his interaction with readers across the world.

A. READING MARK TWAIN IN ENGLAND

In the 1870s, Mark Twain became increasingly international and England was very much in his thoughts. His biographers have often spoken about the special relationship that the author had with England and with his audience there. Among critics, Howard G. Baetzhold, in *Mark Twain and John Bull: The British Connection* (1978), contributed his analysis and many anecdotes to enhance our familiarity with this transatlantic encounter. *The Innocents Abroad* and *Roughing It* appear to have contributed to the beginning of that long relationship. However, the first trip that forged Twain's relationship with English audiences came about because he was concerned that he had been shut out of profits in the British market for *The Innocents Abroad* and "The Jumping Frog of Calavaras County." The lack of international copyright law meant that foreign publishers could reprint Twain's work without payment. One conspicuously did so in England: John Camden Hotten pirated Mark Twain's work and promoted his unauthorized editions. Twain responded sharply to this, concerned about his royalties abroad. In 1872, he wanted to protect the British copyright of *The Innocents Abroad* and *Roughing It*. That meant that he had to be in England to secure the English copyright for his books. British law required that the author be present in Britain on the day of publication. When he announced that he was going to England, Livy thought the separation would be difficult. She decided to go also. They spent Fall 1872 in Britain. This was the beginning of a long relationship between Twain and his British audience.

Most English readers viewed Mark Twain as America's humorist and some saw him as America's chronicler of the West. About twelve different volumes of Twain's writings were in print in England in the 1870s. There were also cheap editions published by Hotten, who pirated copies and capitalized on Twain's works. *Choice Humorous Works of Mark Twain* (1873) included some choice selections of his own writing, or selections that were not from Mark Twain. Wide circulation of such books meant increased reputation for Mark Twain. However, he never made any money at all from these editions that altered the material context in which his work was read. Twain wrote: "My books are bad enough just as they are written, then what they must be after Mr. John Camden Hotten has composed half a dozen chapters and added the same to them?"[2]

People in England often saw Mark Twain in person, beginning in the 1870s. Yet, Twain could not always gauge the responses of his British readers. A familiar anecdote is told that after he arrived in Liverpool, on a train, Twain sat next to a man who was reading *The Innocents Abroad*. As he read, the expression on this reader's face never changed. Twain must have wondered if his humor was not reaching this reader. It was only when he began to lecture to English audiences that he had more direct access to responses from his readers. One audience member, G.W. Smalley, a journalist, thanked Twain for his invitation to a lecture in London:

> Mrs. Smalley and I agreed in thinking the lecture a capital bit in itself and in the manner of its delivery, which was inimitable. I admired your way of leading up to your points & your great good sense in giving a slow-witted English audience time to take them in. That they enjoyed so many of them was a proper tribute to you, for the average Englishman does not take kindly to the peculiar humour in which you excel.[3]

Perhaps that audience member had it right, as he observed the English difference in humor. Twain recognized that members of his English audience could be guarded with respect to their emotions. However, they relaxed this when in a lecture audience.[4] He clearly appreciated letters of this sort and he wrote home of his British reception: "They make a stranger feel entirely at home and they laugh so easily it is a comfort to make after-dinner speeches here. I have made hundreds of friends, and last night in the crush of the opening of the New Guild Hall Library and Museum I was surprised to meet a familiar face every few steps. Nearly 4,000 people of both sexes came and went during the evening, so I had a good opportunity to make a great many new acquaintances."[5]

Twain's time in England brought the issue of international copyright to the foreground of his thoughts. The author made a deal with Routledge to gain protection against other British publishers. He wrote scathingly on "John Camden Hottentot" in the *London Spectator* September 20, 1872, as he sealed his deal with George Routledge, who published *Innocents Abroad* in 1872 in Britain. The book appeared in two volumes, minus illustrations, subtitled *The New Pilgrim's Progress*. In his note at the start of the British edition, Twain says: "I have made a patient and conscientious revision of this book for publication in England and I have weeded out of it nearly, if not quite all, of the most palpable and inexcusable of its blemishes."[6] His need to protect the British copyright of *Roughing It* had led to his 1872 trip.

The American writer was enchanted by his English audience. In late September 1872, Mark Twain was a celebrity in London. At the Guildhall dinner, Twain sat next to Sir John Bennett, one of the many readers of *The Innocents Abroad*. "I was never so taken aback in my life," Twain wrote. "I thought I was the humblest in that great titled assemblage- & behold, mine was the only name in the long list that called forth this splendid compliment [...] I did not know I was a lion." He wrote: "I am by long odds the most widely known & popular American author among the English & the book will be read by pretty much every Englishman."[7]

Twain's comment, while hyperbole, captured well the situation: In England, he had become the most popular of American authors. The English audience in 1872 knew Mark Twain by reputation. Justin Kaplan believes Twain was "adored by the masses" but could only expect "cool tolerance" from "official culture." Yet, in England "there seemed to be no class division in taste as far as humor was concerned."[8] For the English, Mark Twain represented American qualities, traits that were "Western." His time in England gave him a chance to look back across the ocean at American culture. He saw in England responsible government and dignified elites. In contrast, in the Grant administration at home he saw corruption and chicanery. This was the America of progressive energy and unscrupulous scandal that he soon characterized in *The Gilded Age.* He also noticed a difference in his audiences and wrote: "Americans are not Englishmen and American humor is not English humor; but both the American and his humor had their origin in England. . . . "

> English and colonial audiences are phenomenally alert, and responsive. When masses of people are gathered together on England, caste is submerged, and with it the English reserve; equality exists for a moment, and every individual is free; so free from any consciousness of fetters, indeed, that the Englishman's habit of watching himself and guarding himself against any injudicious exposure of his feelings is forgotten and falls into abeyance.[9]

In the 1880s, Katie L. Corbet, the daughter of working class parents in Manchester, encouraged Twain to write on the history of England. She and her brother William were not concerned about distinguishing facts from fiction, if he made it interesting she said:

> My brother and I have read The Adventures of Tom Sawyer, The Adventures of Huck Finn, Life on the Mississippi, and, The Prince and the Pauper, and think them splendid, especially the Prince and the Pauper I think. We have been thinking it would be a delicious History of England, if you wrote it, and made a few variations of corse, like you did in the Prince and the Pauper. It would not matter about you making it true if you made it interesting. We should like you to write it so much, please, do. I am your loving reader.[10]

In the chill of winter, 1886, Mark Twain informed Charles Webster, who was managing his publishing company, that he had "begun a book, whose scene is laid far back in the twilight of tradition."[11] It would be three years before the story would be published as *A Connecticut Yankee in King Arthur's Court.* At the moment, "Mark Twain" was on hiatus and Samuel Clemens was playing billiards, speculating on stocks, and distracted with dreams of success for the Paige typesetter. His dreams of King Arthur took some time to incubate. Twain himself was more like Cervantes' Don Quixote than Sir Lancelot at this time: a man dreaming of success while tilting at windmills. *The Connecticut Yankee* was put on hold in 1886–1887, while Twain was absorbed in business activities: his publishing firm, the Paige typesetter, and stock speculation. He collaborated on a play with William Dean Howells: *Colonel Sellers as a Scientist.* However, he was more concerned with the publishing business and with the

Paige typesetter he had invested in. This investment would prove to be a fiasco. Twain had entered a deal to pay the creator's development costs of three thousand dollars per month. The hope was for a big payoff, once the typesetting machine was in full working order. It was not anticipated that other manufactures would make the Paige typesetter obsolete before it could even be perfected.

Twain's critique of British "culture," in *A Connecticut Yankee in King Arthur's Court*, can be set within this context. His novel was given impetus by Matthew Arnold's comments on Ulysses S. Grant. In a sense, Twain's novel was an assertion of American ingenuity against outworn English traditions. With his book Twain reprised the old world–new world conflict he had dealt with in *The Innocents Abroad*. Twain went to imagined history, implicitly asserting that America indeed had technology, inventiveness, and progressive vigor to offer. He turned, for contrast, to Arthurian legend: that body of chivalric literature which refers to the adventures of King Arthur's court. This was entirely familiar to British audiences, for whom the stories of King Arthur and his knights were something of a national myth. The legends extended from Welsh literature and Geoffrey of Monmouth through Cretien de Troyes. They included *Gawain and the Green Knight* and the grail theme in *Percival*. Most notable was Thomas Malory's *Le Morte d'Arthur*, which was Twain's starting place for his novel. Upon reading Malory, Twain daydreamed of himself as knight in shining armor, displaced from the modern age and alive in the realm of King Arthur. As the next year came, Sir Robert Smith of Camelot soon became Hank Morgan, an engineer from Connecticut.

By Twain's reckoning, being a knight could be quite uncomfortable. Imagine being stuck in a suit of armor all the time, Twain suggested. "Iron gets red hot in the sun- leaks in the rain [...] freezes me solid in the winter. Suffer from lice & fleas [...] Can't dress or undress. Always getting struck by lightning. Fall down, can't get up."[12] Twain's bathos took the knight's heroic chivalric pose and inverted it into humor. Initially opposing aristocracy, Hank Morgan soon joins them and is dubbed "the Boss."

In the summer of 1887, the year of Queen Victoria's Jubilee celebration, Twain returned to writing *A Connecticut Yankee*. He gave to it the sharp edge of critique. His previous admiration for England was tempered with irritation toward everything that breathed of feudalism. Twain told his business agent Franklin C. Whitmore that he believed the new book was "worth thirty or forty thousand when finished" and he was writing furiously. *A Connecticut Yankee* was about modern America. In his novel, Twain was dealing with the "quarrels" between America and Britain. As in *The Innocents Abroad*, he had again taken up the theme of the "new world" and the "old world." Now he added a twist. The United States was fresh and new, industrious and active, a place of energy that had achieved what Britain had not. Twain had long resisted all anti-British talk, as Louis Budd pointed out.[13] However, he now let his distaste for what he considered reactionary, feudal, and antimodern take comic form. Released by Charles Webster and Company, the first hard-cover edition had 575 pages and about 220 illustrations. *A Connecticut Yankee in King Arthur's Court* sold 32,000 copies in its first year. It was a low figure compared with several of Twain's earlier efforts. The book, however, is one of Twain's creations that later increased in sales and continues to sell today.[14]

William Algie, one of the novel's non-British readers wrote in January 1890 from Alton in Ontario, Canada:

> Permit a grateful Canadian to express his hearty thanks for the many pleasures your pen has given him during the past 10 or 12 years. I have just concluded a pleasant perusal of "The Yankee in King Arthur's Court" and you have earned in it the gratitude of every "lover of liber-ty." I trust that the time may speedily come when Chap. XIII will be incorporated in every school book to the end that the "glorious French Revolution" may be understood by the generations to come. . . . [15]

On New Year's Day, 1900, Twain was in London but he was thinking of his family's return home to the United States. "We are all hoping to end our long exile & see you then and have a time," he wrote to Howells.[16] When at last he arrived in New York, America applauded his return. He was photographed, interviewed, and talked about in America's news-papers. Mark Twain was the darling of the media; he was one of the nation's favorites.

The audience in New York City saw him first hand that autumn. With the assistance of Frank Doubleday, the Clemens family established a resi-dence in New York at 14 West 10th Street in Manhattan. William Dean and Elinor Howells lived nearby at 115 East 16th Street. In New York, Mark Twain became an attraction at public events. Mark Twain was now a media event. He contributed to this process, striding down the city blocks of Manhattan as if on parade. He employed a press clipping ser-vice. He gave speeches. At the Waldorf Astoria he greeted Winston Churchill, applauding him, at a time when he was criticizing imperialistic policies. Of England and America, he said, "We have always been kin. Kin in blood, kin in religion, kin in representative government, kin in ideals, kin in just and lofty purposes, and now we are kin in sin, the harmony is complete, the blend is perfect, like Mr. Churchill himself, whom I now have the honor to present to you."[17]

Compliments from English readers continued to be effusive. Edith Draper of Lancashire wrote a heartfelt letter to Mark Twain on December 29, 1906, and she received a reply from him on January 15, 1907.

> I wonder if you would care to hear how much my husband & self appreciate your books. We have been married 4 years & I have bought him one of your works each birthday & at Christmas. He is never tired

of reading them & they keep him at home many a time when he would be out at night. He reads them aloud to me & I enjoy the reading as much as himself. The reason I am writing is to beg a favour of you. Would you be kind enough to give me your photo so that I can give my husband a surprise on his next birthday?

She comments that they do not have much and would "dearly prize" a photo of Twain. "We have a little boy six months & his father says when he is older he will tell him about poor little Huck & Tom Sawyer." She had been reading "some extracts in our paper copied from your articles in the 'North Atlantic Review.'" [18]

Mark Twain's final trip to England came in 1907. On June 17, 1907, Twain received an Oxford honorary doctoral degree, a prestigious recognition, which appears to have been thrilling to him. He proudly wore his Oxford robes on occasions for the rest of his life. In his early years, he had been regarded as only a humorist. Now he was a writer recognized around the world, honored by one of Britain's historic universities. While in London, Twain was also honored at the Savoy Hotel at a luncheon. In London, George Bernard Shaw was introduced to Samuel Clemens by Archibald Henderson at St. Pancras Station. On July 3, 1907, Shaw and his wife had lunch with him at Adelphi Terrace, along with Max Beerbohm. Both Twain and Shaw had written on Joan of Arc. On July 3, 1907, Shaw wrote to Mark Twain:

> My dear Twain—not to say Dr. Clemens (though I have always regarded Clemens as mere raw material—might have been your brother or your uncle) Just a line to excuse myself from running away today. . . . I meant to ask you if you had ever met William Morris. I won't ask you now, because it would put you to the trouble of answering this letter; so let it stand until I look you up in America. But what put it into my head was this. Once, when I was in Morris's house, a superior anti-Dickens sort of man (sort of man who thinks Dickens is no gentleman) was annoyed by Morris disparaging Thackeray. With studied gentleness he asked if Morris could name a greater master of English. Morris promptly said "Mark Twain." This delighted me extremely, as it was my own opinion; and then I found out that Morris was an incurable Huckfinomaniac. This was the more remarkable, as Morris would have regarded the Yankee at the Court of King Arthur as blasphemy, and would have blown your head off for imply that the contemporaries of Joan of Arc could touch your own contemporaries in villainy. [19]

Shaw concluded his letter to Twain: "I am persuaded that the future historian of America will find your works as indispensible to him as a French historian finds the political tracts of Voltaire." He adds that in his play, *John Bull's Other Island*, the priest says, "'Telling the truth's the funniest joke in the world,' a piece of wisdom you helped to teach to me." [20]

Boyhood on the Mississippi readily found its way to England. Early in the twentieth century, British readers recalled their childhood associations with Tom Sawyer. In the Reader's Experience Database (RED), we learn that Neville Cardus read only boys' papers until, quite suddenly in adolescence, he "dove into Dickens and Mark Twain." Cardus, presumably, then is quoted: "Then without scarcely a bridge-passage, I was deep in the authors, who to this day I regard as the best discovered in a lifetime."[21] These authors are Fielding, Browning, Hardy, Tolstoy, "even Henry James." One may ask how Dickens and Twain become an extension of "boys' papers" and why any "bridge-passage" would be necessary from their work to that of the others named here. If there is some causal chain implied here, Twain and Dickens are, perhaps, regarded as a middle-brow intermediary stage in a passage from boys' papers to adult novels, or more elite literary reading experiences. Christopher Grieve from Scotland writes, "The house was behind the post office and below the town library, and in a few years not even the joys of guddling, girning, and angling matched the boy's pleasure in Emerson, Hawthorne, Ambrose Pierce [*sic*], Sidney Lanier, and Mark Twain." This reader is said to have carried washing baskets up the stairs to fill it with books.[22] Quite an avid reader he was, indeed.

Novelist V.S. Pritchett writes that "Bartlett was a good painter in water-colors. When we read *Kidnapped* he made us paint the Scottish moors. We laughed over Tom Sawyer and Huckleberry Finn."[23] In the Great War, in the Somme, the writer Edmund Blunden apparently needed a sense of humor to endure waiting along the edges of battle. Blunden wrote while a member of the 11th Royal Sussex Regiment: "Tom Sawyer's ingenious antics are at present my principal book and bible."[24] R.H. Kiernan, a busied and distracted soldier in the British army, wished that he could "lie down and read or sleep in the quietness." He wrote: "I mean, I could not read for more than a few minutes at a time, and I had Tom Sawyer."[25] These readers of *The Adventures of Tom Sawyer*, under the stark and adult conditions of battle, may have been reaching back to a more innocent time in their own childhoods. Tom Sawyer provided antics and laughter during a most serious time.

In "My Favorite Novel and His Best Book," the British writer Walter Besant admitted that he had "so many favorite novels" but Twain's *Huckleberry Finn* was one that "seized" and enchanted him. Besant, considering readers of the novel, wrote:

> the child, and his elder brother, and his father, and his grandfather, may read it with like enjoyment—not equal enjoyment, because as a man gets older and understands more and more of the world of men and women means, he reads between the lines and see things which the child cannot see and cannot understand. . . . [T]o read the invisible part of the page is one of the compensations of age.[26]

Besant found spontaneity in the book, in which characters "follow each other with unexpectedness belonging to a voyage down the river." In considering the book, he sought to distinguish British traits from American ones. Of the narration, he wrote, "In some places when an English boy would have rolled on the floor with laughing, the American boy relates the scene without a smile." Huck Finn is young and his "experiences of life have not, so far, inclined him to look at things from a humorous point of view," Besant claims. He believes that "there is no character in fiction more fully, more faithfully presented than that of the character of Huckleberry Finn." [27] The boy is "shrewd," says Besant.

> I think that Shrewdness is a more common characteristic of the American than of the Englishman. I mean that he is more ready to question, to doubt, to examine, to understand. He is far more ready to exercise freedom of thought; far less ready to accept authority. His individuality is more intense; he is one against the world; he is more readily on the defensive.

The British author also recognizes that Huckleberry Finn is closely connected with the natural world. He writes:

> he has an immense natural love for the woods and forests; for the open air; for the great river laden with the rafts forever going down the stream; for the night as much as the day; for the dawn as much as the splendor of the noonday. [28]

Twain continued to be read by working class women in Britain as well. For example, Jonathan Rose points to Arnold Freeman's 1918 Sheffield survey, which shows a girl, a machine file cutter, age twenty-five, who has read Dickens's *The Old Curiosity Shop*, *Innocents Abroad*, *The Scarlet Pimpernel*, and the *Bible*. [29]

B. RECEPTION IN EUROPE

In 1891, the author brought his family again to Europe to restore Livy's health and to encourage the education of his daughters. Twain thought that he might write a series of travel articles for *McClure's*, or a book of travel sketches. In 1895, he made a world tour, including western Canada, Australia, New Zealand, India, and South Africa in his travels. While living in Vienna, in the years before the turn of the century, Twain sharpened the edge of his social criticism and he wrote many imaginative sketches, letters, and acerbic critiques.

Increasingly, Twain received letters from young people living in Europe. For instance, seventeen year old Olaf Halvorsen wrote to Twain from Norway in January 1890:

> Letters like this you are sure to receive so many, that you do not read them, but throw them in the paper-basket. However I resolved upon

making a trial, and as you are my favorite author, and I have read all, you have wrote, I hope, you will not take it in bad part, when I beg to ask you for your monogram. You are not able to imagine the delight, it would give me to have your handwriting. I would frame it, and you would ever oblige yours truly Norwegian admirer, Olaf Halvorsen, 17 years old.[30]

As Twain's books entered European culture, they passed through various formats in reprints. His work was published in English by the German firm of Tauchnitz and it was translated into French by many companies in Paris. The reading experience was filtered through French and German print cultures with distinct qualities that reprinted and circulated Twain's books. For example, in its French setting, *The Adventures of Tom Sawyer* was marketed specifically as a children's book. When the same novel appeared in Germany, Austria, and Switzerland, the plain brown cover paperbacks of Tauchnitz made it affordable for readers. Tauchnitz, in a sense, democratized the reading of Twain, making his books widely accessible.[31]

These shifts in marketing, material text, and audience were already well underway when the Clemens family arrived at Le Havre, in France in 1891, and made their way to Paris and then on to Geneva. There was a "dramatic textual metamorphosis" when Twain's books went across the Atlantic to France, observes Ronald Jenn. France had a need for children's books, which had become one aspect of a "policy of mass schooling."[32] The Jules Ferry laws had made school compulsory in 1881. *Huckleberry Finn* became prize or gift book published in France in December 1886. The French publisher A. Hennuyer of Paris first published both *The Adventures of Tom Sawyer* and *The Adventures of Huckleberry Finn*. Here we can see beginnings of the common association of the two novels as they were directed toward the juvenile market. Jenn points out that the material text of Twain's productions changed from their American incarnations to their appearances in France. "From a textual point of view. *Tom Sawyer* and *Huckleberry Finn* were considerably manipulated and adapted," he informs us.[33]

Many French readers were introduced to *The Adventures of Tom Sawyer* and *The Adventures of Huckleberry Finn* through school reading. The novel went into its French edition from the British one, crossing genres as well as languages. As Ronald Jenn points out, "it was turned into a children's book."[34] In France, Jenn notes, it took until 1948 for the book to become widely available to adult readers. There is evidence, of course, that adults bought these children's books and it is likely that some families read these books aloud. However, Jenn points out alterations of Twain's text for those readers. Several of the changes in the text were the work of William Little Hughes, who was an Irish writer and editor who worked for the French Ministere de l'Interieur. Within the text of *The Adventures of Tom Sawyer*, the word "boy" was replaced by the word "student." The word "nigger" became "slave." Hughes changed Huckleberry Finn's father's comment: "Your mother couldn't read and she could write nuther, before she died." Since this hardly encourages student reading, Hughes writes: *"Ma mere m'avait un peu appris a lire et a ecrire."* ("My mother had taught me how to read and write a little.") [35] Jenn observes that these books by Twain "stand for the ritual passage into print culture of an ever growing number of people whose incorporation was achieved thanks to schooling and literacy, with a view to developing their ability to read silently and individually." [36] The absence of international copyright meant that *The Adventures of Tom Sawyer* could be readily reprinted, copied, translated, and adapted in France and elsewhere. The American publication was delayed until late 1876. So, the British edition became the basis for French reprints and cheap reprints from Canada that flooded the American market.

While in France, the Clemens family traveled near Domremy-la-Pucelle, the birthplace of Joan of Arc. [37] Twain would soon write on that unexpected topic. He would later comment that the book was among his favorites of his writings. It was also the favorite of one little American girl, Linda Berle, a high school student in Boscawen, New Hampshire:

> I have just finished reading your "personal recollections of Joan of Arc" for the fourth time, As Joan has always been a favorite character of mine, I am writing to tell you how much I enjoyed it. I reread it about every year, and like it better for each reading. I want to thank you for the pleasure you have given me.
>
> I have also read the "Connecticut Yankee at King Arthur's Court" with very great interest. I am a senior at Salem High School, and for a theme I told the story. The teacher gave me an A, and I learned he had heard of the book but had not read it. Later when we were studying the "Idylls" of Tennyson, I heard him recommending your book to a pupil for a good picture of Arthurian times. [38]

Along with these heroic characters of France and England, Mark Twain's time in Germany brought exposure to the mythical figures of Richard Wagner's music-dramas. [39] Back in the 1870s, Livy, Susy, and Clara had attended nineteen performances of Richard Wagner's operatic works. Twain, writing "At the Shrine of St. Wagner's" swore that he barely survived this. In 1891, the family again visited Heidelberg and they stayed at the Schloss Hotel, overlooking Heidelberg Castle. Years before, Livy had entered German culture wholeheartedly, insisting that her girls learn the German language. Twain wrote that the housemaid was involved in the effort: "From the day we reached German soil we have required Rosa to speak German to the children—which they hate with all their souls." In *A Tramp Abroad*, Twain added an appendix that included notes on his bewilderment with the German language. By the time Twain chose to live in Austria, in the 1890s, he had become fluent in German.

European audiences were treated to Twain's fiction, replete with American regional accents and African American vernacular. His stories became a true heteroglossia of tongues, translated into French, German, Italian, Danish, Russian, modern Greek, and other languages. Germany, Austria, Switzerland, and Italy became important sites of the trade in Twain's works. In Germany, several publishers besides Tauchnitz produced Twain's works, among these Mann in Leipzig, Freytag in Leipzig, and Lutz in Stuttgart. Twain was a recognizable figure in some European circles as the Clemens family traveled from Bad Nauheim in Germany to Florence, Italy. There they had leased the Villa Viviani, an estate with its green shutters open to the fields of Tuscany. From this temporary home they could travel to Venice and to Milan, Lake Como, and on through Switzerland through Germany. As the Clemens family crossed borders, so too did Twain's writings, circulating throughout the world. *McClure's* had printed much of the story that would become *The American Claimant*, which then appeared in a Charles Webster and Company hardcover edition. *Tom Sawyer Abroad* was making its journey to subscribers in America and into bookstores in England.

Twain's European audience also heard the critical voice that entered Twain's *Pudd'nhead Wilson*, written while he was in Europe. During the summer of 1892 Twain had worked on the story, which he was calling "Those Extraordinary Twins." With further writing, the story began to change shape. It became a critique on racial issues and social responses to race and class. He also started a story that featured Tom Sawyer, Huckleberry Finn, and Jim, which became *Tom Sawyer Abroad*. In this story, Tom, Huck, and Jim float eastward in a balloon from St. Louis across the American landscape and the Atlantic Ocean to Africa. Readers traveled with them as they flew over Africa, and heard Huck, the narrator, say: "Jim's eyes bugged out, and he began to stare down with no end of interest, because that was where his originals came from."[40] With this publication, we see variant texts. The story appeared in *St. Nicholas Magazine*, a popular children's magazine edited by Mary Mapes Dodge. Although Twain was irritated by editorial corrections of his punctuation and the omission of his slang, those editorial changes were included when the story was published in book form by Chatto and Windus in London. Charles Webster and Company published the book days later, in what would prove to be one of its last gasps as a publisher.

C. THE WORLD TOUR

A global audience for the work of Mark Twain had emerged long before a worldwide tour was planned in 1895 to revive the author's lagging finances. Twain went forth to meet this audience of the English-speaking world out of necessity. The American economy had been throttled by a depression in 1893, giving Twain's publishing company a final blow from which it would not recover. Twain's investment in the Paige typesetter had similarly reached cataclysmic proportions. Mark Twain, who had lived so well on a crest of prosperity in the 1880s, was now facing financial ruin. Tested by bankruptcy in 1894, he planned to venture on an exhausting world tour to pay back his creditors. The Panic of 1893 in the United States was a severe depression that followed railroad speculation and overbuilding in the 1880s. Economists have cited deflation dating back to the Civil War, a slowdown in railroad expansion, difficulty with the gold standard and U.S. monetary policy, and declines in the European economy. In England, economic indices fell sharply in 1894 and British investment in American businesses fell off. The severity of the depression in the United States is reflected in the rise in unemployment from 3.0–3.7 percent in 1891 to more than 10 percent across five consecutive years, from 1893 through 1897. In 1890 the national GNP had been strong, albeit behind that of Britain. However, by the time Grover Cleveland was inaugurated as president, for a second time, in March 1893, U.S. gold reserves had fallen to a low level. When the gold reserve trembled at 22 million, perilously close to bankruptcy, financier J.P. Morgan intervened. He sold a U.S. bond issue at 3.5 percent to the Rothschild's banks and others in Europe. Although a second recession contracted the economy from about December 1895 to about June 1897, the infusion of capital helped to readjust the economy. Twain, however, saw the necessity of taking extraordinary measures to return to financial solvency. His choice of a world tour was of great benefit to his audience and contributed greatly to his lasting worldwide reputation.

Mark Twain's travel books participated in a trend of international travel that was supported by the growth of commercial trade and steamship lines. Transatlantic trade and travel is characterized by *Harper's* first edition of 1893: a front page picture of a transatlantic steamship on a winter voyage. "Rough Weather at Sea" is a caption that could have likewise been attached to financial markets in America and Europe. The financial preoccupations of the time were captured in one of Twain's stories that year: "The 1,000,000 Bank Note." Twain's *The American Claimant* was now in book form and it was concluding in the *Idler*, after being previously serialized in the *New York Sun*. The climate of hard times tended to increase social sensitivity to public issues and industrial problems. As strikes and populist free silver agitation buffeted the United States, Mark Twain increasingly emerged as a writer of conscience. His writings of the next decade would be laced with barbed social criticism. Ever the entertainer, his popularity would grow as he traveled into a complicated modern world.

Twain's audience in Europe and in America often read notes and fillers about him in the pages of their newspapers. As the year 1895 began, these readers had much to read about. On January 5, Captain Alfred Dreyfus was convicted of treason in a French court and stripped of his rank. The case became a cause célèbre. As a cold winter swept across Europe and America, the moving picture projector was patented and the Lumiere Brothers showed their first film, bringing a new visual dimension to public entertainment. Twain's global lecture tour took place at the same time that Joshua Slocum was traversing the world in a boat alone and the winner of the first automobile race topped a speed of seven miles per hour. In New York, J.P. Morgan offered his infusion of capital to adjust the strained economy, while, in Iowa, Daniel David Palmer was providing the first chiropractic adjustment for strained backs. Mark Twain scribbled with a ballpoint pen, while Frederick Blaisdell patented the pencil. *The Importance of Being Earnest* played in London, even as the play's author, Oscar Wilde, was placed on trial. Mark Twain had introduced fingerprinting into his story, *Pudd'nhead Wilson*, but could little know how important that would become in criminal justice. Nor did he know that the discovery of x-rays would soon be made by Wilhelm Rontgen. And, alas, Mark Twain would never win the Nobel Prize, which Alfred Nobel instituted that year. That probably mattered little to Australian readers of Twain, like sixteen-year-old Miles Franklin. Martyn Lyons, in his case study of her reading, observes that "she thrilled to Mark Twain's Personal Recollections of Joan of Arc."[41] She was not alone. Many Australians anticipated Mark Twain's arrival.

Twain was now off to see the world and he crossed the Pacific on the Canadian–Australian steamer the *Warimoo*. By August 30, he and Livy had reached Honolulu. Australian audiences were well-primed by the news media for Twain's six week lecture tour visit there. As early as April, the newspaper of Zeehan and Dundas was writing: "the celebrated humorist intends to visit the Australian colonies at the end of the year." The *Mercury*, Hobart, Tasmania, wrote on August 27: "Mark Twain, Mr. Samuel Clemens, the American humorist, has suffered seriously with the book selling house of Charles M. Webster and Company New York and now proposes to go on a lecture tour around the world [...]"[42] When Twain reached Australia, enthusiastic audiences were waiting and the newspapers continually placed Mark Twain in front of the Australian public:

> Mark Twain began a series of lectures in Sydney on September 19. The Protestant Hall where the lecture opened was crowded to its utmost capacity with an audience it was evident had a thorough acquaintance with the books of the humorist.[43]

Newspaper accounts carried notes of concern about Twain's financial situation, following the decline of his publishing business and his investment in the Paige typesetter:

> Much sympathy is felt for Mark Twain who is now in Sydney in financial trouble. He was a partner in the publishing house of G.C. Webster [*sic*] which failed in hard times last year.[44]

The *Advertiser* in Adelaide identified Twain with his first bestseller, *The Innocents Abroad*, and suggested that there was much expectation of Twain's arrival: "As the time approaches for the arrival in Adelaide of the author of "Innocents Abroad" public curiosity respecting the celebrated humorist becomes daily greater."[45] Much of the comment in the newspapers suggests that the Australian audience viewed Twain primarily as a humorist. The *Windsor and Richmond Gazette*, for example, was effusive: "Who has not laughed until his eyes grew dim?"[46] An audience member there wrote, thinking of the future for Australian performers:

> To the Editor. Remarks concerning Mark Twain. I don't think that if a freetrader he is speaking consistently. In time to come, no doubt we will be sending some of our native talent to other shores. . . . and I think it only fair that these lecturers from other countries should be treated as we expect to be treated if we ever turn out Mark Twains as Talmages from the cornstalks [...] E.E.T.[47]

Mark Twain arrived in Australia when the Australian book market in the 1890s was experiencing what historians of the book have called "a creative moment, when a specifically Australian literary nationalism took shape."[48] It was also a time, however, of a continuing domination of the market by London products. As Martyn Lyons and Jay Arnold have pointed out, books from Macmillan, Methuen, Unger, Longmans, Heinemann, Lane, and others filled the Australian market. There was the popular Hodder and Stoughton's yellow jacket series at local bookshops, lending libraries, and railway bookstands. Ward, Lock and Company had a strong share of the adolescent market. The firm of Angus and Robertson had only begun its rise to the largest firm in Australia. World trade was organized into trading blocs. Great Britain regulated prices and set fixed trading margins between wholesale and retail prices.[49] British influence remained considerable in the Australian market. Despite his critique of English feudalism in *A Connecticut Yankee*, Twain was still viewed as a friend to Britain. He was read by Australians from all walks of life and he appears to have been viewed by this audience as a performer: a funny American entertainer.

While work focusing on discovering Twain's Australian audience remains to be written, we do have several anecdotes of his encounters with readers and lecture audiences members. Twain recalled a sociable man in Sydney who would often greet him and ask him about the character in one of his stories: "Say—Mark! Is he dead?" Twain says that others asked similar questions:

> A reference to a passage in some book of mine, though I didn't detect it at that time, that that was its source. And I didn't detect it afterward in Melbourne, when I came on the stage for the first time, and the same question was dropped down upon me from the dizzy height of the gallery. It is always difficult to answer a sudden inquiry like that, when you have come unprepared and don't know what it means.[50]

One of the strangest stories of Mark Twain followers is that of a man from Bendigo, Australia, who called himself Mr. Blank. He evidently had no difficulty with reaching Twain by mail. Through the 1870s, he sent Mark Twain more than a dozen letters filled with minutes from the Mark Twain Club and its thirty-two members at Corrigan castle. However, there was no castle. The club had only one member: Mr. Blank, who had invented all of it.[51]

Twain met Mr. Blank in Bendigo, while on his lecture tour, some "twelve or fifteen" years later, by the man's accounting. He refers to Mr. Blank in *Following the Equator* and comments on how diligently the man read his books. He reminded Twain of Corrigan Castle and of their correspondence, including the many questions about passages in the books.[52] Twain wrote: "It was through Mr. Blank—not to go into particulars about his name—it was mainly through Mr. Blank that my stay in Bendigo was made memorably pleasant and interesting.[53] "He was an Irishman; an educated gentleman. . . . He made me like him, and did it without trouble. This was partly through his gentle and winning ways, but mainly through the amazing familiarity with my books which his conversation showed."[54]

Along with these anecdotes, there are other letters from Australian readers. For example, J. Gavan Reilly wrote on October 20, 1895: "Every digger who dwells under the blue sky of Australia is familiar with your imperishable works; yea, as familiar Sir as the English race are with Dickens. . . . " He adds his request for an autograph to assist in a fundraising effort.[55]

Twain stayed in Australia until Christmas, offering a Farewell Lecture at the School of Arts in Sydney on December 24. After a visit to New Zealand, he headed on to India. On January 18, 1896, he and Livy reached Bombay, now Mumbai. "India does not consist of cities," he wrote. "India is one vast farm, one almost interminable stretch of fields with mud fences between them."[56] In August, Twain had written to Rudyard Kipling that he would repay in India Kipling's visit to Elmira years before.

> It is reported that you are about to visit India. This has moved me to journey to that far country in order that I may unload from my conscience a debt long due to you [...] I shall arrive next January and you must be ready. I shall come riding my ayah with his tusks adorned

> with silver bells and ribbons and escorted by a troop of native howdahs
> richly clad and mounted upon a herd of wild bungalows. And you
> must be on hand with a few bottles of ghee, for I shall be thirsty.[57]

Twain in India was a cultural import, who arrived as a lecturer and a
performer. India was an oral culture filled with many languages and
literacy was at about ten percent. Priya Joshi comments, "There was a
remarkable consistency in Indian readers' preference for the most popular forms as they circulated through libraries and reading rooms."[58] She
notes a preference for melodrama and the popularity of G.W.M. Reynolds. If one had done a similar study of American writers imported
into India, Twain might be added to this. Reviewing her book, Henry
Schwartz observed that "the performance of texts . . . was an enormously
productive venue for generating literary pleasure and meaning."[59] Twain
was one of India's first visiting lecturers.

While on his tour of India he said: "I barked at audiences all about
India for six weeks, then the cough expired by statute of limitation."[60]
Twain then made the long journey to South Africa, where some tensions
had been brewing since L.S. Jameson's failed raid in late December 1895.
These tensions, in a few years, would lead to the Boer War. The *Cape
Times* wrote:

> His visit to South Africa has fallen in the midst of exciting times and it
> would have been difficult for anyone interested in the development of
> a new country, as any American naturally would be, and particularly
> such a keen observer of men and manners as Mr. Clemens, to have
> chosen a more suitable period for a peregrination through Austrel Africa than the present year of grace.[61]

From South Africa, Twain traveled north to Europe, arriving in England in September 1896. He had traveled thousands of miles, lecturing to
the English speaking world.

The personal life of Samuel Clemens at this time was largely unknown
to his audience. Newspaper accounts eventually let his audience know of
one of the most crushing blows of his life: the loss of his daughter Susy,
soon after he and Livy arrived in England. While he was in his rented
house in London with Livy and his daughter Clara, he received a telegram from home that his daughter Susy was gravely ill. Livy and Clara
immediately sailed for New York. They did not arrive in time to see Susy
before she died. Twain received a cable from America, informing him
that his daughter had died. He blamed himself for being away in Europe.
He blamed God for having no pity on mankind. To his wife and daughter
Clara he said, "You want me to believe it is a judicious, a charitable God
that runs this world. I could run it better myself."[62] He threw himself into
work on *Following the Equator*, finishing the travel book in seven months.
The writing, perhaps, was a form of therapy. To Howells he wrote that he
was divided, like two persons. He was deeply devastated by the loss of

his daughter, yet he was determined to write. He told Howells that he and his wife were overtaken by grief; they were "dead people who go through the motions of life. Indeed I am a mud image & it puzzles me to know what is in me that writes & that had comedy fantasies & finds pleasure in phrasing them."[63]

In the 1890s, the pain of the loss of his daughter cut much too close for Twain to write about it. Eventually, Twain recalled this difficult loss in one of the periodical installments of his *Autobiography*. A former resident of Elmira, Louise Davis Chubbuck responded to the *Autobiography* and commiserated with Twain upon his loss of his daughter. She recalled the loss of her own daughter Ruth, who was taking a nurse's course in St. John's in Brooklyn.[64]

For now, he threw himself into work, recalling his global journey. Twain's audience appears to have been well-prepared for another travel book. He thought of calling it "Round the World," for indeed he had circumnavigated the globe. When it reached his audience it was known as *Following the Equator: A Journey around the World*. He wrote on April 13: "finished my book today." Then he picked it back up, wrote further, and wrote on May 18: "finished the book again."[65] The American Publishing Company held the rights for many of Twain's books and sought a deal for his travel book. In June 1897, Frank Bliss traveled to London to discuss subscription sales of *Following the Equator*. Chatto and Windus issued the book as *More Tramps Abroad*. The American Publishing Company placed an illustration of an elephant on their cover. Inside the covers were two hundred more illustrations. By 1895, subscription sales were diminishing. However, *Following the Equator* sold well in various editions at the end of the century. By 1900, the book had been circulated around the world.[66]

Financially, Twain was solvent again. Early in 1897, the *New York Herald* had seized upon a rumor that Samuel Clemens and his family was living in poverty in London and started a fund for them. Never remotely near poverty, the Clemens family could afford a fine residence, music lessons for Clara, and doctors for Livy and the youngest daughter, Jean. With the world speaking tour and the assistance of Henry Huddleston Rogers, Samuel Clemens, the man the world knew as Mark Twain, had cleared away all business debts. *Tom Sawyer Abroad* and *Tom Sawyer, Detective, and Other Stories* had been published by Harper and Brothers. *Joan of Arc* had been serialized in *Harper's* and the unsigned contribution was recognized. The book's publication in May 1896 had his name on it. He dedicated it to his daughter Susy.

On June 22, Twain provided an American press syndicate with his perspective on Queen Victoria's Diamond Jubilee. From his seat on the Strand, Twain observed the gala festivities that included a long procession representing the global reach of Britain's colonial possessions. The Clemens family spent the rest of the summer in Switzerland. At Weggis, on Lake Lucerne, Mark Twain wrote for nine hours a day. He dreamed of a Satanic character who visits the earth and sends reports to hell. "Letters to Satan" began the process of a long series of sketches, including "The Chronicles of Young Satan." This was to become Mark Twain's *The Mysterious Stranger: A Romance*, a book edited by Albert Bigelow Paine after Twain's death, which would appear in 1916.

"I would have as soon spent my life in Weggis as anywhere in the geography," Twain wrote in September 1897.[67] During his time at Weggis, Twain began several manuscripts that were never published in his lifetime. His readers would not see "Villagers 1840-3" in which he imagined life back in Hannibal, looking back at the Clemens family and the people of that town. Nor would they see a sketch featuring his brother Orion as one Oscar Carpenter. While his readers were enjoying *Tom Sawyer Abroad*, he also wrote "Tom Sawyer's Conspiracy," which went some ten chapters before drifting away. In this manuscript, Huckleberry Finn once again narrates the story, this time after the Civil War. Tom Sawyer and Jim are central characters. Briefly recapturing the vernacular language of Twain's famous characters, this effort, unfinished, is a novel that never was. The Tom Sawyer stories and this unfinished novel were the most obvious imaginative extensions of his famous trio of characters: Jim, Tom Sawyer, and Huckleberry Finn. By the end of the century they were identified internationally with children's literature and adolescent reading.

D. VIENNA

When the Clemens family reached Vienna in Fall 1897, a new phase of the creative life of Mark Twain began. Some critics have claimed that with *A Connecticut Yankee in King Arthur's Court* (1889) and *Puddn'head Wilson* (1894), Mark Twain's major phase ended. However, much interesting writing lay ahead. His readership also continued to expand.

In September 1897, Vienna learned of the visit of the Clemens family. Carl Dolmetsch tells us: "Bookshops quickly sold out their stocks."[68] Mark Twain would stay for twenty months in Vienna. Austrian news commented upon Twain regularly. The drawing room of the family's corner suite in the Metropole became a place for encounters with distinguished visitors.

Fin de siècle Vienna was a center of music, art, and architecture. It was the capital of the Austro-Hungarian Empire. In Vienna, the neurologist Sigmund Freud was developing his view of the human unconscious. The city's sophistication and artistic brightness mingled with the darkness of latent anti-Semitism and anti-Judaism. Mark Twain responded to this with a strong recognition of Jewish talent and his harshest criticism of anti-Semitism. In "Concerning the Jews," he argued that anti-Jewish sentiment in Vienna was founded in jealousy of Jewish economic success and intellectual ability. Twain, with this essay, served as a voice of conscience on ethnic and racial issues.

Vienna's Jews lived on the edge of social disruption. The so-called "Jewish question" simmered beneath the brilliant orchestral world. Vienna nurtured the talents of both Gustav Mahler, the Jewish director of the Vienna Court Opera, and the conservative Anton Bruckner, whose powerful compositions drew upon Richard Wagner's influence. The city welcomed Anton Dvorak and the young composer Arnold Schoenberg, whose twelve tone scale had yet to be heard. The orchestral life of Vienna also had its impact upon the Clemens family. Clara Clemens met pianist Ossip Gabrilowitsch, a handsome Russian Jew who was a friend of Gustav Mahler. Gabrilowitsch, a pupil of the renowned Theodor Lesechetizsky, was a conductor as well as a concert pianist. Ossip's courtship of Clara was broken off several times, but he would eventually marry her. In 1909, Twain told people that it would take him the rest of his life just to learn how to pronounce his new son-in-law's name.

While in Vienna, Twain and his family attended opera and concert performances. The American foreign minister Charlemagne Tower, an enthusiastic reader of Mark Twain, was among his visitors. On July 4, 1898, the ambassador held a party that Twain attended. He also hosted a gathering for two hundred American medical students who were attending the University of Vienna. Meanwhile, Clara continued her piano education and Jean studied Polish. Twain began referring to his family's time away as "our exile." He wrote in a letter to Thomas Bailey Aldrich: "I like Europe—I like it very much indeed—but I am two or three thousand years old sometimes & I don't like so much puddling around."[69]

Twain once again conceded his reservations about the German language, which is filled with compound words and in which the verb often appears at the end of a sentence. Speaking in German to an audience in Vienna in 1897, Twain said that he would like to reform the language. One of his proposals was that he would "move the verb so far forward that it could be discovered without a telescope."[70] Austrians appear to have been humored by Twain's comments. Twain entertained them at these public events but he also chose times of withdrawal from society to write. While viewed as a humorist, he was a satiric social critic with an acid pen. The "mysterious stranger" kept returning in his imagination and the fragment had now turned into a story set in Vienna. This character lived in sophisticated circles and had a hedonistic taste for pleasures. He represented the surfaces of a city in which authoritarianism affected politics and society and anti-Semitism was in the air. Twain's Satan says of Vienna that it is his favorite city. He claims that he was its patron saint in the early times and still has much influence there and is greatly respected. Twain would return to this manuscript several times with "Schoolhouse Hill" and "No. 44," exploring this mysterious stranger. Six chapters of Schoolhouse Hill brought Satan to St. Petersburg, where he became an admired friend of Huck and Tom. Hannibal was in awe of him. So too was Vienna, in Twain's later version.

The darkness of Mark Twain's writings was generally unfamiliar to his audience. "What Is Man?", a probing work of determinism, was not published until after Twain's death. However, the seriousness in his story *The Man Who Corrupted Hadleyburg* was soon on display. So too were several essays: "Stirring Times in Austria" and his sharply critical essays on Mary Baker Eddy and Christian Science. Critics like Carl Dolmetsch have suggested that the culture of Vienna may have affected his output. Indeed, there was in much of his work the inward turning quality among intellectuals that Carl Schorske has detected in fin de siècle Vienna. Twain's work of this period seems to have moved amid nihilism and the unconscious. *What is Man?* probed the mind and viewed the human as a machine. His stories moved in an impressionistic style. As Dolmetsch has said, there was "more than a cosmetic effect on his writing."[71] Contrary to Everett Emerson's view that the Vienna years "had little effect on how he wrote," it is clear that a number of factors—personal and cultural—moved Twain toward greater introspection during these years.

This is not the Twain that Austrians saw, however. Twain's dark musings were hidden from public view as the Clemens family arrived in London in May 1899. "We are still in exile," he wrote in a letter to I. Brunner on June 6. While in London, Twain worked in the offices of Chatto and Windus. There he wrote some of "Which Was the Dream?" Meanwhile, another rumor arose, which Twain quickly dispelled. The illness of a cousin, a London doctor, had been reported in the news as the possible death of Mark Twain. The editor of the *New York World* sent a reporter, Frank Marshall White, to determine if Twain was dying in poverty. In his *Autobiography*, Twain remembered that he told him: "The report of my illness grew out of his illness; the report of my death was an exaggeration." Twain's response was widely repeated and given various forms. It emerged as the legendary epigram: "reports of my death are greatly exaggerated."[72]

Such epigrams were a feature of Twain's ready contact with the public. Like today's "sound bites," they were taken up by enterprising reporters who filed them with their news bureaus for publication. The result was a wide dissemination of Mark Twain's humor and apocryphal stories from witty journalists. Through them, Mark Twain, the world traveler, was quite alive in many parts of the world, even long after his death, and so were the images of him as a family man. In Australia, the *Queensland Figaro* (February 28, 1931) wrote:

> One day, when Mark Twain was very busy writing in his study, his little daughter asked where Daddy was and was told she must be quiet and not disturb Daddy because he was upstairs writing an anecdote.

Not long after the doorbell rang and the little girl ran to answer it. The caller asked if Mr. Clemens were in, to which the little girl proudly replied: "Yes, sir, he's in, but you can't see him 'cause he's riding a nannygoat."[73]

E. CELEBRITY AND SOCIAL CRITIC

In 1900, Mark Twain was an international figure. Indeed, Twain was, in Daniel Boorstin's terms, "a person who is well-known for his well-knownness."[74] He was ubiquitous, ever-present amid the rise of advertising, new markets, and new forms of communication. Textual and visual technologies of the press rendered Twain heroic: he had triumphed over adversity and outrun financial disaster. He was the subject of human interest stories that validated for his audience the worthiness of their own personal struggles to be happy. Twain was associated with democracy, fighting and rising to its feet again. He was a text consumed by newspaper audiences, an image circulated and given visibility by news media throughout the world. Just as Twain had prompted laughter, now his endurance and tenacity promoted the notion of success in spite of hard times. Indeed, among common readers and American citizens, Mark Twain had become more memorable than many U.S. presidents. The artist Bill Nye had noticed this in 1895 when he wrote to Junius Brutus Pond:

> Tell Mark Twain that if he had not possessed the fatal gift of humor, he might now be President of the United States, and if I could have my way, he should have been anyhow. Mr. Depew told me that (James) Garfield admitted to him many years ago that he, Garfield, was naturally a humorist but had smothered the low, coarse impulse to be amusing in order that he might forward his political ambition. And what was the result? He went to his grave full of laudable puns while Mark Twain will live forever in the glad hearts of a billion people.[75]

Mark Twain was the subject of interviews, news features, comic blurbs, lithographs, drawings, and photographs. Americans saw in him a mirror of themselves. They insisted that they knew his cousin, or had known Twain in school. He was the Westerner, or miner, or the boy they once were. In 1900, Twain's life now was filled with interactions with well-meaning people who assumed acquaintance with him. Often, after speaking in public, Twain shook hands with people. He recalled:

> and the usual thing happened. It always happens. I shake hands with people who used to know my mother intimately in Arkansas, in New Jersey, in California, in Jericho- and I have to seem so glad and so happy to meet these persons who knew in this intimate way one who was so near and dear to me. And this is the kind of thing that turns one

into a polite liar and deceiver for mother was never in any one of those places.[76]

On one occasion, he was met by a young man who said that his mother had taught him in Elmira. The young man said, "you were most troublesome." Twain replied that "those were my last school days." By the time he first saw Elmira, he was already thirty-three years old. He surmised that the young man's mother must have been thinking of one of the Langdons. He told the young man he had never been in a school house in Elmira. However, he says of the young man, "he never heard anything I said [...] If a person thinks that he has known me at some time or other, all I require of him is that he shall consider it a distinction to have known me: and then, as a rule, I am perfectly willing to remember all about it and add some things that he has forgotten."[77]

The turn of the century audience constructed their ideas about Mark Twain in local communities. Mark Twain was news and he appeared in their newspapers in witty epigrams, the kind of filler that could be easily inserted between news articles. Visually, he was a readily identifiable image: a bushy mustache and rumpled hair, bright eyes and a sharp nose. Mark Twain was made available to the public as a commercially produced commodity. Printing technologies continued to make him visible internationally. Readers had read his stories and travel writings. Others had heard him lecture—or their parents had. When people assembled at social clubs or in literary reading circles, readings of Mark Twain's humorous stories were mixed in as part of the entertainment.

Twain looked beyond his temporary notoriety toward the prospects for something more enduring. In the last years of the nineteenth century, he anticipated a uniform edition of his works. Negotiations went on between Henry Harper, Frank Bliss, and Twain, who was represented by the business savvy of Henry H. Rogers. Harper and Brothers intended to develop that uniform edition. A deal was worked out with the Hartford company, so that the uniform edition could include such works as *The Innocents Abroad* and *Roughing It*, which were American Publishing Company properties.

There were hundreds of mentions of Mark Twain in newspapers of this period. Before the turn of the century, readers were often told of Mark Twain's origins, as in "Mark Twain in his Youth," published in the *Salt Lake Herald* (June 5, 1896). He was the subject of illustrations, as when the *San Francisco Call* placed a big drawing of Twain at the center of the page on October 24, 1897.[78] Mark Twain traveled in people's thoughts also. In 1901, the Union Pacific Overland Ltd. Pullman car had a fixed menu with a selection from *Roughing It* by Mark Twain on the menu.[79]

At the end of the century, Mark Twain struck a dissident stance against American involvement in the Philippines and fulminated against the world's social ills. Louis J. Budd points to the "social commitment" of

Mark Twain's final years, in which he operated as a *de facto* statesman. As a social critic, he opposed "privilege, injustice, vested power, political pretense and economic exploitation," observes Bernard De Voto. Twain's writing had become, as Peter Messent observes, "a series of negotiations between national and international spaces."[80] Fred Kaplan and others paint a picture of Twain as disaffected, cynical about human nature and public affairs. However, Twain appears to have wavered between such depressive musings and keen social analysis. As James Cox has pointed out, when Twain was complaining bitterly about humanity in his last years he "was never more loved and acknowledged as the very epitome of his nation's spirit."[81] In contrast, some letters to Twain show that there were readers who reacted negatively to Twain's stand on imperialism. Whereas Walt Whitman, in his last years, launched forth filament like the noiseless patient spider of one of his poems and invited each self into intimacy with the universe as a seeker, Twain launched dissent.

Readers responded in various ways to Mark Twain the social critic, as his critiques appeared in the form of essays. Sharp criticisms greeted Mark Twain's *North American Review* article, "To the Person Sitting in Darkness." He was called traitorous in some editorials, or in letters signed from "students."[82] A.S. Buchanan, of Darlington, Indiana wrote that Twain's essay was

> an astonishing production from one who claims to be sensible. Truly I had always thought you to be a christian! Please excuse seeming impertinence but for the sake of us poor Hoosiers who have been kept busy making apologies for you of late tell us. Were you ever adjudged insane? [83]

However, Twain also had his enthusiastic supporters, who recognized his call for American integrity. William Augustus Crofutt wrote on behalf of the Anti-Imperialist League in Washington, DC, on February 5, 1901:

> My household is in a state of extreme jubilation and warm satisfaction, for we have this moment risen from the round table after reading aloud your analysis in the North American of the case of Persons Sitting in Darkness. The four ladies voted to help me thank you for what they think will do an immense amount of good. [84]

From Peoria, Illinois came Clayton Ewing's letter, on February 23rd:

> I have just read in "The Public" certain extracts from your article "The person Sitting in darkness" written by you for the February North American Review. I think I can realize something of the criticism that may come to you directly or indirectly as a result of your article.
>
> Ever since boyhood—when your writings captivated me—I have regarded you as my favorite humorist. And my regard for you has grown steadily as I have become more familiar with your works. If anything I say may be any encouragement to you or serve counteract in any degree any of the jibes or criticisms, I will gladly say your article

touched my heart deeply and raised you in my estimation even higher than ever before. Men with sufficient moral courage to speak their convictions are not so numerous. Your article has all the marks of genius, and, aside from its humor, is a scathing arraignment of sham and hypocrisy.

The next paragraph of Ewing's letter indicates that he has read widely in Twain's works. A railroad clerk, at age twenty-four he wrote clearly and articulately, punctuating his letter appropriately, and expressing his ardent commitment to the "single tax" and "the principles of the Declaration of Independence."[85]

Gilbert A. Tracy of Putnam, Connecticut, on February 27, wrote:

I am very glad you wrote and published that article in N.A. Review. It's the truth: and truth hurts. The carping censorious editors pecking at you are like a flock of jackdaws pecking at the great American eagle. A man of your comprehensive view need have no fears. Stand by the courage of your convictions.[86]

There was praise from Edwin Brenholtz in Turnersville, Texas, who wrote:

Praise to the Eternal! A voice has been found. Praise that a man whose honesty no man doubts; who possesses the love and admiration of his fellow countrymen, who has stood face to face with truth, and heard her words, has dared to repeat the message in tones which encircle the earth, and which will go ringing down through the ages.[87]

Twain's publications of the 1890s and the early years of the twentieth century likewise received comment in the British press. William Archer's review of "The Man Who Corrupted Hadleyburg" appeared in the London *Morning Leader* on September 22. The November issue of the *Critic* called his story "a fable designed to drive home an ethical lesson." The *Academy* on September 29 said "Mark Twain censor and critic is rapidly taking the place of Mark Twain, fun maker." *Blackwood's* wrote: "He is too fond of being didactic, of pointing morals, of drawing lessons." *Book Buyer* noted "the more serious papers that have come from his pen in recent years [...] Mark Twain's humor has grown more quiet with the passing of the years, but more subtle as well, more philosophical, with a substratum of wisdom that gives a higher value [...]"[88]

The ethical aspect of Twain's comedy had been present from the time of his earliest books. Yet, the public barely knew at this time the acerbic social critic and the introspective determinist. The ever popular Twain was engaged in writing social justice essays that were later banished to obscurity by A.B. Paine and Clara Clemens, who wished to preserve his public image as a kindly gentleman. This affected how Twain was viewed by the public and how he was portrayed by biographers and critics who wrote about him shortly after his death. More recent biographers, however, note that in December 1898 Twain was reading in the psychology of J. F. Herbart that the individual consists of multiple selves. Sometime between April to June 1899, Twain wrote: "Man's proudest possession- his mind- is a mere machine [...] so wholly independent of him that it will not even take a suggestion from him, let alone a command."[89]

In February 1901, Twain's essay "To the Person Sitting in Darkness," appeared in the *North American Review*. This social satire questioned the work of missionaries in the interest of "Progress and Civilization." The *New York Times* criticized the "austere moralist." However, Twain, ignoring such criticism, wrote more socio-political articles; "To My Missionary Critics," "A Defense of General Funston," and "The Czar's Soliloquy," appeared in the *North American Review*. There was also "King Leopold's Soliloquy," which only appeared as a pamphlet, and the unpublished "The War Prayer," which only appeared many years later. For George B. Harvey, who had purchased the *North American Review* in 1899, this style of essay from Mark Twain seemed too inflammatory for print. At this time, Twain also wrote "The Great Dark," which he never completed. He wrote against the practice of lynching in "The United States of Lyncherdom," an essay that would not be published until 1923. "What Is Man?" was published privately. "Which Was the Dream?" was not published in his lifetime. To show humanity's "miniscule place in the vastness of the universe," he considered a story about microbes and microscopes.

Most readers at the turn of the century did not view Mark Twain as a social critic. In 1898, Mark Twain had initially fully supported America's entry into the Spanish-American War. He believed that the United States was liberating Cuba from an oppressor. Joseph Twichell's son had enlisted in the army and he wrote to his friend: "For this is the worthiest one that was ever fought, so far as my knowledge goes. It is a worthy thing to fight for one's own freedom: it is another sight finer to fight for another man's. And I think this is the first time it has been done."[90] With the explosion of the battleship Maine, from unknown causes, the United States entered a war with Spain. Theodore Roosevelt's "rough-riders" engaged their enemy in San Juan Harbor. Commodore Perry's warships forced Spain to turn back. With the signing of the Treaty of Paris on December 10, Spain left Cuba and America seized Puerto Rico. In the Pacific, U.S. territories were made of the Philippines and Guam. Of this, Mark Twain said: "When the United States sent word to Spain that the Cuban atrocities must end she occupied the highest moral position ever taken by a nation since the Almighty made the earth. But when she snatched the Philippines, she stained the flag."[91]

Some American readers objected to this side of Twain, who had become an image of America to the world. Twain questioned what he began to view as excesses of colonialism. He respected Britain despite its colonialism and he upheld his hopes for America despite his disagreements with its actions in the Philippines. However, he declared himself to be an anti-imperialist. "To the Person Sitting in Darkness," as Fred Kaplan notes, ironically addressed non-Christian natives to say that the "forces of civilization" were doing wonderful things for them.[92] Theodore Roosevelt expressed anger at Twain's writing about American aggression in the Philippines. If Roosevelt had seen Mark Twain's opinions in his notebooks and personal letters, he might have been angrier. To Joseph Twichell, Twain wrote that Roosevelt was "All pow-wow, all bluster, all gas." Twain wrote in another letter: "Theodore the man is sane; in fairness we ought to keep in mind that Theodore, as statesman and politician is insane and irresponsible."[93] In his notebooks he wrote:

> I think he is distinctly and definitely the representative American gentleman of his day. Roosevelt is the whole argument for and against in his own person. He represents what the American gentlemen ought not to be, and does it as clearly, intelligibly, and exhaustively as he represents what the American gentleman is. We are by long odds the most ill-mannered nation, civilized or savage, that exists on the planet today, and our President stands for us like a colossal monument visible from all the ends of the earth.[94]

When the *North American Review* appeared in February, with Twain's article on missionaries, Twain received letters from across the United States, Canada, England, and Australia. He marked favorable letters with + or # says Hamlin Hill. Negative ones were marked with a cross or circle or "against." Hamlin says that "roughly" fifty letters survive. Of these "almost all were enthusiastically favorable."[95]

Twain's audience learned in their newspapers that Twain had experienced another personal crisis in 1904: the loss of his wife, Livy. Early that year, he brought his wife to Europe, hoping that a Mediterranean climate would be helpful to her. Olivia Clemens passed away on Sunday, June 5, 1904, while in Florence, Italy. Her funeral was July 14 in Elmira, in the same room of the family house in which she and Samuel Clemens had been married. The newspapers took account of Twain's loss. In the *Tacoma Times* (September 6, 1904) one reads that George Gregory Smith, a wealthy scientist recently returned from Florence where he had spent time with the Clemens family, claims "the cheeriness" of his disposition despite his wife's death. The reality, in private, was quite different. With Livy gone, Mark Twain was adrift emotionally. He returned to New York and was assisted by his daughter Clara and his new literary scribe, Albert Bigelow Paine. The *Pullman Herald* of Washington State wrote on Twain's *Autobiography* (December 29, 1906): "Twain is one of the few who can smile when everything goes dead wrong and can keep plugging away." The newspaper noted his period of near-bankruptcy and wrote: "Since that time he has worked harder probably than he ever did before and kept on smiling."[96] Nothing was said by the newspaper about his loss of the woman who was the love of his life.

There appears to be a distance between Twain's personal reality and public perception at this time. On October 9, 1905, Twain wrote to Frederick A. Dunecka of the *New York World* to, in effect, syndicate his responses to newspapers. One reader, Reverend L.M. Powers, offered to send Twain expensive cigars. Twain wrote back (November 9, 1905) that he preferred cheap ones.[97] He remained busy, attending a White House dinner party in November 1905 and expressing fierce opposition to the African enterprise of King Leopold of Belgium. He spoke at a New York Press Club dinner in memory of Charles Dickens on February 8, 1906, for Dickens's birthday. Between November 10, 1905, and April 11, 1906, he spoke on at least twenty-five occasions.[98] On March 15, 1906, a restless crowd became a problem at the doors of the Majestic Theater, where Mark Twain was set to lecture. Members of the West Side Y.M.C.A. "had a close resemblance to a football match" as police held them back from entering.[99] Twain carried on as a public figure despite his personal losses, which have been amply documented by critics and his biographers. Clearly, he could still be flamboyant and self-promotional. At a December 1906 congressional hearing on copyright, Twain startled Congress with his white suit as he sat in the legislative chambers.[100]

The Innocents Abroad was still being widely read at this time. Notions of vicarious travel and discovery appear to have provided an appeal for Len G. Westland of London, Ontario, in Canada who, on September 4, 1905, commented in a letter to Twain on this vicarious travel afforded by his works:

> I feel that I have no right to intrude into your life, but ever since the days when I read "Tom Sawyer" "Inocense Abroad," "Roughing It," New Pilgrims Progress and A Yankee at King Arthurs Court down to the present time, when I am following the Equator with you I have wanted to thank you for the pleasure and instruction you have given me. I really think the knowledge to be gained from the above works is invaluable to one who has not had the advantages of treaval.[101]

Readers continued to be emotionally affected by Twain's stories. Lillian R. Beardsley of Connecticut was saddened by "A Horse's Tale" in *Harper's* (August–September 1906), in which Soldiers Boy, a former U.S. cavalry horse, is stolen from its orphan owner Cathy Allison in Spain. Rushing to save the horse during a bull fight, both she and the horse are gored by a bull. "Please don't write any more such heart-breaking stories," Beardsley wrote. Twain wrote back: "I know it is a pity to wring the poor human heart & it grieves me, to do it; but it is the only way to move some people to reflect. "The Horse's Tale" has a righteous purpose. It was not written for publication here, but in Spain . . . . "[102]

That same year, another reader much moved by Twain was thirty-five-year-old Cally Ryland of Richmond, whose father was a book store owner and a Confederate veteran. She wrote to Twain, December 13, 1906, calling him "the greatest man on earth": "Ever since I read, in my childhood, my first story from your pen, it has been the great desire of my life to meet Mark Twain." Twain replied:

> I am thankful to say that such letters as yours do come- as you have divined—with a happy frequency. They refresh my life, they give it value; like yours, they are always welcome, and I am grateful for them.[103]

The audience of Mark Twain continued to be fostered by a flurry of press items. These continued throughout the year. The *Washington Times* featured a story about the author meeting Miss Quick, a young girl, at the docks. In a photograph, Twain appears under a broad brim bowler hat. Miss Quick also wears a hat, a white blouse with a ribbon pinned to the left. She is the daughter of Mrs. E.G. Quick of 63 Eighth Avenue in Brooklyn. "Her hair is hazel, her eyes blue [...]" "I'm eleven going on twelve," she told Twain.[104] The *Washington Times* (October 6, 1907) wrote under a large illustration of him, "One Day in the Life of the King of Humorists." The article noted Twain's summer home in Tuxedo Park, New York, near the railroad. The caption read, "A journey on the Erie is like preparing for the hereafter." The Sunday edition of the *New York Tribune* of October 27 offered a large drawing of Mark Twain on page one. In New Mexico, under an ad that read "Railroad Men Attention!" the *Tumcari News* (November 2, 1907) announced that "The Autobiography of Mark Twain, the greatest literary sensation of the century begins exclusive publication in the illustrated magazine of the *Sunday News Times*." Clearly, they must have thought the railroad men might have been interested. For Thanksgiving, the cover of the Sunday magazine of the *New York Tribune* featured a drawing of a Pilgrim with a musket alongside a turkey. It carried a selection from Mark Twain's *Autobiography*.[105]

On April 26, 1908, Twain told Eden Phillips that he wished he had energy enough to return to "one of two" of his book projects and write but he recognized that "this is a dream and won't ever come true."[106] In 1908 he abandoned "Chronicles of Young Satan" and a novel that had begun to emerge: "No. 44, The Mysterious Stranger." In the story, a young boy with extraordinary powers is in a medieval village in Austria. He becomes friends with the narrator, August Feldner, and lets him know all the secrets of his dream self. However, Twain never finished the story.

Twain's readers would have to wait one hundred years for his final great work: his autobiography. Twain dictated his memories to Albert Bigelow Paine and Josephine Hobby. He wrote: "in this frank way I am a dead person speaking from the grave [...]" Paine conscientiously developed the autobiography, portions of which appeared in editions prior to the popular recent volumes from the MTP at the University of California.[107]

The public dimensions of Mark Twain in the final decade of the nineteenth century and the first decade of the twentieth century were indicated by public polls. In 1893, in a poll by the *Critic*, Mark Twain was fifteenth among the runners-up in a survey of favorite writers. He was preceded by Nathaniel Hawthorne, William Dean Howells, Harriet Beecher Stowe, and Lew Wallace (the Civil War general who wrote *Ben Hur*). Henry James, Edgar Allan Poe, and Herman Melville were not on this list. In *Literature*, in February 1899, the magazine's editor John Kendrick Bangs published the results of a poll that had been taken of the magazine's readers. Bangs was a friend of Twain and imitated his lecture style. He asked: "What ten authors do the readers of *Literature* consider to be the most worthy to become charter members of the American Academy?" William Dean Howells, John Fiske, and Mark Twain received the most votes. There were 84 for Howells, 82 for Fiske, and 80 for Mark Twain. The focus was on contemporary, living writers. The list was reprinted by the *Dial*. It is curious that Thomas Bailey Aldrich (74) and Frank Stockton (59) received more votes than Henry James (56).

A Hall of Fame of American writers was instituted in New York in 1900, with a New York University office at Morningside Heights. Twain become part of the select group in 1920, ten years after his death. (Whitman did not get there until 1930. Emily Dickinson and Herman Melville languished among the electors. They were still not recognized as of 1950.) Twain and Howells were elected to the American Academy of Arts and Letters.[108]

NOTES

1. Thomas M. Baker has recognized the trans-Atlantic context in which celebrity emerged in the nineteenth century. See Blake, *Walt Whitman and the Culture of American Celebrity*. New Haven: Yale University Press, 2006. p. 29. Twain entered this international context with his books and with his frequent trips to England and the European continent.

2. Mark Twain Letter to Mrs. Mary Fairbanks, quoted by Fred Kaplan, *The Singular Mark Twain*. Garden City: Doubleday, 2003. p. 328.

3. G.W. Smalley, Letter to Mark Twain, December 9, 1873, from Hyde Park Square West, London. MTP, UCCL 00999; *Mark Twain Letters*, Mark Twain, Letter to Jane Clemens and Pamela Moffett, November 6, 1872.

4. *Mark Twain Letters*. Fred Kaplan concludes that Twain has "gotten little sense of his British readership" in *The Singular Mark Twain*, p. 152, 282. He suggests that Twain thought little about British readers who thought his humor unsophisticated and who equated this with being "idiosyncratically American," p. 286. Justin Kaplan points out that "his encounter with the English was of critical importance" in *Mr. Clemens and Mr. Twain*. New York: Simon and Schuster, 1966. p. 152.

5. Mark Twain, *Following the Equator: A Journey around the World*, 130. *Mark Twain Letters*, Vol. V, 183–84, 196, quoted by Fred Kaplan, *The Singular Mark Twain*, pp. 284–85.

6. Mark Twain preface to *The Innocents Abroad*, 1872. See also *Mark Twain Letters*, Vol. V.

7. Mark Twain, Letter to Olivia Clemens, September 28, 1872. This comment appears as a caption in Peter Messent, "'Not an Alien but at Home': Mark Twain in London," in *Cosmopolitan Twain*, ed. Ann M. Ryan and Joseph B. McCullough, Columbia: University of Missouri Press, 2008, p. 187. It also appears in Ron Powers, *Mark Twain: A Life*. New York: The Free Press, 2006.

8. Justin Kaplan, *Mr. Clemens and Mr. Twain*, 152–53. Kaplan suggested that England provided Twain with a "baseline" by which he could measure his discontent with his own country. p. 154.

9. Mark Twain, *Following the Equator*, p. 130–31.

10. Katie L. Corbett, Letter to Mark Twain, Manchester, England. MTP, University of California. Rasmussen, 131–132.

11. Mark Twain Letter to Charles Webster, Winter 1886. MTP, University of California.

12. *A Connecticut Yankee in King Arthur's Court*, see pp.1–3.

13. Louis J. Budd, *Our Mark Twain: The Making of His Public Personality*. Philadelphia: University of Pennsylvania Press, 1983. p. 118.

14. Sales figures are noted by Ron Powers in *Mark Twain: A Life*. pp. 529–30.

15. William Algie, Letter to Mark Twain, January 1890. Alton, Ontario. MTP, University of California. Rasmussen, *Dear Mark Twain*, 144.

16. Mark Twain, Letter to W.D. Howells, *Letters of Mark Twain*, ed. A.B. Paine, Vol. 2: p. 677.

17. Mark Twain speech, December 12, 1900, Grand Ballroom, Waldorf Astoria, New York. The essays in Ann M. Ryan and Stephen McCullough's *Cosmopolitan Twain* (University of Missouri Press, 2008) point out the urban identity of Twain, who lived in New York longer than he lived in Hannibal.

18. Edith Draper, Letter to Mark Twain. Rasmussen notes that the Chatto and Windus editions of Mark Twain sold for two shillings (or fifty cents in the United States), which was more than half her husband's daily salary. MTP, University of California. See Rasmussen, 240–241.

19. Twain's letter to George Bernard Shaw is noted in the *Autobiography*, p. 697. On July 3, 1907, August Rodin was a guest for Mrs. Charlotte Shaw later that day. Morris, in *News from Nowhere*, wrote of a future utopia.

20. Ibid.

21. Neville Cardus, Reader's Experience Database (RED 5279).

22. Christopher Grieve, Reader's Experience Database (RED 8959).

23. V.S. Pritchett, *A Car at the Door: An Autobiography, Early Years*. London, 1968. Reader's Experience Database, (RED 3381) places this writing as written in between December 16, 1910–January 1, 1918.

24. Edmund Blunden, Royal Sussex Regiment. Battalion Headquarters. Mailly. Reader's Experience Database (RED 29768.)

25. Reginald H. Kiernan, *Little Brother Goes Soldiering*. London, 1930. Reginald Kiernan was at Catterick Camp in Yorkshire (RED 29768, 32062).

26. Walter Besant, "My Favorite Novel and His Best Book," *Huck Finn Among the Critics*, ed. M. Thomas Inge. Frederick, MD.: University Press, pp. 43–45.

27. Walter Besant, p. 46.

28. Walter Besant, p. 52. Chatto and Windus were the British publishers of the book that Besant read. The first British edition preceded the American edition by a few weeks. Andrew Lang saw *Huckleberry Finn* as the masterpiece that American critics were overlooking as they sought their great novel. *American Illustrated News of the World*, February 4, 1891. 222. rpt. *Mark Twain: Selected Criticism*, ed. Arthur L. Scott, Dallas: Southern Methodist University Press, 1955. pp. 38–40.

29. Jonathan Rose, *The Intellectual Life of the British Working Class*. New Haven: Yale University Press, 2001.

30. Olaf Halvorsen, Letter to Mark Twain, January 1890, Norway. MTP, University of California. Rasmussen, 146.

31. Tauchnitz became the principal publisher of British and American books in Europe based upon the recognition of intellectual property in an 1846 Anglo-German treaty. Readers on the continent who could read English often read Twain in Tauchnitz authorized editions.

32. Ronald Jenn, "From American Frontier to European Borders," *Book History* 9, 235–60. p. 238.

33. Ibid, 239.

34. Ibid, 240

35. Ibid, 242.

36. Ibid.

37. *A Tramp Abroad*, p. 31. *Joan of Arc* was serialized in *Harper's*. The unsigned contribution was recognized as Twain's writing. The book publication on May 1, 1896 would have his name on it. Twain's writing on Joan of Arc, while dear to him, was an unexpected topic for his audience. Albert Stone Jr. has recognized how Twain's audience had to adjust to topics like Joan of Arc. "For a professional writer this choice of theme sometimes ran counter to the expectations of Twain's audience." p. 71.

38. Lina Wright Berle, Letter to Mark Twain, 1908, Boscawen, New Hampshire. MTP, University of California. Rasmussen, 255.

39. The appendix for *A Tramp Abroad* includes comments on the German language. See also *Mark Twain's Notebooks*, University of California Press. In Germany, in 1891–1892, his daughter Clara's music teachers encouraged the thought that she might become a concert pianist. Twain, aware of the issues of performing onstage, facing negative reviews, and courting the public was not keen on the idea of this life for his daughter. In Bad Nauheim, Germany, in a hotel dining room, Mark Twain met Oscar Wilde. Livy recalled the large carnation in Wilde's jacket lapel.

40. Mark Twain, *Tom Sawyer Abroad*, ed. Shelley Fisher Fishkin. New York and Oxford: Oxford, 1996.

41. Martyn Lyons, p. 356; Zeehan and Dundas, Australia (April 29, 1895): 2.

42. *Mercury*, Tasmania, Australia (August 27, 1895): 3.

43. *Australian Town and Country Journal*, NSW (September 28, 1895): 1.

44. Ibid.

45. *Advertiser*, Adelaide SA (September 1895): 5.

46. *Windsor and Richmond Gazette* (October 5, 1895): 5.

47. 'E.E.T.' Letter to the Editor, *Windsor and Richmond Gazette* (October 18, 1895): 11.

48. Martyn Lyons and Jay Arnold, *History of the Book in Australia*, University of Queensland Press, xvi.

49. Martyn Lyons pp.7–9.

50. Mark Twain, *Following the Equator*, p. 167.

51. Mark Twain Letter to Charles Casey, May 15, 1876, Mark Twain Papers, University of California, Berkeley.

52. Mark Twain, *Following the Equator*, p. 245–52.

53. Mark Twain, *Following the Equator*, p. 242.

54. Mark Twain, *Following the Equator*, p. 244.

55. J. Gavan Reilly, Letter to Mark Twain, October 20, 1895, Creswick, New York. MTP, University of California. Rasmussen, 167.

56. Mark Twain, *Following the Equator*, p. 29. Writing in 1897, Mark Twain reviewed his recent world travels. He thought of calling the book "Round the World," for indeed he had circumnavigated the globe. The book became *Following the Equator: A Journey around the World*. For this, he incorporated regional history from other authors. He wrote on April 13, 1897: "finished my book today." Then he picked it back up and wrote on May 18: "finished the book again." See *Mark Twain's Notebooks*, p. 327. The American Publishing Company placed an illustration of an elephant on the cover.

Inside the covers were two hundred more illustrations. Chatto and Windus issued the book as *More Tramps Abroad.*

57. Letter to Rudyard Kipling. See Charles Neider ed., Mark Twain, *Autobiography,* p. 234.

58. Priya Joshi, *In Another County: Colonialism, Culture and the English Novel in India* (2002), pp. 45, 81–92.

59. Henry Schwartz, *Modern Language Quarterly* (March 2005): 136–42.

60. Mark Twain, *Autobiography,* p. 191.

61. "Mark Twain On Tour in Cape Town," *Cape Times,* South Africa. See, *Mark Twain: The Complete Interviews* ed. Gary Scharnhorst, Tuscaloosa: University of Alabama Press, p. 313.

62. *Mark Twain-Howells Letters: The Correspondence of Samuel L. Clemens and William Dean Howells, 1872–1910,* Vol. II, p. 664.

63. *Mark Twain's Notebooks,* p. 327.

64. Louise Davis Chubbuck, Letter to Mark Twain. Winter 1907–1908, Harrisburg, Pennsylvania. MTP, University of California. Rasmussen, 248–249.

65. Twain announced the completion of his book in a letter to William Dean Howells.

66. See Dennis Welland for a discussion of Twain's personal and business relationship with Andrew Chatto whose firm put "1,150,000 copies into English hands" and made Twain some 20,500 pounds. Dennis Welland, *Mark Twain in England.* London: Chatto and Windus, 1978.

67. *Mark Twain's Notebooks,* 338; Ron Powers, Mark Twain, 589.

68. Carl Dolmetsch, *Our Famous Guest: Mark Twain in Vienna.* Athens and London: University of Georgia Press, 1992. p. 1. Dolmetsch adds that "until recently (1992), Twain's late years and the works of his old age were of less interest to both scholars and the general reader than were his more colorful, adventurous early years and the popular works of his major phase." p. 12–13. Dolmetsch argues that culture in Vienna affected Twain's outlook: nihilism, hedonism, and "impressionistic" style. R. Kent Rasmussen in *Dear Mark Twain* offers a note and illustrations from a Viennese girl, Elsa Hinterleitner, p. 169–70.

69. Mark Twain, Letter to Thomas Bailey Aldrich, June 29, 1898.MTP, University of California.

70. *New York Times* (November 27, 1897).

71. Carl Dolmetsch, p. 14; Carl Schorske, *Fin de Siecle Vienna: Politics and Culture.* New York: Vintage, 1981.

72. Twain sent a cable from London upon hearing of a false obituary in the *New York Journal.* His phrase has been adapted in a variety of ways.

73. *Queensland Figaro,* Brisbane, Australia, February 28, 1931. p. 16.

74. Daniel J. Boorstin, *The Image: A Guide to Pseudo-Events in America* (1962), rpt. New York: Vintage, 1992. Eric Eisner, in *Nineteenth-Century Poetry and Literary Celebrity* (Palgrave, 2009) observes: "The celebrity, that is, emerges over the course of the nineteenth century as a new social category, a new kind of public person." p. 3.

75. Mark Twain, Letter to Junius Brutus Pond. May 23, 1895. See Edward L. Tucker, "A New Letter by Bill Nye," *American Quarterly* (ANQ) 17.1 (Winter 2004): 43.

76. Mark Twain, *Autobiography,* p. 309.

77. Mark Twain, *Autobiography,* p. 310. David Haven Blake writes, "Fans may feel that they 'know' a star, but they almost always comprehend that relation exists outside any social context." *Walt Whitman and the Culture of Celebrity,* New Haven: Yale University Press, 2006. p. 168.

78. *Salt Lake Herald* (June 5, 1896), p. 16; *San Francisco Call* (October 24, 1897): 1.

79. New York Public Library, Frank E. Buitolf Menu Collection. During this time, Twain spoke at several public dinners in New York City and was a much in demand after dinner speaker. At Delmonico's he was evidently fed well before he spoke on "As It Strikes Me," at the Sixth Annual Dinner of British Schools and Universities Club. Delmonico's menu for November 4, 1901 included lobster bisque for an appetizer.

Entrees included Saddle of Mutton, English Style, Brussels Sprouts with chestnuts, mushrooms sauté on toast, and sherbet with kirsch. Or, one might have fish: Bass with white wine, cucumbers, laurette potatoes and French peas. A third option was Redhead Duck, Hominy and Jelly, and a Lettuce salad. For dessert there was "Fancy Ice Cream," assorted cakes, cheeses, and coffee.

80. Louis J. Budd, *Our Mark Twain*, p. 165. Bernard De Voto, MCV 25; Peter Messent, *Mark Twain Annual*, Vol. 9 (2011): 54. Peter Messent, *Cambridge Introduction to Mark Twain*, Cambridge: Cambridge University Press, 2007, p. 116. See also Louis J. Budd, *Mark Twain: Social Critic* (1950) and Bernard De Voto, *Mark Twain's America* (1932).

81. Quoted in Fred Kaplan, *The Singular Mark Twain*, New York: Anchor, Doubleday, 2003, p. 601. See James Cox, *The Fate of Humor*, Princeton: Princeton University Press, 1966.

82. See R. Kent Rasmussen, *Dear Mark Twain*, p. 191.

83. A.S. Buchanan, Letter to Mark Twain, March 26, 1901. Darlington, Indiana. MTP, University of California, 190–191.

84. William Augustus Crofott, Letter to Mark Twain, February 5, 1901. MTP, University of California. Rasmussen, 183.

85. Clayton Ewing, Letter to Mark Twain, February 23, 1901. MTP, University of California. Rasmussen, 185–186.

86. Gilbert A. Tracy, Letter to Mark Twain, February 27, 1901. Putnam, Connecticut. MTP, University of California.

87. Edwin Brenholtz, Letter to Mark Twain, March 5, 1901, Turnersville, Tennessee. MTP, University of California. Rasmussen, 188.

88. William Archer, *London Morning Leader* (September 22), *Academy* (September 29), *Critic* (November 1901) appears in *Contemporary Reviews*, p. 504, *Blackwoods* Vol. 55, No. 339, Arthur Hoeber, *The Book Buyer* (1901) Vol. 20, p. 120. See *Contemporary Reviews*, ed. Louis J. Budd, Cambridge: Cambridge University Press, 1999.

89. Mark Twain is quoted by Justin Kaplan, *Mr. Clemens and Mr. Twain*, New York: Simon and Schuster, 1966. p. 340.

90. Mark Twain, Letter to Joseph Twichell, June 17, 1898. MTP, University of California.

91. Albert Bigelow Paine, *Mark Twain: A Biography*, Vol. 2, Part 2, New York: Harper's 1912, p. 99. Edgar Lee Masters, *Mark Twain: A Portrait*, New York: Charles Scribners and Sons, 1938. p. 218.

92. Fred Kaplan, *The Singular Mark Twain*. pp. 518–19, 527–28.

93. Mark Twain, Letter to Joseph Twichell, 1905. *Mark Twain Letters*, Vol. II, University of California Press, p. 766. 98.

94. Bernard De Voto, *Mark Twain in Eruption*, p. 33.

95. Hamlin Hill, *Mark Twain: God's Fool*, Chicago: University of Chicago Press, 1973. pp. 24–25.

96. *Pullman Herald* (December 29, 1906): 1–2.

97. Mark Twain's letter to Frederick Duneka is cited in Charles Neider, pp. 296–97. The letter to Rev. L.M. Powers is cited by Charles Neider, p. 299.

98. Mark Twain, *Autobiography*, p. 546.

99. Mark Twain, *Autobiography*, p. 409–10.

100. Washington, DC, in December 1906. News accounts covered this on December 8.

101. Len G. Westland, Letter to Mark Twain, September 4, 1905. MTP, University of California, Berkeley. See Rasmussen, 218. See the letters that R. Kent Rasmussen has collected in *Dear Mark Twain* (2013).

102. Lillian R. Beardsley, Letter to Mark Twain, August 25, 1906. MTP, University of California. Rasmussen, 231.

103. Cally Ryland, Letter to Mark Twain, December 13, 1906. MTP, University of California. Rasmussen, 237–238.

104. "Mark Twain, Home, Flirts with Girl Going on Twelve," *Washington Times* (July 23, 1907). "Little Miss Quick Amuses Humorist," *New York Tribune* (July 23, 1907).

105. "One Day in the Life of the King of Humorists," *Washington Times. New York Tribune* (October 27, 1907): 1. "Railroad Men Attention!" *Tumcari News* (November 2, 1907). *New York Tribune* (November 1907).

106. Mark Twain, Letter to Eden Phillips (April 26, 1908). MTP, University of California.

107. See Bernard De Voto, *Mark Twain in Eruption* (New York: Harper's, 1940) p. 201. Twain's final years included his dictations of his *Autobiography*. He notes its spontaneous manner: "Finally in Florence, in 1904, I hit upon the right way to do an Autobiography: Start it at no particular time in your life; wander at your free will over all your life; talk only about the thing which interests you for the moment; drop it at the moment its interest threatens to pale; and turn your talk upon the new and more interesting thing that has intruded itself into your mind meantime." Preface, *Autobiography* Vol. I, Paine, p. 193.

108. American Academy of Arts and Letters. Columbia University, New York. Offices are currently at the Miller Theatre in Washington Heights.

NINE

Mark Twain's Audience and his Afterlife

When Twain died in 1910, newspapers in every corner of the United States and around the world paid their respects with tribute articles. The uniform edition of Mark Twain's works, or Author's National Edition, was promoted by *Harper's*. A sixteen-page publicity flyer was circulated. The three-volume biography by Albert Bigelow Paine (1912) cast a comfortable and interesting Twain before the public, leaving out much of the sharp satire and irascibility, the personal issues of family struggle, pessimism, and depression, and numerous other details. The portrait of a genial, fully alive, imaginative writer emerged, the image of a family-centered man, with affection for people and a desire for riches. Reviewers cast Twain as an "epic of the soil, the history of a century, the growth of a nation and the characterization of most of the great men of thought and action of that time."[1]

There were numerous tributes in newspapers. For example, on April 22, 1910, the *Tacoma Times* in the state of Washington provided a tribute to Mark Twain, announcing his death under a large drawing of the author. This was jammed on a busy page between "Wezler Returns Tonight," "26 Bodies Found in Mine," and a call to recount ballots in a recent election. The *Citizen* of Berea, Kentucky, on April 28, 1910, offered its tribute with a drawing in the top left column: "Life of Mark Twain, The Great American Humorist." It gave its readers a short biography, with "Kentucky Gleanings." This was one of the several places across the country, Hartford, Elmira, St. Louis and Hannibal, and San Francisco, that claimed Mark Twain as its own.[2]

The image and works of Mark Twain had now entered a new era. The twentieth century cast lights into the night sky and automobiles crossed distances. On the sides of buildings commercial advertisements appeared. Printed ads appeared in books and throughout periodicals. They intersected with news, illustrations, and stories and became a part of discourse. Advertising agencies emerged, selling ad space in magazines, newspapers, and on buildings and in public areas. Commercial technique became an aspect of cultural discourse and Mark Twain became an image for advertising. "Who Will Succeed Mark Twain?" asked James L. Ford in the *New York Tribune*, November 13, 1910. Two years later, the *Day Book* in Chicago noted "Twain's Fun":

> Mark Twain's spontaneous fun was irresistible. When a joke of his had fallen and had been received in silence by his audience, he remarked, "A crowd like that can make a good deal of silence when they combine." It was Twain who said, "reader, suppose you were an idiot. And suppose you were a member of Congress. But I repeat myself." [3]

Between 1910 and 1920, Twain is visible everywhere. In popular terms, he clearly had not died. Mark Twain's readership was considered in a *San Francisco Call* book review by Porter Garnett. His "Literary Notes and Comments" (October 20, 1912) reviews *The Life of Mark Twain* by Albert Bigelow Paine:

> This is an important as well as a highly interesting contribution to American literary history. No figure in American life has had so wide, so varied, so loyal and, above all, so intimate a following as the subject of this work [...] It would be difficult to find another American writer whose life was more full than was Mark Twain's. [4]

Mark Twain was a multifaceted figure and he became what people wanted to make of him. He was also lauded as the quintessential American and readers saw him in that light. In *Century Magazine* (1910) George Ade wrote his tribute:

> [...]Mark Twain was probably the best of our emissaries. He never waves the starry banner and at the same time he never went around begging forgiveness. He knew the faults of his home people and he understood intimately and with a family knowledge all of their good qualities and groping intentions and half-formed plans for big things in the future [...] [5]

Twain's books were advertised as a form of solace during the Great War. In an ad on December 2, 1917, in the *New York Tribune* one reads "Mark Twain—His Spirit Cheers and Comforts a Tired World." In an illustration to the right, Mark Twain's arms are around Tom Sawyer and Huckleberry Finn, implying comfort for the boys who have gone off to war. Tom Sawyer and Huckleberry Finn became everyone's boys. "Take Huckleberry Finn and Tom Sawyer by the hand and go back to your own boyhood," urged an ad in the *New York Tribune* (October 13, 1918). Under an illustration of two boys fighting, Mark Twain's name appears in capitals:

No wonder our soldiers and sailors like Mark Twain. No wonder the boys at Annapolis told Secretary Daniels that they would rather have Mark Twain than anyone else. To them, as to you, Mark Twain is the spirit of undying youth- the spirit of real Americanism [...]"[6]

Innocence surrounds these images of boyhood. "Hello Huck" and "Hey Tom, Tom Sawyer" ads appeared in the *New York Tribune* throughout 1917. In October 1918 a "Hello Huck" ad appeared across three columns of a newspaper in Lincoln, Nebraska (the *Commoner*, October 1, 1918).[7] In the illustration, a boy with a smile on his face lies on his stomach while reading a book that is resting on the ground. His head is propped up in the palm of his right hand and his feet, which dangle playfully in the air, cross at the ankles.

Common readers continued to regard Twain as a source of humor. Their comments indicate that he was most frequently noted for his tales of boyhood. Assessed critically, Twain would gradually come to be regarded as a distinctively American literary voice, a writer who made use of American characters and subjects and vernacular speech. Many critics have pointed out that prior to 1900, few American writers departed markedly from European models, or contributed greatly to literary theory. Whitman, Twain, and Henry James were exceptions.[8] In 1879, Henry James' essay *Hawthorne* was added by the Macmillan Company to its English men of letters series. Emerson, Bryant, Prescott, Whittier, and Whitman entered the series in the early twentieth century. Twain did not. Critics focused upon a canon of mostly New England writers. Twain was not among them. Yet, he was among America's most popular authors at the time.

A. MISSOURI READERS IN THE TWENTIETH CENTURY

Missouri called Mark Twain back home in June 1902, when the University of Missouri awarded him with an honorary doctorate. The *St. Louis Republic* announced "Mark Twain's Return to Hannibal and the Haunts of Huckleberry Finn."[9] There are illustrations of Twain across the top of the article. The energy of Twain's Missouri audience is highlighted by his journey home to that state in 1902. At that time, Henry Wysham Lanier was comparing the U.S. economy to a boat on Mark Twain's river:

The prodigious development of resources, which went on at an accelerating rate, enabled the country as a whole to progress in spite of all mistakes; and while we apparently had to learn the dangers as Mark Twain learned the Mississippi snags, by running on them, it was impossible to wreck a nation so dowered with natural wealth and human energy.[10]

In May 1902, Twain went to Hannibal, about one hundred miles north of Columbia. On Thursday, May 29, 1902, he arrived by train from St. Louis. Robertus Love, a young book reviewer from the *St. Louis Post-Dispatch*, reported on the visit. In Hannibal, Twain saw a modern town and he was greeted by many people he did not recognize who insisted they had known him as a boy. At Farmers and Merchants Bank there was a reception. He handed out diplomas to the graduates of Hannibal High School that night. He spoke with a reporter from the *St. Louis Star* on his way to Columbia: "The colossal part of this is my degree will cost me nothing, whereas other folks have to earn theirs."[11] The *St. Louis Republic* reported that "Being a humorist, it was apparent that many persons expected Mark Twain to be funny." A *St. Louis Dispatch* photo was taken in front of his former Hill Street home in Hannibal (May 30 1902). That evening, he dissolved into tears while speaking, realizing that he would probably never see Hannibal ever again. On Sunday morning, he posed for photographs at the train station and then he was on his way.

Two days later, the *Akron Daily Democrat* (June 2, 1902) announced "Mark Twain Goes Back to Hannibal"; there was a report on the Memorial Day speech. "If we had known he was aboard that train," remarked a citizen, "the union depot would not have been big enough to hold the chairmen of committees." The article states that Twain will visit the cave where Becky was lost. It presents a man who says to Twain, "I never saw you before but I recognized you by your picture in newspapers." Another says, "I'm a railroad engineer and my mother in law went to school with you." Even so, there is nothing said by anyone about having read his books.[12]

Along with the people who believed they had known Twain in Hannibal were the many readers elsewhere who continued to associate him with the Mississippi River. Theodore Roosevelt on board the S.S. *Mississippi*, October 1, 1907, wrote to his son Kermit:

> After speaking at Keokuk this morning we got on board this brand new stern-wheel steamer of the regular Mississippi type and started downstream. I went up on the Texas and of course felt an almost irresistible desire to ask the pilot about Mark Twain. It is a broad, shallow, muddy river [...] [13]

In Hannibal, Missouri, Tom Sawyer and Huck Finn seem to live somewhere around every corner. Mark Twain has been a household name there for many years. In 1916, the *Daily Missourian* noted "A Visit to Mark Twain's Home" in Florida, Missouri, by Reverend H.B. Barnes:

> Near the building the state of Missouri has placed a monument to the memory of Mark Twain. It consists of a base and square shaft of Carthage stone mounted by a bronze head, the whole standing twelve feet high [...] Florida has not yet become a mecca for lovers of good literature and admirers of great authors and one reason is the condition of

the roads in the region. It is, instead a good place for hunting, fishing, and scenery.[14]

For decades after Twain's death, his memory was kept alive in the University of Missouri alumni publication. In a March 1914 edition alumni read "We even got solemn over Mark Twain."[15] In 1917, they read: "That brilliant Missourian Mark Twain said in ending his *Innocents Abroad*: Broad, wholesome and charitable views of men [...]"[16] College alumni were haunted by Twain's spirit: "[This is] said to be received from Mark Twain by way of the Ouija board."[17] In 1920 the alumni publication repeats Twain's quote that reports of his death have been greatly exaggerated.[18] The University of Missouri's honorary LLD to Mark Twain, which he received in January 1902, is noted several times, including in June 1923. There are many references to Twain in a university speech in September 1923. The alumni publication in May 1925 recalls that they looked upon a concert of a boy's choir "as Mark Twain looked upon the ocean."[19]

The state of Missouri, likewise, has remained a proverbial hotbed of Mark Twain readers. In the Truman Presidential Library, one finds Twain's name coming up often in oral history interviews. When people have been asked to talk about their lives, they have taken the opportunity to mention Mark Twain.

In the 1970s, Professor Leland D. Peterson claimed that he was drawn to Missouri by reading Twain: "One of the reasons I had gone to Missouri before that was a lifelong interest in Mark Twain, and I wanted to visit the country a little bit."

John A. Earp of Missouri was a cable operator in the sound car for Truman's election campaign. He cited Mark Twain as he recalled Harry Truman's election and the "Dewey Wins" newspaper headline. "Harry must have felt very much like Mark Twain, when he said, "The reports of my death are greatly exaggerated."

In a variation on one of Twain's comment, Stephen J. Springarn, who served in the Truman White House, begins his interview: "I think I'll start off by quoting Mark Twain. As I get older, I remember less and less of past events, and most of what I remember isn't true."

Naval officer Robert L. Dennison, a naval aide to President Truman, graduated from the US Naval Academy in 1923. He became the commander of the S.S. *Missouri* from 1947 to 1948, after being Assistant Chief of Naval Operations, 1945–1947. Dennison says: "I remember one time we were talking about Mark Twain. I think I mentioned Mark Twain as being such a great writer, or something, and the President took out after Mark Twain."

Eben A. Ayres, assistant press secretary to President Truman, believes that Harry Truman read much Twain. On one of their trips together on the *Williamsburg*, someone asked what book he found most valuable and interesting in his life. And Truman said, "History, the old Greeks, and other satirists and so forth." Ayres adds: "Mark Twain, whose writings he had read extensively."[20]

These comments remind us of how thoroughly Twain has been adopted by Missouri. His connection with Hannibal and the Mississippi has remained vivid, and his characters Tom Sawyer and Huckleberry Finn have become familiar characters of popular culture. Twain's writings interested Professor Peterson in seeing Missouri. President Truman's associates kept Twain in mind as they discussed the Missouri-born president with their interviewers. They mentioned Truman's own reading of Twain. Such associations remain strong. The 2010 edition of Twain's autobiography sold rapidly in Missouri. *USA Today* (May 7, 2010) noted the enthusiasm of some people for Hannibal, where the Twain boyhood home is a national historic site.

Mark Twain's trip to Missouri was his final journey west. He began to decline offers to travel and speak at locations beyond New York City. However, newspapers across the nation continued to maintain his presence in all regions. For example, the *Houston Daily Post*, December 7, 1902, notes "Samuel Clemens will be sixty-seven years old tomorrow." The Houston newspaper repeats the description of the birthday party for him by St. Clair McKehay, editor of the *Brooklyn Eagle*.[21] People in Missouri, perhaps inspired by Twain's recent visit, sought to give him further honors. On May 30, 1903, he replied that to name a day at the St. Louis World's Fair "Mark Twain Day" was an honor not for the living but only for those who had died. "I hope that no society will be named for me while I am still alive," he wrote in a letter to T.F. Gatts.[22]

Mark Twain's popularity apparently retarded his entry into the American literary canon. With the exception of scholars like Brander Matthews, critical acceptance from critics came slowly. In 1911, George Santayana wrote in "The Genteel Tradition in American Philosophy" that in the humorists there were "some indications of a truly native philosophy." Both Whitman and the humorists, including Twain, had made efforts "to escape from the genteel tradition, and to express something worth expressing behind its back."[23] Yet, as Jay B. Hubbell points out: "Critical suspicion of the popular author for many years kept the literary historians from seeing that Mark Twain was a major American writer."[24]

The 1920s shows a turn in critical appreciation of Mark Twain. Van Wyck Brooks's important study *The Ordeal of Mark Twain* (1920) appeared at this time. Twain's considerable impact upon American culture was also beginning to be publicly recognized by America's progressive historians. Along with them, some other astute readers saw value in Twain the social critic. In 1920, Senator James A. Reed of Missouri, following a stage production of *The Prince and the Pauper* asserted that Mark Twain was a much needed voice for social justice:

Mark Twain gave us pleasing fantasies but he also gave to America and to the world one of the most direct visions it had ever known. He saw instantly through sham and pretense of every sort. Sometimes a nation deliberately deceives itself and worships its delusion. Mark Twain, the American, was a caustic solvent for delusion. He was wholesome. We need his mentality today in America and in the world.[25]

In 1927, when Vernon Parrington (1871–1929) produced the first volume of *Main Currents of American Thought*, his book was filled with reflections on America's writers. For Parrington, a writer with liberal leanings, Walt Whitman was the apogee of American writers and Mark Twain was "individual and incomparable." Cooper, Howells, Melville, Thoreau, and Whitman all received his emphasis. In his second volume, he gave new attention to America's writers of the South: William Gilmore Simms, John Pendleton Kennedy, Beverley Tucker, and others. Parrington set Twain among America's most significant writers. The gradual development of Twain's critical reception, from the time of Albert Bigelow Paine to Van Wyck Brooks' *The Ordeal of Mark Twain* and Bernard De Voto's *Mark Twain's America*, complemented this.[26] The writer of *Innocents Abroad*, western adventures, steamboats, and Missouri boys entered the American canon.

Twain the social critic became particularly important in the 1930s. This decade brought yet another resurgence of public interest in the author. Tom Sawyer arrived in film in 1930 and American schools began teaching *The Adventures of Tom Sawyer*. Bernard De Voto's *Mark Twain's America* (1932) responded to Van Wyck Brooks *The Ordeal of Mark Twain* (1920), with a new critical assessment. Franklin Roosevelt's use of the term "the New Deal" was traced to Twain's phrase in *A Connecticut Yankee in King Arthur's Court*. When President Roosevelt dedicated the Mark Twain Memorial Bridge in Hannibal, he said:

No American youth has knowingly or willingly escaped the the lessons, the philosophy and the spirit which beloved Mark Twain wove out of the true life of which he was a part along this majestic river.[27]

Charles Compton, when he did his study on reading at the St. Louis Library in the early 1930s, found that Mark Twain was the author the library patrons most liked to read. Inquiring into reader preferences, he found that, "taste was not related to age, class, or occupation." Compton assembled his study by first looking at library cards and writing letters to the people whose names he found on them. In *Who Reads What?* (1934), Compton offered a careful study of the St. Louis library system. That Mark Twain was the author that St. Louis readers liked most may have had partly to do with local publicity regarding Twain's own Missouri heritage. However, Twain's stories were shown to be popular across age, occupation, and class.[28]

Twain clearly maintained a strong popular audience. Louis Budd (1983) pointed out that in the 1930s the professoriate "had yet to develop a dignifying rationale for Twain's lasting readership."[29] As Budd observed, "[t]he great bulk of his audience has evidently ignored the shifts of critical opinions."[30] What did clearly occur is that *The Adventures of Huckleberry Finn, The Adventures of Tom Sawyer,* and *A Connecticut Yankee in King Arthur's Court* began to outpace *The Innocents Abroad, Roughing It,* and other books in sales.

The search for Mark Twain's popular audience was visible in quests like Charles Compton's library study. However, most surveys from the 1930s that record reader appreciation of Twain do not tell us a great deal. In each case, one must ask who is being surveyed. The drift of critical opinion regarding the canon of American literature may provide us with some clues. Yet, critical estimates may be historically situated responses and they are different from popular reception. Twain was represented as a pillar of American democracy during the heyday of the progressive historians Charles Beard and Vernon Parrington. To American common readers in the 1920s and 1930s, he was more likely known as the writer of *Tom Sawyer* and *Huckleberry Finn.*

Public surveys of readers in the 1920s and 1930s indicate that Twain was primarily recognized as the creator of Tom and Huck. Teachers were the selected group for a survey in 1926. *The Adventures of Huckleberry Finn* and *The Adventures of Tom Sawyer* both were on the *Golden Book Magazine*'s list by Henry W. Lanier in 1926 (Million Books and Best Books). This survey drew about four hundred responses from men and women who taught high school and college English. The top choices among them were for Poe's stories, Hawthorne's *The Scarlet Letter,* and Twain's *Huckleberry Finn.* Cooper's *Last of the Mohicans,* Joel Chandler Harris's *Uncle Remus* and Melville's *Moby Dick* followed. Howell's *The Rise of Silas Lapham* received half the votes that *Moby Dick* received. Recent novelists like Sinclair Lewis and Theodore Dreiser were not on the list.

The editor of the *Saturday Review,* writing "An American Canon" in 1927, did not include Mark Twain as a pivotal author. However, he conceded that "in one book" his work might be recognized: *Huckleberry Finn.* We read in these pages that Melville's *Moby Dick* is a novel "we probably must omit from the canon," although why it is to be omitted is never said. Likewise, Thoreau's *Walden* is mentioned, but omitted. The editor writes of Walt Whitman, but then says "we must exclude" him. Instead, he includes Franklin, Irving, Cooper, Emerson, and Longfellow. Of twentieth-century writers, he only adds Sinclair Lewis and his novel *Babbitt.*[31] Female writers are not represented.

Another contemporary survey was the work of Asa Don Dickinson, the young Brooklyn librarian, we recall, who had corresponded with Twain. As the University of Pennsylvania librarian, Asa Don Dickinson developed his list of *The Best Books of Our Time* (1925). To this he added volumes in 1937 and 1948, to bring the list up to date to the mid-1930s and the mid-1940s. His objective was to cull a list of books from library associations and to connect these with lists produced by newspapers and periodicals and in critical essays and literary histories. Twain was no longer alive and was not recognized in the top ten on any of these lists. In Dickinson's top ten of living writers there were only three American authors. Nine, including Twain, were present in the next fifteen selections.[32]

Louis Budd notes that Twain was "assigned" in classrooms after World War II.[33] Among these classrooms were many in the Missouri school system. The Missouri Association of School Librarians had a Mark Twain Reader's Award for grades four through six. It gave children a reading list, including some of Twain's less controversial fiction. The assigning of Twain's fiction in elementary and secondary education was duplicated in many school systems nationally. When Jay Hubbell, in 1958, polled sixteen students who would become teachers, Mark Twain topped their list.[34] *Huckleberry Finn* was second only to *The Scarlet Letter* and *Moby Dick* among their choices for the greatest American novel.

A strong response to *The Adventures of Tom Sawyer* and *The Adventures of Huckleberry Finn* is indicated in many of the school surveys of the 1930s and 1940s. However, overall, Mark Twain does not appear high on most lists other than those taken of young, school-aged readers. Graduate students and professors do point to *Huckleberry Finn* but they mention little else in the Twain catalog.

For example, a 1949 UNESCO poll was supported by the MLA's American literature section. This gathered the selections of twenty-six professors and men of letters. Indeed, they were all men and their average age was sixty; the selectors did not include women. Female authors Willa Cather, Emily Dickinson, and Edith Wharton were recognized among their choices for the American literary canon. The professors were asked to choose their top twenty works "which you would select as the best representatives of the literary art of our country." Hawthorne's *The Scarlet Letter* was the work most often mentioned, followed by Poe's collected works. Then there followed Mark Twain's *Huckleberry Finn*, Melville's *Moby Dick*, and James's *Portrait of a Lady* and Emerson's *Essays*. Thoreau, Whitman, Frost and Cooper all received more than one hundred points in this survey. Cather and Dickinson followed at eighty-five and eighty-one respectively.

Huckleberry Finn did not make the list in Eric Goldman's *Books That Changed America* (1953), in *Saturday Review of Literature* on July 4, 1953. There are two works of fiction on Goldman's list: *Babbitt* and *Uncle Tom's Cabin*. Likewise, when Robert B. Downs compiled a list of twenty-five *Books That Changed America* (1970), *Huckleberry Finn* followed that twenty-five as a runner-up. His previous list, *Molders of the American Mind* (1961) did not include Twain's novel. It included Emerson's *Essays* and Whitman's *Democratic Vistas*, but these were inexplicably dropped in the later publication. [35]

B. MARK TWAIN TODAY

We still recall Mark Twain through the 1908 portraits by Alvin Langdon Coburn and the photos of Albert Bigelow Paine, Dorothy Quick, Isabel Lyon, and others. We see the white suit and white mane of hair, the whimsical look, the beaming yet rakish appearance despite the proudly worn Oxford gown. Twain sits in a nonchalant pose, sea-pilot's cap on his head, with his feet propped on the rail of a ship that will take him around the world. He lives photographically, as Albert E. Stone wrote in a book review, "somewhere between art and document" with that prop of a pungent cigar in his mouth, its fiery glow dwindling in a way that Twain's image itself never does. [36]

Mark Twain is conspicuously present in a multimedia age and his electronic life among us is pervasive. His virtual presence is sustained not only via e-books and films but as a result of his gift for pithy remarks. He is a perennial source of the witty sound-bite. The search term "Mark Twain quotations" yields two million-thirty thousand hits on a Google search. He remains among the most quoted and quotable people in the world. He has widely been quoted—sometimes accurately, sometimes not. Twain's quips have often been repeated, with variations. These witticisms keep him alive in the public sphere. For example, at the dedication of Union Theological Seminary buildings at Broadway and 120th Street in New York in 1910, a speaker asserted: "We need to follow Mark Twain's effective counsel, 'When in doubt, tell the truth.'" [37] Further upstate in New York, there was the use of Mark Twain by William Sulzer, a gubernatorial candidate asserting his honesty, at a banquet at the Hotel Ten Eyck in Albany on March 13, 1913: "You remember Mark Twain once said, 'When in doubt, take a drink.' My policy as governor is a little different: when in doubt I shall confide in the people." [38] In an address to the Illinois Historical Society, one of its editors recalled Twain as he spoke of delays in the publication of the Illinois Centennial History: "But first of all, let me assure you that the very optimistic report in the newspaper of recent date, that the history was on the point of being ready for distribution is, to quote a well-remembered remark of Mark Twain's upon the report of his death, greatly exaggerated." [39] In an interview with the Federal Writers Project, Robert Wolfe Isaacs, a businessman from Australia, said that he was quoting Mark Twain: "Place your eggs in one basket, but watch the basket." [40]

A homey wisdom has often been found in Twain by some of his audience. When Nancy Holt, whose mother was Cherokee and whose father was Scots-Irish, was interviewed for a southern oral history project, she thought of a phrase from Twain:

> And then, like Mark Twain says [...] when he was sixteen his father was rather dumb and didn't know anything, and when he was eighteen he was amazed at how much the old man had learned, in such a short time. Well, I'm kind of that way too.[41]

William Dean Howells once said of Mark Twain: "He was a youth to the end of his days, the heart of a boy with the head of sage." More than one hundred years after his death, Twain is still that boy, Huckleberry Finn and Tom Sawyer, and the sage: a man in a white suit with a wink in his eyes.

When Mark Twain left this world one hundred years ago, he had an extraordinary public future still ahead of him. In 1910, a Salt Lake City newspaper was curious about the future of Mark Twain:

> A wise writer in the East gravely reviews the works of Mark Twain and decides that only two or three of his productions will be read in a hundred years hence [...] Who can tell what is to be seen a hundred years hence? Someone may dig them out 500 years from now and translate them into the language of the future. The frontier and the simple home are passing away. The humor Mark Twain had these. . . . Will men catch the spirit of that humor? [42]

Our interaction with Mark Twain "a hundred years hence" from that article is far from over. The spirit of his humor endures. As Louis Budd pointed out, "He keeps bobbing up" in a wide variety of forms.[43] There are texts, pictorial images, stage productions, films, television shows, cartoons, and all manner of designations of public places bearing the names of Mark Twain and his famous characters. In 1960, *Newsweek* focused upon American nostalgia in "Mark Twain: Yearning for Yesterday." *Newsweek* wrote: "as dispensed by the mass media he seems to be a bit of Americana rather than an artist."[44] At the centenary of his death in 2010, this comment appears to have been equally true. It is clear that each generation recreates Mark Twain and that the popular response to Twain's writings is something besides the critical response. His books are alive in the cultural memory of the English speaking world and beyond it. The curling white hair, beak nose and mustache and white suit are easy to caricature and easily remembered. This is a "national grandfather figure" according to Hal Holbrook, whose dazzling recreations of Twain on the stage have supported the enduring image of Mark Twain.

Overall the majority of Mark Twain's popular readers have always valued his humor and his storytelling. The critical record shows a gradual recognition by critics of Twain's literary merits. In 1963, Henry Nash Smith pointed out that Mark Twain's books had been examined through the lens of "the general course of American criticism." Critics in the first decade of the twentieth century considered Twain's novels via impressionism, Smith observed. In the 1920s, there was a search for "a usable past" and Twain was a key American figure. In the 1930s came "the cult of realism and social significance." Then attention to technique emerged in the late 1930s and 1940s and there was an interest in symbolism.[45] Mark Twain's common readers have usually not read him within these categories. Rather, they have generally read his stories in less analytical ways, sometimes relating Twain and his characters to their own lives.

For example, one twentieth-century scientist saw his research in periodicals for a history of science as being similar to time travel in Twain's novel *A Connecticut Yankee in King Arthur's Court*. Arthur L. Shawlow, who worked at Bell Laboratories and at Stanford, had a strong interest in the history of science. While at Stanford, at the age of seventy-five, he recalled how he and his colleagues investigated past scientific inquiries: "It's sort of like time travelling, almost like the *Connecticut Yankee in King Arthur's Court*. And we did that. We'd go back to old issues of *Physical Review* or other journals."[46]

The common readers of Mark Twain, while they have interpreted Twain in various ways, often suggest that they have read Twain with amusement and appreciation. The records left by Mark Twain's American audience suggest that they saw him as one of their own. His characters reflected their own lives. Twain's use of an American vernacular made him different than many other authors. From the folksy yet worldly cynicism of the narrator of *The Innocents Abroad* and the tall tales of the South and West in his sketches, to the rollicking anecdotes of *Roughing It* and the indigenous Midwestern dialects and African American speech of *Huckleberry Finn*, Twain's voice was a unique contribution to American letters. People have recognized that uniqueness. They have been entertained by Twain's stories. When documenting the stories of their own lives, some autobiographers or interviewees have remembered him.

Twain remains popular today largely as an image and through adaptations of his works. Jay B. Hubbell, in 1972, recognized that the professors of English now maintain the reputation of older American writers by selecting those who are to be studied or anthologized.[47] One may wonder how often Mark Twain is read these days for the sheer delight of his prose. That was the question, we may recall, that was asked by one Twain reader, Mabel Bates Back. Students read now, in print or on electronic devices, for their classes and term papers. Professors read specialized studies by other professors or critics. Twain, like Charles Dickens and some other popular authors of the nineteenth century, is most often sustained by film, television, and theatre. Even with the considerable recent sales of Twain's *Autobiography*, one may wonder how often present readers, like their predecessors, turn to Mark Twain for entertainment and read Twain on their Kindles and Nooks. The popular Mark Twain is an image, a name, a figure presented to the world. The celebrity has become larger than his works, even as the characters of his imagination are transposed into film or drawn into comic books. Yet, his marvelous books are reprinted, distributed, and read—and some audiences still see that pauper as a prince, that industrialist as a knight, and those boys casting off on a raft into the unknown promise of a river.

A further assessment of Mark Twain's audience can reach toward an additional degree of scientific accuracy with further data collection and attention to the methodology of book historians. This study, hopefully, has provided a resource that other researchers may build upon. Twain, while prominent in public imagery and legend, remains a somewhat elusive figure. His audience is even more difficult to track. Indeed, the journey of those who investigate the history of readers may feel a bit like heading west for Nevada on a train and a stagecoach, as Samuel Clemens did as a young man. One searches the geography for signposts of the audience and yes, there are trees but few paths have been carved out in the wilderness. One looks to the mountains of Twain biography and to the peaks of Twain scholarship with hopes for future research on his readers. It will be a painstaking but curiosity-driven panning for archival gold that will further map the frontier.

Mark Twain has achieved a kind of near-eternal life on earth that his nineteenth-century readers, largely forgotten, have not. In legend, his life is made into something like a cosmic force when it is equated with the long afterglow of Halley's Comet. Samuel Clemens did not exactly arrive or leave with the comet. Yet, he was born while Halley's Comet was in transit of earth and died during the time it had again appeared in the heavens. When this astronomical phenomenon arrived again in 1986, Mark Twain still remained a notable part of popular culture. The comet is visible to people on earth every seventy-five or seventy-six years. It will next appear in about 2061 or 2062. Amid all the changes in social life, technology, commerce, and reading by 2061, the chances are that Mark Twain will still be alive and well.

NOTES

1. *North American Review* 197 (January 1913): 136. See Louis J. Budd, *Our Mark Twain*, 231.

2. *Tacoma Times*, April 22, 1910; Rev. H.B. Barnes, "A Visit to Mark Twain's Home"; "Mark Twain: The Great Humorist" and "Kentucky Gleanings," *Citizen*, Berea, Kentucky, April 28, 1910.

3. *Day Book*, Chicago, November 20, 1912.

4. Porter Garnett, "Literary Notes and Comments," *San Francisco Call*, October 20, 1912.

5. George Ade, *Anthology*, ed. Shelley Fisher Fishkin, Library of America, 2010, p. 126.

6. *New York Tribune* (October 13, 1918): 4.

7. "Hello Huck" advertisement, *Commoner*, Lincoln, Nebraska, October 1, 1918.

8. Jay Hubbell, *Who Are the Major American Writers?* Durham: Duke University Press, 1972. 168. 1958 poll, pp. 226–27.

9. *St. Louis Republic* (June 8, 1902): 45. Magazine section.

10. Henry Wysham Lanier, *A Century of Banking in New York*. George Doran 1922. p. 201.

11. *St. Louis Star* (May 29, 1902): 1, 7. (p.185); *St. Louis Republic* (May 30, 1902): 1–2. *Mainly the Truth: Interviews with Mark Twain*. ed. Gary Scharnhorst. Tuscaloosa: University of Alabama Press, 2009, p. 187. *St. Louis Post-Dispatch* photo (May 30, 1902): 1.

12. *Akron Daily Democrat* (June 2, 1902): 1.

13. Theodore Roosevelt Letter to Kermit Roosevelt, pp. 202–03. *Theodore Roosevelt's Letters to His Children*. New York: Scribner's, 1919.

14. *Daily Missourian*, Wednesday, (September 20, 1916): 6.

15. University of Missouri Alumni Publication, March 1914, p. 197.

16. University of Missouri Alumni, February 1917, p. 155.

17. University of Missouri Alumni, May 1917, p. 271.

18. University of Missouri Alumni, December 1920, p. 76.

19. University of Missouri Alumni, September 1923, p. 171.

20. Leland D. Peterson, University History, Professor at Old Dominion. Interviewed, July 19, 1977, Truman Library, Missouri. John A. Earp, Stephen J. Springarm, Robert L. Dennison, Truman Library. Interview, November 2, 1971; Eben A. Ayres, Truman Library. Assistant Press Secretary and Special Assistant at the White House. Truman Library Archives.

21. *Houston Daily Post* (December 7, 1902) reprint of St. Clair McKehay article from the *Brooklyn Eagle*.

22. Mark Twain, Letter to T.F. Gatts quoted by Charles Neider, p. 276. To Edward L. Dimmit of St. Louis, he wrote on July 19 from the Adirondacks, declining an invitation to celebrate Missouri's eightieth anniversary. "Fifty years ago I might have eagerly gone across the world to celebrate anything that might turn up," he wrote, thanking him for "the prized honor [...] of asking me to be present." Thinking back to his Missouri boyhood, Twain wrote: "The whole scheme of things is turned wrong end to. Life should begin with age and its privileges and accumulations, and end with youth and its capacity to enjoy such advantages." Quoted by Charles Neider, p. 264.

23. George Santayana, "Genteel Tradition in American Philosophy"; Jay Hubbell, *Who Are the Major American Writers?* Durham: Duke University Press, 1972. pp. 265, 335.

24. Jay Hubbell, *Who Are the Major American Writers?* Durham: Duke University Press, 1972.

25. Senator James A. Reed, *New York Times* (December 1, 1920).

26. Vernon Parrington, *Main Currents of American Thought*, 1927. Van Wyck Brooks, *The Ordeal of Mark Twain*, 1920. Bernard De Voto. *Mark Twain's America*, 1932. In the first part of the twentieth century, Mark Twain became an image, the progressive historians' hope for America. This appears much like the point in Kim Sturgess' *Shakespeare and the American Nation* (Cambridge University Press, 2004) or Lawrence Levine's *Highbrow/Lowbrow: The Emergence of Cultural Hierarchy in America* (Harvard University Press, 1988) that nineteenth-century Americans fit Shakespeare into their own cultural needs. See Levine p. 240.

27. President Roosevelt's remarks were recorded by the Associated Press and appeared in the *New York Times*, September 5, 1936. When Cyril Clemens presented Roosevelt with a "great orator" medal on in December 1933, the president acknowledged that the phrase had appeared in Twain's novel. See *New York Times* (December 5, 1933). *Evening World*, December 1, 1920. p. 11.

28. Charles Compton, "Who Reads What?" (1934); Gordon Hunter, *What America Reads, Taste, Class and the Novel, 1920–1960*, Chapel Hill: University of North Carolina Press, 2009. p. 142. Louis Adamic, in response, wrote "What the Proletariat Reads," to try to assess what sort of books working class and immigrant readers were turning toward. His survey showed newspaper reading and an interest in periodicals like *True*

Stories, Screen Romances, Wide West Tales. See Louis Adamic, *True Stories, Screen Romances, Wide West Tales.*

29. Louis J. Budd, *Our Mark Twain: The Making of His Public Personality*, p. 234.

30. Ibid, 235.

31. "An American Canon," *Saturday Review.* See also Jay Hubbell, *Who Are the Major American Writers?* Durham: Duke University Press, 1972.

32. Asa Don Dickinson, *Best Books of Our Times* (1925), rpt. Garden City: Doubleday, Doran, 1929.

33. Louis Budd, *Our Mark Twain: The Making of His Public Personality*, Philadelphia: University of Pennsylvania Press, 1983. pp. 235–236.

34. Jay Hubbel, *Who Are the Major American Writers?* (1958) Durham: Duke University Press, 1972.

35. Unesco Poll, 1949; Eric Goldman, "Books That Changed America," *Saturday Review of Literature* (July 4, 1953). Robert B. Downs, *Books That Changed America*, 1970; *Molders of the American Mind*, 1961, p. 20; "The Best Ten American Books," *The Critic* (April 22, 1893): 255; (May 27, 1893): 335; *Literature* (February 1899).

36. Albert E. Stone, *The Innocent Eye: Mark Twain and Childhood Imagination*, New Haven: Yale University Press, 1962.

37. Union Theological Ceremonies. November 27–29, 1910. New York Public Library pamphlet, p. 88.

38. Illinois Historical Society, Vol. 24, 1918. p. 76.

39. Robert Wolfe Isaacs, Federal Writer's Project, Library of Congress. Interview in Clayton, New Mexico, December 15, 1939.

40. Nancy Holt, Frances E. Webb Interview, October 27, 1985. Documenting the American South. Oral History, K-0010. #4007.

41. William Dean Howells, *My Mark Twain.* Baton Rouge: Louisiana State University Press, 1967.

42. "A Leap of History," *Goodwin's*, Salt Lake City, Vol.17, Is. 10 (June 25, 1910): 1.

43. Louis J. Budd, *Our Mark Twain*, p. 230. Laura Skandera Trombley calls Mark Twain "America's First Modern Celebrity" in an article for "Book Beast" (2012) (The Daily Beast.com). She comments on his white outfit and his persona, his 1908 incorporation of his nom de plume, and his copyright of his image, which sold many items. In the creation of popular culture, social legitimacy is given to the public spectacle. The performance or product is set in a framework where there is a correlation between crowd numbers, circulation, and potential wealth. Celebrity sells. The image of Mark Twain, in his lifetime, and in ours, has been used in this manner.

44. "Mark Twain: Yearning for Yesterday," *Newsweek. Time* magazine (July 14, 2008) wrote of "The Dangerous Mind of Mark Twain": "Why he was ahead of his time on race. What his writing can teach America today." (Stephen I. Carter, "Getting Past Black and White")

45. Henry Nash Smith, *Mark Twain: The Development of a Writer.* Cambridge: Harvard University Press, 1963.

46. Arthur L. Shawlow, Regional Oral History Office. Bancroft Library, University of California, Berkeley.

47. Jay Hubbell, *Who Are the Major American Writers?* Durham: Duke University Press, 1972. p. 322.

Bibliography

"A Day With Mark Twain," *Rollingpen's Humorous Illustrated Annual*, May 1882.

"A Leap of History," *Goodwin's*, Salt Lake City, Vol.17, Is. 10 (June 25, 1910): 1.

"A Picture of Memory: Settlement in Oakland County," Speech at Supervisor's Picnic, Oakland County, August 24, 1892, *Michigan Pioneer Collections*, 22. Lansing: Robert Smith and Company, 1894. p. 407.

Ack, George. *In Pastures New*. New York: McClure, Phillips, 1906.

Akron Daily Democrat (June 2, 1902): 1.

Alcott, Louisa May. *Little Women*. Ed. Madelon Bedell. New York: Modern Library, 1983.

Anderson, Benedict. *Imagined Communities: Reflections on the Origin and Spread of Nationalism*. London: Verso, 1991.

Anderson, Frederick, ed. *Mark Twain: The Critical Heritage*. London: Routledge, Kegan and Paul, 1971.

Andrews, Kenneth. *Nook Farm: Mark Twain's Hartford Circle*. Cambridge: Harvard UP, 1950.

Annual Report of the Michigan State Library Commissioners. Lansing: Robert Smith Printing, 1900.

Atlantic, "Recent Literature," Mark Twain Letters, Vol. 5, 95.

Atlantic, (May 1876): 105.

Australian Town and Country Journal, NSW (September 28, 1895): 1.

Back, Mabel Bates. Knott County Farmer, Kentucky Family Farm Oral History Collection. Interview, June 1991. Louie B. Nunn Center for Oral History. University of Kentucky Library, Lexington, Kentucky.

Badia, Jane, and Jennifer Phegley. *Reading Women: Literary Figures and Cultural Icons from the Victorian Age to the Present*. Toronto: University of Toronto Press, 2005.

Baetzhold, Howard G. *Mark Twain and John Bull: The British Connection*. Bloomington and London: Indiana University Press, 1970.

Baker, Franklin T. "High School Reading," *English Journal* (1918): 474–485.

Baldwin, Martha. "What Women Did for Oakland County," pp. 261, 266. Oakland County, Michigan Pioneer Collections. Lansing: Robert Smith and Company, 1894.

Baltimore American (November 29, 1884): 2.

Baltimore Gazette (April 27, 1877): 1.

Barcus, Clyde, and Edith Barcus Scrapbook, page 15, University of Nevada.

Barlow, Dudley. "Why We Still Need Huckleberry Finn," ed. Stephen K. George. *Ethics, Literature, Theory: An Introduction*. Lanham: Rowman and Littlefield, 2005.

Barnes, H.B. "A Visit to Mark Twain's Home"; "Mark Twain: The Great Humorist" and "Kentucky Gleanings," *Citizen*, Berea, Kentucky, April 28, 1910.

Basbanes, Nicholas A. *Patience and Fortitude: A Roving Chronicle of Book People, Book Places, and Book Culture*. New York: Harper Collins, 2001.

———. *A Splendor of Letters*, New York: Harper, 2003.

Beedle, John Hanson. *The Undeveloped West, or Five Years in the Territories*. Philadelphia and Chicago: National Publishing, 1873, p. 54.

"Belles Lettres, Poetry, and Fiction," *British Quarterly Review* 78 (July 1883): 226–27.

Bender-Slack, Delane. "The Role of Gender in Making Meaning of Texts," Feminist Teacher, Vol. 20, No.1 (2009): 15–27.

Besant, Walter. "My Favorite Novel and His Best Book." In *Huck Finn among the Critics: A Centennial Selection.* Ed. M. Thomas Inge, 43–52, Frederick, MD.: University Publications of America, 1985.

Billington, Ray Allen. *Frederick Jackson Turner: Historian, Scholar, Teacher.* New York: 1973.

Bird, John. "Mind the Gap: A Reader Reading The Adventures of Huckleberry Finn." In *Twain's Omissions: Exploring the Gaps as Textual Context.* Ed. Gretchen M. Martin, 9–20. Newcastle-on- Tyne: Cambridge Scholars Publishing, 2013.

Blake, David Haven. *Walt Whitman and the Culture of American Celebrity.* New Haven: Yale University Press, 2006.

Blake, Faye M. University of California, Bancroft Library, Regional Oral History.

Blunden, Edmund. Royal Sussex Regiment. Battalion Headquarters. Mailly. Reader's Experience Database (RED 29768.)

Boorstin, Daniel J. *The Image: A Guide to Pseudo-Events in America* (1962), rpt. New York: Vintage, 1992.

Bowden, Witt, Michael Karpovich, and Abbot Payson Usher. *An Economic History of Europe Since 1750.* New York: Howard Fertig, 1970.

Bridgeman, Richard. *Traveling in Mark Twain.* Berkeley: University of California Press, 1987.

Brodhead, Richard H. *Cultures of Letters: Scenes of Reading and Writing in Nineteenth-Century America.* Chicago: University of Chicago Press, 1993.

Brooklyn Daily Union (November 22, 1871).

Brooklyn Eagle (May 11, 1867): 3.

Brooklyn Eagle (Tuesday, March 16, 1869).

Brooklyn Daily Eagle (November 22, 1871).

Brooklyn Eagle, "Local Brevities," (February 27, 1873).

Brooklyn Eagle, (November 11, 1875).

Brooklyn Eagle, (Saturday, May 6, 1876): 6.

Brooklyn Eagle, "Literature and Music: Second Annual Reception of the South Brooklyn Literary Society," (Friday May 25, 1877).

Brooklyn Eagle, (December 9, 1877): 3–4.

Brooklyn Eagle, (February 20, 1878).

Brooklyn Eagle, (Sunday, March 31, 1878): 3.

Brooklyn Eagle, "Tuscan Lodge, The Second Annual Parlor Entertainment," (November 22, 1878): 4.

Brooklyn Eagle, (November 9, 1883): 2.

Brooklyn Eagle (September 23, 1888): 3.

Brooklyn Eagle (December 29, 1891): 2.

Brooklyn Eagle, (July 1, 1892): 2

Brooklyn Eagle (April 7, 1893): 4.

Brooklyn Eagle (Tuesday, March 24, 1896): 11.

Brooklyn Eagle, (June 9, 1896): 6.

Brooklyn Eagle, (October 27, 1896): 5.

Brooklyn Eagle, (January 25, 1897): 4

Brooklyn Eagle (Thursday, January 28, 1897): 4.

Brooklyn Eagle (Friday, June 18, 1897): 5.

Brooklyn Eagle (Tuesday, January 25, 1898): 13.

Brooklyn Eagle, (February 13, 1898): 3.

Brooklyn Eagle (May 29, 1899): 4.

Brooklyn Eagle (May 24, 1902): 7.

Brooklyn Eagle (Sunday, October 19, 1902): 5.

Brooklyn Eagle, (February 10, 1901): 18, 42.

Brooklyn Eagle, (June 8, 1901): 18.

Brooklyn Eagle "Royal Arcanum," (Saturday, September 13, 1902).

"Brooklyn Notes," *Freeman,"* (February 27, 1886).

Brooks, Van Wyck. *The Ordeal of Mark Twain.* New York: E.P. Dutton, 1920.

Brooks, W.S. "What a Black Man Saw," *Methodist Episcopal Church Review*, Vol. 17. No. 4 (April 1901): 298. Ohio Historical Society, African American Collection.

Brown, Janet. "Looking at Darwin: Portraits and the Making of an Icon," *Isis*. Vol. 100, No. 3 (September 2009): 542–570.

Brown, Henry Collins. *In the Golden Nineties*. Hastings-on-Hudson: Valentine's Manual, 1928.

Browne, Ray B. *Journal of American Culture*. Vol. 32, No. 2 (June 2009): 168–69.

Budd, Louis J. *Our Mark Twain: The Making of His Public Personality*. Philadelphia: University of Pennsylvania Press, 1983.

———. *Mark Twain: Social Philosopher*. Bloomington: Indiana University Press, 1962.

———. "A Talent for Posturing: The Achievement of Mark Twain's Public Personality." In *The Mythologizing of Mark Twain*. Ed. Sara de Saussure and Phillip D. Beidler. Tuscaloosa: University of Alabama Press, 1984.

———. *Mark Twain: The Contemporary Reviews*. Cambridge: Cambridge University Press, 1994.

———. *Critical Essays on Mark Twain 1867–1910*. Boston: G.K. Hall, 1982.

Budd, Louis J., and Edwin H. Cady, eds. *On Mark Twain: The Best from American Literature*. 1982.

Bush, Jr., Harold K. *Mark Twain and the Spiritual Crisis of His Age*. Tuscaloosa: University of Alabama Press, 2007.

———. "Acting Like Mark Twain: Performance in Nineteenth-Century American Culture and W.D. Howells' *A Chance Acquaintance*," *American Quarterly*, Vol. 49, No. 2 (June 1947): 429–437.

———. "The Mythic Struggle behind East and West: Mark Twain Speech at Whittier's 70th Birthday Celebration," *American Literary Realism*. Vol. 27, Is. 2 (Winter 1995): 53–73.

Cardus, Neville. Reader's Experience Database (RED 5279)

Carson, G. "Get the prospect seated. . . . and keep talking," *American Heritage*, IX, 5 (1958): 38-41, 77–80.

Cassuto, Leonard, Clare Virginia Eby, and Benjamin Reiss, eds. *The Cambridge History of the American Novel*. New York and Cambridge: Cambridge University Press, 2011.

Catholic World. Vol. 51, Issue 302 (May 1890): 275.

Catholic World. Vol. 59, Is. 353 (August 1894): 715.

Cavallo, Gugliemo, and Chartier, Roger, eds. *A History of Reading in the West*. Trans. Lydia G. Cochrane. Cambridge: Polity, 1995.

Cherches, Peter. "Star Course: Popular Lectures and the Marketing of Celebrity in Nineteenth-Century America," PhD dissertation, New York University, 1997.

Chumard, Barbara C. *Thrall Library, 1901–1960: A Historical Study of a Small Town Library*. SUNY-Albany, MLS thesis, 1996.

Clemen, John. *George Washington Cable Revisited*. Boston: Twayne, 1976.

Clemens, Clara. *My Father, Mark Twain*. New York: 1931.

Clemens, Cyril "A Visit to Mark Twain Country," *Overland and Monthly*, 7 (April 1929): 116–17, 127

Clemens, Susy. *Papa: An Intimate Biography of Mark Twain*. Ed. Charles Neider. Garden City: Doubleday, 1978. pp. 221–22.

Cleveland Gazette (July 14, 1888).

Compton, C.H. "Who Reads Mark Twain?" In *Who Read What?: Essays on the Readers of Mark Twain, Hardy, Shaw, William James, The Greek Classics*, 15–34. New York: H.W. Wilson, 1934.

———. *American Mercury* (April 1934): 465–471.

Coran, James E. "Twain in San Francisco. *Cosmopolitan Twain*. Columbia: University of Missouri Press, 2008.

Cox, James M. *Mark Twain: The Fate of Humor*. Princeton: Princeton University Press, 1966.

———. "Mark Twain: The Triumph of Humor." In *The Chief Glory of Every People: Essays on Classic American Writers*. Ed. Matthew J. Bruccoli, 211–230. Carbondale and Edwardsville: Southern Illinois University Press, 1973.

Covici, Pascal, ed. "Dear Master Wattie: The Mark Twain-David Watt Bowser Letters," *Southwest Review* (Spring 1960): 106–108.

Crawford, R.C. "Itinerant Life in the Michigan Conference of the M.E. Church," Michigan Historical Collection, Vol. 22, 1883.

The Critic, "The Best Ten American Books," (April 22, 1893): 255; (May 27, 1893): 335.

Cummings, Sherwood. *Mark Twain and Science: Adventures of a Mind*. Baton Rouge: Louisiana State University Press, 1988.

Cutter, Charles Ami. *Rules for a Dictionary Catalogue*. Washington, D.C.: U.S. Government Printing Office, 1891, p. 18.

Daily Missourian (Wednesday, September 20, 1916): 6.

Danky, James P., and Wayne Wiegand, eds. *Print Culture in a Diverse America*. Urbana: University of Illinois Press, 1998.

Darnton, Robert. *The Case for Books: Past, Present, and Future*. New York: Public Affairs, Perseus, 2009.

———. *The Kiss of Lamourette: Reflections in Cultural History*. New York: W.W. Norton, 1991, rpt. 1996.

———. "What is the History of Books?" *Daedelus* 111 (Summer 1982): 65–83.

Davidson, Cathy. *Revolution of the Word: The Rise of the Novel in America*. Oxford and New York: Oxford University Press, 1986.

Davis, Thomas A. Letter to Mark Twain. AME Zion Church, February 6, 1880, Harry Ransom Center, University of Texas.

Day Book, Chicago (November 20, 1912): 1.

De Saussure, Sara and Phillip Baedler. *The Mythologizing of Mark Twain*. Tuscaloosa: University of Alabama Press, 1984.

De Voto, Bernard. *Mark Twain's America* (reprint). University of Nebraska Press: 1997.

———. "Introduction," *The Portable Mark Twain*. New York: Viking Press, 1974.

———. *Mark Twain: Modern Critical Views*, Chelsea House, 2006.

———. *Mark Twain in Eruption*. New York: Harper and Brothers, 1940.

Devoy, Robert. *A Tale of Palmyra Massacre*. Civilian of Missouri Collection, 1903.

Diamond, Suzanne. *Compelling Confessions: The Politics of Personal Disclosure*. Madison: Fairleigh Dickinson University Press, 2010.

Dickinson, Asa Don. Sheepshead Bay Branch, November 19, 1905. *Humanities*, Vol. 21, Is. 1 (January/February 2000).

———. *The Best Books of Our Times*. Garden City: Doubleday, Doran, 1925, rpt. 1929.

Dickinson, L.T. "Marketing a Best Seller: Mark Twain's *Innocents Abroad*. " New York: The Papers of the Bibliographical Society of America 41 (1947): 107–122.

Dolmetsch, Carl. *Our Famous Guest: Mark Twain in Vienna*. Athens and London: University of Georgia Press, 1992.

'E.E.T.' Letter to the Editor, *Windsor and Richmond Gazette*, October 18, 1895, p. 11.

Eisner, Eric. *Nineteenth-Century Poetry and Literary Celebrity*. Basingstoke: Palgrave, 2009.

Elementary School Journal (1935) p. 11. Elementary School Journal, "Voluntary Reading," Grades IV-VIII. University of Chicago Press (1928) rpt. 1931: p. 15.

Eliot, Simon, and Jonathan Rose. *A Companion to the History of the Book*. Malden, MA: Blackwell, 2007.

Emerson, Everett. *Mark Twain: A Literary Life*. Philadelphia: University of Pennsylvania Press, 2000.

———. *The Authentic Mark Twain*. Philadelphia: University of Pennsylvania Press 1984.

Engleman, J.O. "Outside Reading, Decatur, Illinois Schools," *English Journal* (January 1917): 20–27.

"English as She is Taught," *Cleveland Gazette* (March 20, 1887).

English Journal (1918): 474–487.

Evening World (December 1, 1920): 11.

Fader, Regina. "Changing Old Institutions: Race in the Mark Twain Museum," *Arkansas Review*, Vol. 40, No. 1 (April 2009): 5–17.

Farwell, Willard B. "The Society of California Pioneers, Part II," *Overland Monthly*, Vol. 29, Is. 171, (March 1897): 292–302.

Fatout, Paul. ed. *Mark Twain Speaks for Himself*. West Lafayette, IN: Purdue University Press, 1978. rpt. *Mark Twain Speaking*. University of Iowa Press, 2006.

Ferris, G.L. *Appleton's Journal*, Vol. 12, Is. 276 (July 4, 1874): 15–18.

Fetterley, Judith. *The Resisting Reader: A Feminist Approach to American Fiction*. Bloomington: Indiana University Press, 1978.

———. "Reading About Reading: 'A Jury of Her Peers,' 'The Murders in the Rue Morgue,' and 'The Yellow Wallpaper.'" In *Gender and Reading: Essays on Readers, Texts and Contexts*. Ed. Elizabeth Flynn and Patrocinio P. Schweickhart. Baltimore: Johns Hopkins University Press, 1986.

Fishkin, Shelley Fisher. *Lighting Out for the Territory: Reflections on Mark Twain and American Culture*. Oxford University Press, 1997.

———. *Was Huck Black?: Mark Twain and African American Voices*. New York and Oxford: Oxford University Press, 1993.

Fitzgerald, F. Scott. *Flappers and Philosophers*, New York: Charles Scribner's Sons, 1920.

Flint, Kate. "Afterword: Women Readers Revisited." In *Reading Women: Literary Figures and Cultural Icons from the Victorian Age to the Present*. Ed. Janet Badia and Jennifer Phegley. Toronto: University of Toronto Press, 2005.

Forrest, Jay W. *Tammany's Treason*. Albany: Fort Orange Press, 1913.

Frank, Waldo. "The Land of Our Frontier," *Our America*. New York: Boni and Liveright, 1919.

Garnett, Porter. "Literary Notes and Comments," *San Francisco Call*, October 20, 1912.

Garvey, Ellen Gruber. *Writing with Scissors*. New York and Oxford: Oxford University Press, 2012.

Gentry, Jimmy. Oral History Interview, University of Tennessee, Knoxville. Center for the Study of War and Society; Thomas T. Adams, Oral History Interview, Rutgers University History Department Oral Archives of World War II. Interviewed on May 18, 1997.

Gerber, John C. *Mark Twain*. Twayne Series. Cengage-Gale, 1988.

———. *The Mythologizing of Mark Twain*. Tuscaloosa: University of Alabama Press, 1984.

Gilligan, Carol. *In A Different Voice* Cambridge: Harvard University Press, 1982.

Giles, Todd. "Twain and Audience." In *Mark Twain's Adventures of Huckleberry Finn*. Ed. Harold Bloom, 193–202. New York: Chelsea House, Infobase, 2007.

Gilmore, William. *Reading Becomes a Necessity of Life*. Amherst: University of Massachusetts Press, 1989.

Glassberg, David. *Sense of History: The Place of the Past in American Life*, Amherst: University of Massachusetts Press, 2001.

Gohdes, Clarence. "Mirth for the Million." *Literature of the American People*. Ed. A.H. Quinn. New York: Appleton-Century-Crofts, 1951.

Goldman, Eric. "Books That Changed America," *Saturday Review of Literature* (July 4, 1953).

The Golden Era (March 11, 1866).

Grieve, Christopher. Readers Experience Database (RED 8959)

Hackenburg, Michael. "The Subscription Publishing Network in Nineteenth-Century America." In *Getting the Books Out: Papers of the Chicago Conference on the Book in 19th-Century America*. Ed. Michael Hackenburg, 45–75. Washington, DC: Library of Congress, 1987.

Hall, John. *God's Word through Preaching*. New York: Dodd and Mead, 1875.

Hart, Fred. *The Sazerac Lying Club: A Nevada Book*. San Francisco: S. Carson, Boston: Lee and Shephard. New York: C.T. Dillingham, 1878.

Hart, James D. *The Popular Book: A History of America's Literary Taste*, 1950, rpt. Berkeley: University of California Press, 1961.

Hellwig, Harold. *Mark Twain's Travel Literature*. Jefferson, NC: McFarland, 2008.

Henderson, Archibald. "The International Fame of Mark Twain." In *Critical Essays on Mark Twain, 1910–1980*. Ed. Louis J. Budd. Boston: G.K. Hall, 1983.

Henshall, May Dexter. "Reading in the Rural Districts," Bulletin of the American Library Association, Vol. 9. *English Journal* (1915): 190.

Hill, Hamlin. *Mark Twain and Elisha Bliss*. Columbia, MO: University of Missouri Press, 1964.

———. *Mark Twain: God's Fool*. Chicago: University of Chicago Press, 1973.

———. "Mark Twain: Audience and Artistry," *American Quarterly*, 25–40, Vol. 15, No. 1 (Spring 1963): 25.

Hochman, Barbara. *Getting at the Author*. Amherst: University of Massachusetts Press, 2001.

———. *Uncle Tom's Cabin and the Reading Revolution: Race, Literacy, Childhood and Fiction, 1851–1911*. Amherst: University of Massachusetts Press, 2011.

———. "Readers and Reading Groups." In *The Cambridge History of the American Novel*. Ed. Leonard Cassuto, Clare Virginia Eby, and Benjamin Reiss. New York and Cambridge: Cambridge University Press, 2011.

Hoeber, Arthur. *The Book Buyer*, Vol. 20 (1901): 120.

Hoffmann, Andrew. *Inventing Mark Twain: The Lives of Samuel L. Clemens*. New York: William Morrow, 1997.

Holland, J.G. "Star Lecturing," *Scribner's* 8 (May 1874): 110.

Homer. *The Iliad of Homer*, Book I- VI, Introduction, Robert A. Keep. Boston: J. Allyn, 1887.

Honey, Emily Hamilton. "Guardians of Morality: Librarians and American Girls' Series Fiction, 1890-1950," *Library Trends* Vol. 60, Is. 4 (Spring 2012): 765–785.

Horn, Jason Gary. *Mark Twain and William James*. Columbia and London: University of Missouri Press, 1996.

Howells, William Dean. *My Mark Twain*. Baton Rouge: Louisiana State University, 1967.

Hsu, Hsuan L. "Sitting in Darkness: Mark Twain and America's Asia," *American Literary History*, Vol. 25, No. 1 (Spring 2013): 69–84.

Hubbell, Jay B. *Who Are the Major American Writers?: A Study of the Changing Literary Canon*. Durham: Duke University Press, 1972.

Hume, Beverly A. "Mark Twain's Mysterious Duplicate in *Pudd'nhead Wilson*," *Nineteenth-Century Literature*, Vol. 68, Is. 1 (June 2013): 90–112.

Hunter, Gordon. *What America Reads, Taste, Class and the Novel, 1920–1960*. Chapel Hill: University of North Carolina Press, 2009.

Illinois Historical Society. Vol. 22. Springfield: Illinois Historical Society, 1916. p. 37.

Illinois Historical Society, Vol. 24, 1918. p. 76.

Indian Advocate, Sacred Heart, Oklahoma (March 1, 1906): 77.

Inge, M. Thomas, ed. *Huck Finn among the Critics*. Frederick, MD: University Publications, rpt. Praeger, 1995.

Ingersoll, Ernest. *Knocking about the Rockies*. New York: Harper and Brothers, 1883.

Ingham, Mary B. "Alexis: His Home and His Religion," *Ladies Repository*, Vol. 9, Is. 3 (March 1872): 216–22. p. 218.

Isaacs, Robert Wolfe. Federal Writer's Project, Library of Congress. Interview in Clayton, New Mexico, December 15, 1939.

Iser, Wolfgang. *Prospecting: From Reader Response to Literary Anthropology*. Baltimore: John Hopkins University Press, 1993.

It's a Wonderful Life, dir. Frank Capra, 1946.

Jackson, Leon. *The Business of Letters: Authorial Economies in Anti-bellum America*. Palo Alto: Stanford University Press, 2008.

Jacobs, Wilbur R. *The Historical World of Frederick Jackson Turner, With Selections from His Correspondence*. New Haven: Yale University Press, 1968.

James K. Hosmer Collection, Minneapolis Public Library. Hoag Mark Twain Collection.

Jay, Gregory. *America the Scrivener: Deconstruction and the Subject of Literary History.* Ithaca: Cornell University Press, 1990.

———. *American Literature and the Culture Wars.* Ithaca: Cornell University Press, 1997.

Jenkin. Stephen. *The Greatest Street in the World.* New York: G.P. Putnam, 1911.

Jenn, Ronald. "From American Frontier to European Borders: Publishing French Translations of *Tom Sawyer* and *Huckleberry Finn*," *Book History*, Vol. 9 (2006): 235–260.

Johnston, Carrie. "Mark Twain's Remarkable Achievement: Effacing the South for Northern Audiences," *Rocky Mountain Review*, Vol. 67, Is. 1 (2013): 66–74.

Joshi, Priya. *In Another County: Colonialism, Culture and the English Novel in India* (2002), pp. 45, 81–92.

Kaplan, Amy. *The Anarchy of Empire in the Making of U.S. Culture.* Cambridge: Harvard University Press, 2002.

Kaplan, Fred. *The Singular Mark Twain.* New York: Doubleday, 2003.

Kaplan, Justin. *Mr. Clemens and Mr. Twain.* New York: Simon and Schuster, 1966.

Kelley, Mary. *Learning to Stand and Speak: Women, Education and Public Life in America's Republic.* Chapel Hill: University of North Carolina Press, 2006.

Keokuk Daily Gate City (January 16, 1885).

Kiernan, Reginald H. *Little Brother Goes Soldiering.* London, 1930. Reginald Kiernan was at Catterick Camp in Yorkshire (RED 29768, 32062).

King, Edward. *The Great South: A Record of Journeys in Louisiana.* Hartford: American Publishing, 1875.

Kirk, Eleanor. *Washington Bee* (February 25, 1887).

———. *Washington Bee* (March 5, 1887).

———. *Washington Bee* (March 22, 1887).

Kneeland, Samuel. *Wonders of the Yosemite Valley and of California.* Boston: A. Moore; New York: Lee, Shephard and Dillingham, 1871.

Knoper, Randall. *Acting Naturally: Mark Twain and the Culture of Performance.* Berkeley: University of California Press, 1995.

Lanier, Henry Wysham. *A Century of Banking in New York.* New York: George H. Doran, 1922.

Launer, John, *The Inventions of Mark Twain: A Biography.* New York: Hill and Wang, 1990.

Lear, Bernadette A. "Were Tom and Huck on the Shelf?: Public Libraries, Mark Twain, and the Formation of Accessible Canons, 1869–1900," *Nineteenth-Century Literature* 64 (September 2009): 189–224.

Leftwich, Mary Ellen. University of Mississippi Oral History Project, Hattiesburg, Mississippi.

Levine, Lawrence. *Highbrow/Lowbrow: The Emergence of Cultural Hierarchy in America.* Cambridge: Harvard University Press, 1988.

Library Door, Vol. 1. No. 3 (December 1930).

Likins, Mrs. J.W. *Six Years Experience as a Book Agent. San Francisco, 1874 in California as I Saw It: First Person Narratives of California's Early Years, 1849–1900.* San Francisco, 1874. California State Archives. Library of Congress. www.memory.loc.gov.

Literature in the Elementary School Classroom. University of Chicago Press, 1913–1914, p. 161. rpt. 1925, p. 705.

Long, Elizabeth. *Books Clubs, Women and the Uses of Reading in Every Day Life.* Chicago: University of Chicago Press, 2003.

Lorch, Fred. "Mark Twain's Public Lectures in England in 1873," *American Literature.* Vol. 29, No. 3 (November 1957): 294–304.

———. "Mark Twain's Lecture Tour of 1868–1869: The American Vandal Abroad" pp. 39–51.

———. *The Trouble Begins at Eight.* Ames: Iowa State University Press, 1968.

Lott. Eric. *Love and Theft: Blackface Minstrelsy and the American Working Class*, New York: Oxford Press, 1992.

Loving, Jerome. *Confederate Bushwacker: Mark Twain in the Shadow of the Civil War*. Concord, New Hampshire: University Press of New England, 2013.

Lyons, Martyn. *Reading Culture and Writing Practices in Nineteenth-Century France*. Toronto: University of Toronto Press, 2008.

Lyons, Martyn, and Jay Arnold. *History of the Book in Australia, 1891–1948: Toward a National Culture in a Colonized Market*. St. Lucia: University of Queensland Press, 2001,

Lystra, Karen. *Dangerous Intimacy: The Untold Story of Mark Twain's Final Years*. Berkeley: University of California Press, 2004.

Machor, James L. *Readers in History: Nineteenth-Century American Literature and the Contexts of Response*. Baltimore: Johns Hopkins University Press, 1993.

———. "Fiction and Informed Reading in Early Nineteenth-Century America," *Nineteenth-Century Literature* 47 (1992): 320–48.

"Mark Twain in His Youth," *Salt Lake Herald* (June 5, 1896): 16.

"Mark Twain's Beginnings" in *St. Paul Globe* (January 13, 1901): 22.

Marshall, P. David. *Celebrity and Power: Fame and Contemporary Culture*. Minneapolis: University of Minnesota Press, 1997.

McGill, Meredith. *American Literature and the Culture of Reprinting, 1834–1853*. Philadelphia: University of Pennsylvania Press, 2004.

McHenry, Elizabeth. *Forgotten Readers: Recovering the Lost History of African American Literary Societies*. Durham: Duke University Press, 2006.

McKay, Janet Holmgren. "Tears and Flapdoodle: Point of View and Style," *Style* 10 (Winter 1976): 41–50.

McKenzie, Compton. *The Early Life Adventures of Sylvia Scarlett*. New York: Harper and Brothers, 1918.

McMurray, Thomas "Pet." Letter to Mark Twain, Mark Twain Project, 31816.

McFarland, Philip. *Mark Twain and the Colonel: Samuel Clemens, Theodore Roosevelt and the New Century*. Lanham: Rowman and Littlefield, 2012.

McPhee, Claire. "An Experiment in Reading in the Seventh and Eighth Grades," *Elementary School Journal*. p. 532.

McWilliams, Cary. *Honorable in All Things*. California Digital Library. Online Archive. Japanese American Relocation Archive.

Mearns, Hughes. "Unsupervised Reading," *Creative Youth: How a School Can Set Free the Creative Spirit*. Garden City: Doubleday, Doran. 1930.

Melton, Jeffrey Alan. *Mark Twain, Travel, Books and Tourism: The Tide of a Great Popular Movement*. Tuscaloosa: University of Alabama Press, 2002.

Mencken, H.L. "The Man Within," *Smart Set*, 60 (October 1919): 138–43.

The Mercury, Tasmania, Australia, August 27, 1895. p. 3

Messert, Peter. "Not an Alien but at Home: Mark Twain and London." In *Cosmopolitan Twain*. Ed. Ann M. Ryan and Joseph McCullough, 187-210. Columbia: University of Missouri Press, 2008.

———. "A Re-Evaluation of Mark Twain Following the Centenary of His Death," *Mark Twain Annual*, Vol. 9, (2011): 44–64.

———. "Tension over the Changing American Culture." In *Readings on the Adventures of Tom Sawyer*. Ed. Katie de Koster. San Diego: Greenhaven, 1999.

Michelson, Bruce. *Printer's Devil : Mark Twain and the American Publishing Revolution*. Berkeley, Los Angeles and London: University of California Press, 2006.

———. "On Twain and the Mississippi and Missouri." In *Cosmopolitan Twain*. Ed. Ann M. Ryan and Joseph McCullough. Columbia: University of Missouri Press, 2008.

———. "Mark Twain the Tourist: The Form of the Innocents Abroad," *American Literature* (November 1, 1977): 385–87.

Miller, C.E. "Give the Book to Clemens," *American History* 34 (1999): 40–44.

Miller, Elizabeth Smith. December 31, 1910. NAWSA Suffragette Scrapbook, Library of Congress, Rare Books and Special Collections, Washington, DC.

Miller, John Fulenwider. "The Effects of Emancipation upon the Mental and Physical Health of the Negro of the South," p. 2. Documenting the American South, University of North Carolina, Chapel Hill.

Mondlin, Marvin, and Roy Meador. *Book Row: An Anecdotal and Pictorial History of the Antiquarian Book Trade*. New York: Carroll and Graf, 2004.

Nader, Jennifer. "Mark Twain in Australia: Two New Interviews," *American Literary Realism*, Vol. 45, Is. 2 (Winter 2013): 166–173.

Napier, Irene Ponder. University of Southern Mississippi, Civil Rights Documentation Project, Oral History and Cultural Heritage.

Neider, Charles. ed. *The Autobiography of Mark Twain*. New York: Harper, 1959.

———. *The Selected Letters of Mark Twain*. New York: Cooper Square Press, 1999.

"Netayahu's Embrace of Mark Twain," *New York Times* (May 20, 2009).

New York Times (November 27, 1897).

New York Times (December 5, 1933).

New York Times (November 20, 2010): C1.

New York Tribune, "Luncheon Given by the Pilgrims in Honour of Mark Twain," (June 20, 1907).

New York World (April 28, 1877).

New York World (September 4, 1895).

Nordlok, David J., ed. *American Literary Scholarship: An Annual, 1989*. Durham: Duke University Press, 1989.

North American Review 197 (January 1913): 136.

Obenzinger, Hilton. *American Palestine: Melville, Mark Twain and the Holy Land*. Princeton: Princeton University Press, 1999.

O'Connor, Elizabeth Paschal. *I, Myself*. New York: Brentanos, 1911. pp. 329–31.

———. *My Beloved South*. New York: G.P. Putnam's, Knickerbocker Press, 1914.

O'Hara, D.P. "Book Publishing in the United States to 1901. Chapter IV. Subscription Books and Their Publishers," *Publisher's Weekly* 115 (May 11, 1929): 2344–2246.

Ong, Walter J. *Orality and Literacy: The Technology of the Word*. London and New York: Methuen, 1982.

Ouchita Telegraph, Monroe, Louisiana (September 19, 1885).

Overland and Out West Monthly "Current Literature," 571–81,Vol. 8, Is. 6 (June 1872): 580.

———. (May 1929): 145–46.

Paine, Albert Bigelow. *Mark Twain: A Biography*. 3 vols. New York: Harper and Brothers, 1912.

———. *Mark Twain's Letters, Complete*. New York: Evergreen Review, 2007.

Parrington, Vernon. *Main Currents of American Thought*, 3 vols. *The Beginnings of Critical Realism in America, 1860–1920*. New York: Harcourt, Brace, 1927, 1930. rpt. Norman: Oklahoma University Press, 1987.

Partridge, Henry Morton. *The Most Remarkable Echo in the World*. New York: Privately Printed, Cosmo, 1933.

Pawley, Christine. *Reading Places: Literacy, Democracy, and the Public Library in Cold War America*. Amherst: University of Massachusetts Press, 2010.

Peterson, Harry C. "Ghost Towns on '49 Tour: Historic Spots to Live Again in Story," *Call* (May 15, 1922).

Peyser, Thomas. "Mark Twain, Immigration, and the American Narrative," *ELH*, Vol. 79, No 4 (Winter 2012): 1013–1037.

Phelan, James. "A True Book, with Some Stretches: Twain's Huck and the Reader's Experience of Huckleberry Finn," *Foreign Language Studies*, Vol. 32, No. 4 (August 2010): 13–23.

Powers, Ron. *Mark Twain: A Life*. New York: The Free Press, 2006.

Price, Leah. "Reading: The State of the Discipline," *Book History* 7 (2004): 305.

Pritchett, V.S. *A Cab at the Door: An Autobiography, Early Years*. New York: Random House, 1968. Readers Experience Database, (RED 3381).

"Prominent People," *The Leader* (December 14, 1883): 3.

Pullman Herald (December 29, 1906): 1–2.

Queensland Figaro, Brisbane, Australia (February 28, 1931): 16.

Radway, Janice A. *Reading the Romance: Women, Patriarchy, and Popular Literature*, 1984. Rpt. Chapel Hill: University of North Carolina Press, 1991.

Railton, Stephen. "Getting Tom to Market."

———. *Mark Twain: A Short Introduction*. Malden, MA, and Oxford: Blackwell, 2004.

———. *Mark Twain in His Times*. http://etextlib.virginia.edu/railton.

Raleigh, John Henry. *Matthew Arnold and American Culture*. Berkeley: University of California Press, 1957.

Rasmussen, R. Kent. *Critical Companion to Mark Twain*, New York: Facts on File, 2007.

———. *Dear Mark Twain: Letters from his Readers*. Berkeley: University of California Press, 2013.

Read, Opie Percival. *Mark Twain and I*. New York: Rand McNally, 1940. Openlibrary.org/authors/OL159298A/Opie_Percival_Read.

"The Reader," *Graphic* (London) 28 (September 1, 1883): 231.

Reed, James A. "Twain's Birthday: Senator Reed Extols the Author," *New York Times* (December 1, 1920).

Regan, Robert. "The Reprobate Elect in The Innocents Abroad." In *On Mark Twain: The Best from American Literature*. Ed. Louis J. Budd and Edwin H. Cady. Durham: Duke University Press, 1987.

Repplier, Agnes. *Catholic World*, Vol. 36 (1882): 127.

———. *Catholic World*, Vol. 51, Is. 304 (July 1890): 550–58.

———. *Harper's Weekly* (December 23, 1905).

Robinson, A.J. *Memorandum and Anecdotes of the Civil War: In Remembrance of the Boys Who Fought to Maintain One Flag, One Country and One People, 1860–1865*, Chapter VII, Vicksburg Campaign. Privately Printed, 1910.

Roland Record, Roland, Iowa. (March 6, 1901).

Roosevelt, Theodore. *Theodore Roosevelt Letters to His Children*. Ed. Joseph Bucklin Bishop. New York: Charles Scribner's Sons, 1919.

Rose, Jonathan. *The Intellectual Life of the British Working Class*. New Haven: Yale University Press, 2001.

Ryan, Barbara, and Amy M. Thomas, eds. *Reading Acts: U.S. Readers Interactions with Literature, 1800–1950*. Knoxville: University of Tennessee Press, 2002.

Ryan, Ann M., and Joseph McCullough. *Cosmopolitan Twain*. Columbia: University of Missouri Press, 2008.

Sandrock, Louise. "Another Word on Children's Reading," *Catholic World*, Vol. 51, Is. 305 (August 1890): 679.

———. *Mainly the Truth: Interviews with Mark Twain*. Tuscaloosa: University of Alabama Press, 2009.

Schorske, Carl. *Fin de Siecle Vienna: Politics and Culture*. New York: Vintage, 1981.

Schwartz, Henry. *Modern Language Quarterly* (March 2005): 136–142): 136–42.

St. Louis Globe Democrat (March 17, 1885).

St. Louis Post-Dispatch (May 12, 1882): 2.

St. Louis Post-Dispatch photo (May 30, 1902): 1.

St. Louis Republic (May 30, 1902): 1–2.

St. Louis Star (May 29, 1902): 1, 7.

San Francisco Bulletin (March 14, 1881): 1 (CR 269).

San Francisco Call (March 10, 1907): 12.

Sattlemeyer, Robert. *American Literary Scholarship: An Annual, 1989*. Ed. David J. Nardlack. Durham: Duke University Press, 1989.

Sattelmeyer, Robert, and J. Donald Crowley, eds., *One Hundred Years of Huckleberry Finn*. Columbia: University of Missouri Press, 1985.

Scharnhorst, Gary, ed. *Mark Twain: The Complete Interviews*. Tuscaloosa: University of Alabama, 2006. p. 168

Scofield, F.A. "Outside Reading," *English Journal* (1918).

Seelye, John. *Mark Twain in the Movies: A Meditation with Pictures*. New York: Viking, 1977.

Shawlow, Arthur. Bancroft Library, University of California, Berkeley, Regional Oral History Office.

Sheehan, Donald. *This Was Publishing: A Chronicle of the Book Trade in the Gilded Age*. Bloomington: Indiana University Press, 1952.

Shelden, Michael. *Mark Twain: Man in White—The Grand Adventures of His Final Years*. New York: Random House, 2010.

Sherman, Mrs. L.A., Hastings, Nebraska, Federal Writer's Project, October 1938. Library of Congress.

Sherman, Stuart P. "Review of Albert Bigelow Paine, *Mark Twain: A Biography*," *Nation*, 95 (November 14, 1912): 457–59.

Sicherman, Barbara. *Well Read Lives: How Books Inspired a Generation of American Women*. Chapel Hill: University of North Carolina Press, 2011.

———. "Reading and Middle Class Identity in Victorian America: Cultural Consumption, Conspicuous and Otherwise." In *Reading Acts: U.S. Readers Interactions with Literature, 1800–1950*. Ed. Barbara Ryan and Amy M. Thomas, 137–160. Knoxville: University of Tennessee Press, 2002.

———. "Reading and Ambition: M. Carey Thomas and Female Heroism," *American Quarterly*, Vol. 45, No. 1 (March 1993).

Simmons, Sarah. March 22, 2000, Virginia Polytechnic Oral History Interviews.

Sloane, David E.E. "Huck's Helplessness: A Reader's Response to Stupefied Humanity." In *Making Mark Twain Work in the Classroom*. Ed. James Leonard, 140. Durham: Duke University Press.

Smalley, G.W. Letter to Mark Twain (December 9, 1873) from Hyde Park Square West, London. Mark Twain Project, UCCL 00999;

Smedes, Susan Dabney. *Memorials of a Southern Planter*. Baltimore: Cushings and Bailey, 1888, p. 273.

Spiller, Robert. *The Cycle of American Literature*. New York: Signet, 1953.

———. *Late Harvest: Essays and Addresses in American Literature and Culture*. Westport, CT. and London: Greenwood, 1981.

Smith, Henry Nash. *Mark Twain: The Development of a Writer*. Cambridge: Harvard University Press, 1962.

Smith, Henry Nash, and William M. Gibson, eds., *Mark Twain-Howells Letters*, 2 vols. Cambridge: Harvard University Press, 1963.

Starkies, W.J.M. *The Archarians of Aristophanes*. London: Macmillan, 1909. Note #164, p. 177.

Stedman, Edmund Clarence. *The Life and Letters of Edmund Clarence Stedman*. London: Moffatt, Yard and Company, 1910.

Sterling, C.F. Letter to Mark Twain (January 21, 1871) Mark Twain Project, University of California, UCLC 31744.

Stern, Madeline B. "Dissemination of Popular Books in the Midwest and Far West During the Nineteenth Century." In *Getting the Books Out: Papers of the Chicago Conference on the Book in 19th-Century America*. Ed. Michael Hackenburg, 76–97. Washington, DC: Library of Congress, 1987.

Stone, Albert E. "Mark Twain's Joan of Arc: The Child as Goddess." Ed. Louis J. Budd and Edwin Harrison Cady. Durham: Duke University Press, 1987.

———. Review. *Nineteenth-Century Fiction*. Vol. 34, No. 3 (December 1979).

———. *The Innocent Eye: Mark Twain and Childhood Imagination*. New Haven: Yale University Press, 1962.

Storey, Mark. "Huck and Hank Go to the Circus: Mark Twain under Barnum's Big Top," *European Journal of American Culture*, Vol. 29, No. 3 (March 2011): 217–228.

Strong, Edward W. Bancroft Library. Oral History, "Freedom of Speech" Movement. University of California, Berkeley.

Sturgess, Kim. *Shakespeare and the American Nation*. Cambridge: Cambridge University Press, 2004.

Sweeney, Michael. Interviewed by Richard Burks Verrone, Texas Tech University Archive. Oral History.

Syracuse Standard (October 5, 1869): 12.

Tacoma Times (April 22, 1910): 4.

Talley, Robert T., Jr. "Bleeping Mark Twain? Censorship, Huckleberry Finn and the Function of Literature," *Teaching American Literature: A Journal of Theory and Practice*, Vol. 6, No. 1 (Spring 2013): 97–108.

Taper, Bernard, ed. *Mark Twain's San Francisco.* New York: McGraw-Hill, 1963.

Taylor, Benjamin Franklin. *The World on Wheels and Other Sketches.* Chicago: S.C. Griggs, 1874.

Tebbel, John. *A History of Book Publishing in the United States.* Vol. 1. The Creation of an Industry. New York: R.R. Bowker, 1972.

Thomas, Amy. "There is Nothing So Effective as a Personal Canvass: Reevaluating Nineteenth-Century American Subscription Books," *Book History* 1 (1998): 140–155.

Thomson, William. "Romance of the Gold Fields," Vol. 34, Is. 283, *Overland and Out West Monthly* (November 1899): 488.

Thompson, M. Jeff. Letter to Charles Dudley Warner, February 20, 1874. Mark Twain Project, University of California. UCLC 39061.

Tillinghast S. Scrapbook, University of California, Santa Barbara Archives, SC 843.

Tolland County Press (August 31, 1876).

Traubel, Horace. *With Walt Whitman in Camden,* Vol. 5. Carbondale: University of Southern Illinois Press, 1964. 481.

Trombley, Laura Skandera. *In the Company of Women.* Philadelphia: University of Pennsylvania Press, 1999.

———. *Mark Twain's Other Woman: The Hidden Story of His Final Years.* New York: Knopf, 2010.

Tucker, Edward L. "A New Letter by Bill Nye," *American Quarterly* (ANQ) 17.1 (Winter 2004): 43.

Tucker, Susan. "Reading and Re-reading: The Scrapbooks of Girls Growing into Women, 1900–1930." In *Defining Print Culture for Youth: The Cultural Work of Children's Literature.* Ed. Anne Lendin and Wayne A. Wiegand. Westport, CT: Librarians Unlimited.

Turner, Frederick Jackson. "On the Significance of the Frontier in American History," Annual Report of the American Historical Association for the Year 1893. Washington, D.C.: GPO and American Historical Association, 1984. pp. 199–227.

Twain, Mark. *Autobiography of Mark Twain.* Vol. 1. Ed. Harriet Elinor Smith et. al., Mark Twain Project. Berkeley: University of California Press, 2010.

———. *Autobiography of Mark Twain.* Vol. 2. Ed. Benjamin Griffin, et. al., Mark Twain Project. Berkeley: University of California Press, 2013.

———. *Autobiography.* Ed. Charles Neider. New York: Harper and Row, 1959.

———. Mark Twain Papers. Bancroft Library, University of California, Berkeley.

———. *Twain-Howells Letters, 1872–1910.* Ed. Henry Nash Smith and William M. Gibson. 2 vols. Cambridge: Belknap Press, Harvard UP, 1960. II, 778–80.

———. *Mark Twain: Life as I Found It.* Ed. Charles Neider. Garden City, N.Y.: Hanover House, 1961. p. 340.

———. *Mark Twain's Letters.* Vol. 1, 1853–1866. Ed. Edgar Marquess Branch, Michael B. Frank, and Kenneth Anderson. Berkeley: University of California Press, 1998–2002.

———. Vol. 2, 1867–1868. Ed. Harriet Elinor Smith and Richard Bucci, Berkeley: University of California Press, 1998–2002.

———. Vol. 3, 1869. Ed. Victor Fischer and Michael B. Frank, Berkeley: University of California Press, 1988–2002.

———. Vol. 4, 1870-1871. Ed. Victor Fischer and Michael B. Frank, Berkeley: University of California Press, 1988–2002.

———. Vol. 5, 1872-1873. Ed. Lin Salamo and Harriet Elinor Smith; Berkeley: University of California Press, 1988–2002.

———. Vol. 6, 1874-1875. Ed. Michael B. Frank and Harriet Elinor Smith, Berkeley: University of California Press, 1988–2002.

———. *The Love Letters of Mark Twain*. Ed. Dixon Wecter. New York: Harper and Row, 1949.

———. *Mark Twain-Howells Letters: The Correspondence of Samuel L. Clemens and William Dean Howells*. Ed. Henry Nash Smith and William M. Gibson. 2 vols. Cambridge: Harvard University Press, 1960.

———. *Mark Twain's Letters to His Publishers, 1867–1894*. Ed. Hamlin Hill. Berkeley: University of California Press, 1967.

———. *Mark Twain's Notebooks and Journals*. Vol. 1. 1855–1873. Ed. Frederick Anderson, Michael B. Frank, and Kenneth M. Sanderson.

———. Vol. 2. 1877–1883. Ed. Frederick Anderson, Lin Salamo, and Bernard J. Stein.

———. Vol. 3. 1883–1891. Ed. Robert Pack Browning, Michael B. Frank, and Lin Salamo. Mark Twain Papers. University of California, Berkeley.

———. Oxford Mark Twain. 29 vols. Ed. Shelley Fisher Fishkin. New York and Oxford, 1996.

———. *The Innocents Abroad* (1869)

———. *Roughing It* (1872)

———. *The Gilded Age* (1873)

———. *The Adventures of Tom Sawyer* (1876)

———. *A Tramp Abroad* (1880)

———. *The Prince and the Pauper* (1882)

———. *Life on the Mississippi* (1883)

———. *The Adventures of Huckleberry Finn* (1885)

———. *The Adventures of Huckleberry Finn*, Gribben, Alan. ed., New South Books, 2011.

———. *A Connecticut Yankee in King Arthur's Court* (1889)

———. *Puddn'head Wilson* (1894)

———. *The Personal Recollections of Joan of Arc* (1896)

———. *Following the Equator* (1896)

———. "Concerning the Jews," *Harper's* (March 1898)

———. "How the Author Was Sold in Newark" (1869) in *Sketches, New and Old*, Uniform Edition, Vol. XIX New York: Harper and Brothers, 1903.

University of Missouri Alumni Publication, March 1914, p. 197.

University of Missouri Alumni, February 1917, p. 155.

University of Missouri Alumni, May 1917, p. 271.

University of Missouri Alumni, December 1920, p. 76.

University of Missouri Alumni, September 1923, p. 171.

Wadsworth, Sarah. *In the Company of Books: Literature and Its "Classes" in Nineteenth-Century America*. Amherst: University of Massachusetts Press, 2006.

Wadsworth, Sarah, and Wayne A. Wiegand. *Right Here I See My Own Books*. Amherst: University of Massachusetts Press, 2012.

Wagenknecht, Edward. *Mark Twain: The Man and His Work* (1935). Norman: University of Oklahoma Press, 1961.

Wald, Lillian. *The House on Henry Street*. New York: Henry Holt, 1915.

Wecter, Dixon, ed. *The Love Letters of Mark Twain*. New York: Harper and Brothers, 1949.

Welland, Dennis. *Mark Twain in England*. London: Chatto and Windus, 1978; Atlantic Highlands, N.J.: Humanities Press, 1978.

Weisbuch, Robert. *Atlantic Double-Cross: American Literature and British Influence in the Age of Emerson*. Chicago: University of Chicago Press, 1986.

West, Ray B. "Mark Twain's Idyll of Frontier America," *University of Kansas City Review*, XV (Winter 1948): 92–104.

"What Middletown Read," Ball State University, Muncie, Indiana. Website at www.bsu.edu/libraries/wmr.

White, William Allen. *The Autobiography of William Allen White*. New York: Macmillan, 1946.

Wieck, Carl F. *Refiguring Huckleberry Finn*. Athens and London: University of Georgia Press, 2000.

Williams, Jeremiah. *History of Washtenaw County*. Chicago: Charles C. Chapman, 1881. p. 670.

Williams, Penina. "The Plaint of a Commonplace Person," *Appleton's Journal*, Vol. 10, Is. 226 (July 17, 1873): 82.

Windsor and Richmond Gazette, Australia (October 5, 1895): 5.

Winship, Michael. "Publishing in America: Needs and Opportunities for Research." In *History of the Book: America, 1639–1876*. Ed. David D. Hall and John Hench, 61–102. Worcester: American Antiquarian Society, 1987.

Wonham, Henry B. *Mark Twain and the Art of the Tall Tale*. Oxford and New York: Oxford University Press, 1993.

———. "The Disembodied Yarnspinners and the Reader of the Adventures of Huckleberry Finn," *American Literary Realism*, Vol. 24, No. 1 (Fall 1991): 2–22.

Wouk, Herman. "This World," *San Francisco Chronicle* (August 5, 1956): 20.

Zboray. Ronald J., and Mary Saracino Zboray, "Have You Read...? Real Readers and Their Responses in Antebellum Boston and Its Region," 139-170, *Nineteenth-Century Literature*, Vol. 52, No. 2 (September 1997): 142.

Zeehan and Dundas News, Australia (April 29, 1895): 2.

Zeublin, Charles. Letter to Elizabeth Smith Miller (December 31, 1910), Library of Congress Rare Books and Special Collections, Digital Archive.

Ziff, Larzar. *Return Passages, Great American Travel Writing, 1780– 1910*. New Haven: Yale University Press, 2001.

Index

About the Author

Robert McParland is Associate Professor of English at Felician College in New Jersey, where he has served as the chair of the Department of English. He is the author of *Charles Dickens's American Audience* (Lexington Books, Rowman & Littlefield 2010).

CPSIA information can be obtained at www.ICGtesting.com
Printed in the USA
BVOW01*1547140914

366588BV00002B/2/P